About the author

Penelope Leach, a trusted source of child-development information and childcare advice for parents all over the world, is a research psychologist specializing in child development and a passionate advocate for children and parents. She is also a mother and grandmother.

After a first degree in history from Cambridge University, a graduate degree in social work, and then a PhD in psychology from the University of London, she studied many aspects of child development and parent-child relationships under the auspices of the UK's Medical Research Council. Penelope also holds an honorary doctorate in Education and is an honorary senior research fellow at the Tavistock Clinic and the Institute for the Study of Children, Families and Social Issues at Birkbeck, University of London. In recent years she co-directed the UK's largest-ever program of research into the effects of various kinds of childcare on children's development in the first five years. Her most recent book, *Child Care Today* (Knopf) was published in 2009.

With five years of research already behind her, though, the births of her own children made her aware of the gulfs between theory and practice, professionals and parents, adults and children, and even men and women. As much of her subsequent work has been devoted to building bridges across these gulfs from both sides as to academic research. Accordingly, she is a past President and Chair of the Child Development Society, Fellow of the British Psychological Society, and a founding member of the Association of Infant Mental Health-UK, yet she also works for parents' and children's organizations, and until 2008 was President of the National Child Minding Association. Her classic book *Your Baby & Child* (Knopf) has sold over three million copies.

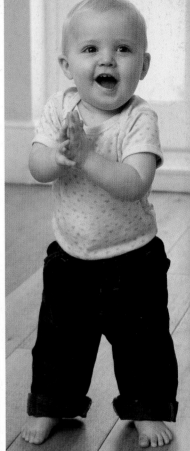

the Essential First Year

Penelope Leach

LONDON, NEW YORK, MUNICH, MELBOURNE, DELHI

Project Editor Claire Tennant-Scull
US Editors Beth Landis Hester, Shannon Beatty
US Editorial Consultant Lisa Fields
Project Designer Carolyn Hewitson
Editors Emma Maule, Terry Moore
Senior Art Editor Nicola Rodway
Senior Production Editor Jennifer Murray
Senior Production Controller Man Fai Lau
Creative Technical Support Sonia Charbonnier
Photography Vanessa Davies
Art Direction for Photography Peggy Saddler
Publishing Manager Anna Davidson
Managing Editor Penny Warren
Managing Art Editors Glenda Fisher, Marianne Markham
Publisher Peggy Vance

Every effort has been made to ensure that the information in this book is complete and accurate. However, neither the publisher nor the author is engaged in rendering professional advice or services to the individual reader. The ideas, procedures, and suggestions contained in this book are not intended as a substitute for consulting with your healthcare provider. All matters regarding the health of you and your baby require medical supervision. Neither the publishers nor the author shall be liable or responsible for any loss or damage allegedly arising from any information or suggestion in this book.

First American Edition, 2010
Published in the United States by
DK Publishing, 375 Hudson Street
New York, New York 10014

10 11 12 13   10 9 8 7 6 5 4 3 2 1
176462—5/2010

A catalog record for this book is available
from the Library of Congress

ISBN: 978-0-7566-5799-4

DK books are available at special discounts when purchased in bulk for sales promotions, premiums, fund-raising, or educational use. For details, contact: DK Publishing Special Markets, 375 Hudson Street, New York, New York 10014 or SpecialSales@dk.com.

Printed and bound by Star Standard, Singapore

Discover more at **www.dk.com**

Contents

About this book

Why a book that's only about babies in the first year, especially when *Your Baby and Child* covers the first five? And where's the sense in calling it *The Essential First Year* when there's obviously got to be a first if there's going to be a second or third? The answer is that while we've known for a long time that the first year of life is important, it's only in this generation that we've begun to understand just how important it is and why. Human babies are born at a much earlier stage in their development than most baby mammals, and their brains are among the least developed parts of them. Those baby brains don't just grow according to genetic instructions, and get more efficient with age. Brain development—structural and biochemical—and function depend on a baby's environment and experience in that essential first year, and especially on warm, secure, responsive relationships with mothers, fathers, or the caring adults who stand in for them.

So your baby's first year with you will go a long way toward shaping the child, adolescent and adult (perhaps parent) she becomes. Of course even the most idyllic first year can't prevent bad things from happening to children later on, but we know much more than we did about what makes a first year good, and we know that it can

and does help to give children the resilience to cope with whatever life may throw at them.

There are many influences on your baby that you cannot control, such as the genes she was passed at conception, her experiences in the womb and at birth, and things that happen later on, too. But although you can't prevent negative events, your relationship with your baby is a major influence on how powerfully and how lastingly she is affected by them. Her genetic inheritance is a good example: We all carry millions of genes and more and more specific ones are being identified for everything from breast cancer to an ear for music. But while you and her father can do nothing to change the genes she got from you both, you certainly influence the impact they have on her. Many of those millions of genes, desirable and undesirable, are only likely to be "expressed" in particular circumstances or environments—otherwise they sit silently in the DNA. Since the relationships your baby has with you are the most important aspect of her environment, those relationships are bound to affect some of the ways her genetic inheritance plays out.

Likewise, your baby's experiences in the womb and at birth are mostly out of your control, but although you can't do anything to prevent a traumatic forceps delivery from stressing your baby (as well as yourself), you may be able to

moderate, even head off, longer-term effects by understanding her extra crying and irritability in the first days and handling it sensitively. Even when babyhood is long past, the security of children's earlier relationships remains vital. Any child will certainly be thrown off course by horrific happenings when she is two or seven years old—such as losing a parent or being abused—but how deeply an individual child is affected, how well she manages her feelings at the time, and how completely she bounces back onto her previous developmental track, depends on resilience that's rooted in that essential first year.

"Parents matter" is not a new message. Women have always known that babies' survival depends on being mothered. But this is the first generation to understand that it is not solely the relationship a mother makes with her baby that matters; the ongoing relationship between the baby and her father matters, too, and both are responsible not only for her immediate health and well-being, but also for her whole growth and development as a person, now and in the future. It's also in this generation that many parenting issues that have always been matters of opinion and open to argument, are beginning to be resolved by scientific evidence that parents should be aware of. This is not a "how to" book like *Your Baby and Child*; it is a "why?" book. Some of the issues are similar, but the viewpoints are different. Most parents don't have time to follow child development arguments or look up scientific papers, though, so some of the most interesting are encapsulated in boxes headed "From research" and "You may hear…" and some parents' voices can be heard in "Parents talking about…". Similar boxes highlight some useful tips for parents of twins.

Stressing the lifelong impact of your relationship with your baby piles extra responsibility on you when you're only just coming to terms with having a baby at all. But the information is there, and since this is a no-punches-pulled kind of book it doesn't try to sugar-coat it. Once you can get your heads around your own enormous influence on this new person's whole way of being, though, the downsides of being a parent may fall into a different perspective. Being woken in the night again and again for three months can seem overwhelmingly awful, but when you understand why babies are so inclined to wake, you'll ignore anyone who says yours is doing so to "manipulate" you and know that she won't go on doing it forever. And when you realize that how you react (or decide not to react) when she cries for you tonight may still play a part in how she reacts to stress next year, and 30 years on when she's mothering your grandbaby, the torment of those awakenings may pale beside the brilliance of the smile with which she greets you.

Penelope Leach

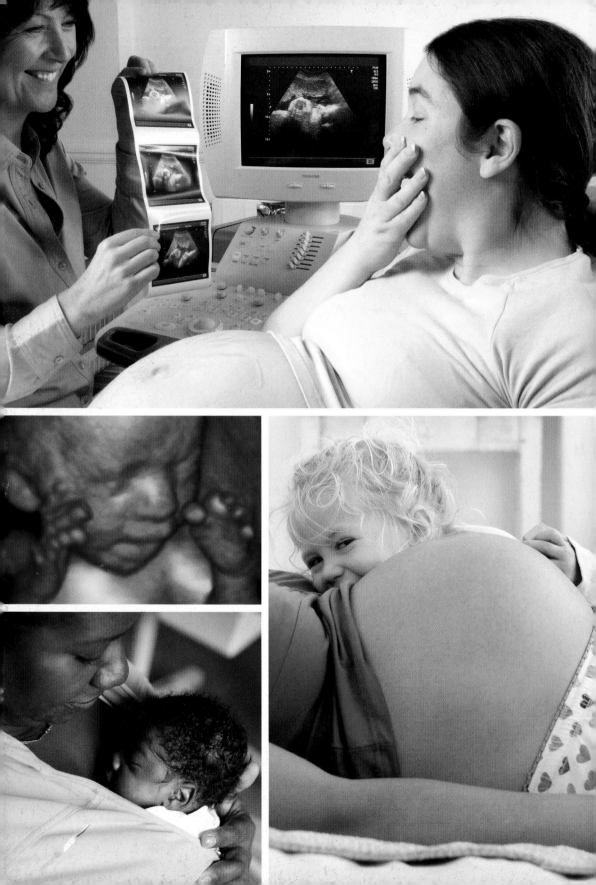

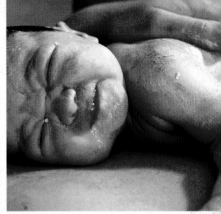

Pregnancy and birth

Preparing to be parents

Each time your watch ticks, hundreds of pregnancies are established and babies born in every part of the world. Childbirth is not just an everyday but an every-second business, yet for all those women, and for many of their partners, a birth, especially a first birth, is life's biggest landmark.

Parents? Us parents? Once you have your baby, neither of you will ever be the same again. Prenatal care and classes can explain the bodily upheavals of pregnancy and birth; friends and family can help you foresee changes in your lifestyle, but nobody can fully prepare you for the most important aspect of becoming parents: an upheaval in feelings so radical that it will change you into different people. Like it or not, you are going to be emotionally involved with this baby in a way you have never been involved before, and having this unique relationship of new parent to new child is going to change the way you think and feel about yourselves, each other, your own parents, your jobs, your community…

A different kind of getting ready for birth

While it is safe to predict that you are going to experience intense and far-reaching feelings,

since you are unique individuals, it would be idiotic for any outsider to try to tell you *what* you will feel. You cannot even entirely prepare yourselves, because you are both so used to the way you feel about things, as separate people and as a pair, that it is difficult to imagine feeling differently. Still, it's valuable to be aware of the emotional climate into which you are moving so that you can be alert to what's going on, for yourselves and each other, and look for positive ways through or around any rough patches.

Couples who don't think beyond the delivery, perhaps especially women who pride themselves on carrying on exactly as usual all through pregnancy, or those who let pregnancy impinge, but behave as if it was going to culminate in a birth, rather than a child, are sometimes caught completely off-guard by the storm of emotions the increasingly imminent prospect of a new baby evokes. Sometimes they then try to fight those feelings down rather than work with and through them. They struggle to hold onto their past equilibrium and to convince themselves (and each other) that they are still the people they used to be, rather than search for a new balance, for people who are suddenly parents and a partnership that is suddenly a family.

Fighting off strong feelings is seldom a good idea, and it certainly isn't in pregnancy. Feelings you refuse to acknowledge are liable to turn themselves inside out and sneak past your defenses in a new guise. The child who dreads school and tries not to think about it during the weekend may wake on Monday morning

From research

Pregnancy exhaustion. There's a physical reason for the overwhelming exhaustion many women feel in the first three months: Their bodies are not just supplying the baby with oxygen and nutrients through the placenta as they will do right up to the delivery, they are actually making the placenta, which is a big drain on their energy and resources. By the fourth month, the placenta is complete, and most women then get a surge of energy.

Having fun with the bump is a good start toward making friends with the baby brother or sister inside it.

with a tummy ache. She is not pretending to have a tummy ache so as not to have to go to school. The ache is real. It truly hurts. But, unbeknownst to her, it is that same anxious dread in a new form. Unease very easily disguises itself as disease. Deny significant anxieties in pregnancy and they may similarly break through, perhaps in depression. More women (and some men) suffer from depression before birth (prenatal depression) than from the more familiar, postpartum depression; both are bad for babies.

Having a baby—especially a first baby—is always an anxious business because a minute, helpless, brand-new person is a tremendous responsibility and it feels heavy. You can manage it, though. Whoever you are and whatever your circumstances, you can carry and birth and rear this baby to be the healthiest and happiest he can possibly be. You will do it better from the baby's point of view if you do it with pleasure, and you will do it more easily from your own point of view if you enter wholeheartedly into being parents.

Who's in there?

Of course you know that what's inside you is a baby (or two), but in early pregnancy it can be difficult to think of that baby as a real person, or yourself as a mother, and even more difficult for your partner to think of himself as a father. In fact, even if you don't actually throw up, the collection of physical symptoms that are typical of this stage of pregnancy may tempt you to feel as if you're sick rather than having a baby. Ultrasound scans have made it far easier for parents to be aware of their babies from early on. If you have a "dating scan" at around 12–13 weeks, the baby will be so tiny that its whole body fits on the screen. You'll see movements (weeks before you can feel them for yourself)

and hear the heartbeat loud and clear. At this early stage the ultrasound operator will be able to tell you if you are carrying twins, but she won't be able to tell you whether the baby is a boy or a girl, even if you desperately want to know, because the external genitals are not yet fully formed.

If you have further scans after mid-pregnancy, though, it will be possible for the operator to see whether the baby is a girl or a boy (unless the legs happen to be crossed). So do decide, and remember to tell her in advance, whether or not you want to know.

Scans, including 3-D and 4-D scans carried out by research teams, have recently made it possible to study fetal behavior in detail. By 20 weeks the baby inside you will be able to move his fingers and may suck his thumb. He may yawn, and once his eyes are able to open, at around week 25, he may blink (though why he should blink in darkness nobody knows). Pictures have also been taken of remarkably mature-looking facial expressions including smiling (which was something babies were thought to learn from their parents, two or three months after birth) and crying. We don't yet know whether a fetus's smiles or crying mean that he is happy or unhappy; these facial expressions could be random or "practice" for later.

It is clear, though, that babies in the womb do react to what goes on outside it. Fetuses as young as 16 weeks have been seen to startle when the mother had a fall, and by 18–20 weeks a loud buzzer sounded against mothers' abdomens makes them immediately straighten their backs and limbs and turn their heads before curling

Twin tip

Nobody can tell whether your babies are identical (monozygous) or non-identical fraternal (dizygous) from the placenta alone, either before or after birth. Identical twins almost always share a placenta but may occasionally have one each. Fraternal twins have a placenta each but occasionally the two fuse into one. The ultrasound operator will probably be able to tell you how many sacs there are: If the two babies share a sac they are definitely identical and that means, of course, that they are of the same sex. If they are in separate sacs they are not identical; one may be a boy and the other a girl, or they may both be the same sex.

Why it matters...

whether you know in advance if it's a boy or a girl.
◆ It's traditional (some people say "natural") to find out a baby's sex only as it emerges.
◆ It can be part of the excitement of the delivery.
◆ Knowing the sex before the baby is born makes it easier to think of the baby as a person.

◆ If one of you especially wants one sex or other and isn't going to get it, knowing in advance may give you time to get over the disappointment so it doesn't spoil the welcome you give the baby.
◆ Knowing the sex of a coming sibling may make it easier for older children to imagine and look forward to the baby—and if it's the "wrong" sex for the older child, he, like his parents, has time to get used to the reality.

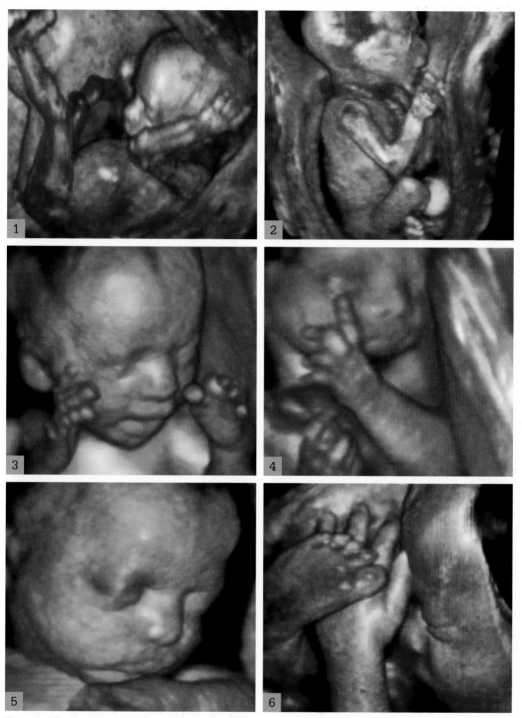

These are 3-D color scans. (1) & (2) were taken at 16 and 18 weeks. They are so tiny almost the whole fetus can be seen, and so folded up, that length measurements are taken top to bottom. (3) & (4) were taken at 26 weeks. Length is now measured head to toe. The fetus on the right is blinking. (5) & (6) were taken at 31 and 32 weeks. The fetuses are getting short of space. On the left, a face alone fills the screen; on the right, face, hands and feet are packed together.

back down into the "fetal position". There is evidence that by mid-pregnancy fetuses notice and remember sounds that they have heard often and react to them after birth. It is widely accepted that newborn babies recognize their mother's (and perhaps their father's) voice and distinguish it from strangers' voices, and that they react with interest (perhaps by stopping crying) to advertising jingles they have heard many times over several months but not to new ones. In the last weeks of pregnancy, lights and sounds that are new and unexpected may make your baby jump, but over a few days he gets used to them and no longer takes any notice.

Bearing the baby in mind

By the middle of the pregnancy you will be more aware that your just-noticeable bulge is a real baby because he'll begin to make his presence (and personality!) felt as he swims and trampolines inside you. You're likely to feel movements for the first time at around 17–19 weeks if you are slim, a couple of weeks later if you are not. At this stage the baby only weighs about 3 ounces (100 g), so the movements are so light and fluttery that they are easy for you to miss and impossible for your partner or older children to feel. By 20 or 22 weeks though, you'll probably feel acrobatics going on in there (babies have been filmed doing somersaults in the

Twin tip

Early birth is normal. It's probable that twins will be born before they reach term, and even if you stay healthy and have no problems such as high blood pressure, it is likely that you will need to give up work by the middle of your third trimester. Your two babies and their luggage will reach the size and weight of a full-term single baby by about 28 weeks, and this might fool your body into thinking it's time to go into labor. You'll be monitored every two weeks and will probably be advised to take it easy. Your babies will be considered mature enough for delivery at 37 weeks.

womb), and as his growth reduces the space available to him, you'll begin to feel the baby kicking out with his legs and feet and pushing with hands and elbows. His father will be able to feel his movements too.

Fetuses vary in their levels of activity. Boys are not more active than girls and very active babies are not more likely to be hyperactive in childhood. Whatever their overall level of activity, though, fetuses are usually quiet—perhaps asleep—for about half the time and active the other half, alternating the two over roughly two-hour cycles. As your pregnancy progresses you may find that your baby is quietest when you are most active, as perhaps he is soothed and rocked by your movements, and that he starts doing gymnastics as soon as you lie down to rest or sleep.

Towards the end of pregnancy anything you put on your belly—such as a bar of soap in the bath—is likely to get kicked off. This trick is guaranteed to make a small sibling laugh.

From research

Stress in pregnancy. The less for you, the better for your baby. Anxieties that are potentially damaging to babies include anxiety about the pregnancy and the wellbeing of the fetus; general anxiety; depression, with or without anxiety; spousal discord or cruelty; life events, such as bereavement; daily hassles, such as being bullied at work or having problems with neighbors; involvement in natural disasters or living in a war-zone.

Working is not a damaging stress in itself although of course a job in which a woman is unhappy may be stressful.

Enjoying your pregnancy is better for you all

Your overall happiness and good spirits affect the environment your womb provides for the baby via hormonal and chemical messages. In fact, babies in the womb may be permanently affected by their mothers' long-term emotional state. Generations of women all over the world have talked about babies being influenced by their mothers' moods. Yours is the first generation to have scientific evidence that it's true. Of course it's not only positive feelings that can affect your baby; anxiety and depression can too. It used to be thought that babies were affected because women who were anxious in pregnancy became over-anxious mothers. In fact, anxiety in pregnancy affects babies while they are still in the womb and matters to their development whatever happens at or after the birth. Occasionally a baby's long-term development may actually be altered in a process known as "fetal programming".

Any anxiety, depression, or stress may reduce the quality of a fetus's environment, but studies have shown that the anxieties that are most likely to affect that environment are worries about the pregnancy itself and about the baby's wellbeing, and stress caused by problems in the relationship with the father. These can affect development in the womb and may even increase the (small) chances of the baby being born early or at low birth weight, having reduced scores on developmental tests, and having a range of behavioral difficulties during childhood. The most stress-free pregnancy possible is therefore a mother's right and a father's duty, because it is an obligation to their child. Don't let the idea of "spoiling yourself" or "being spoiled" come into your mind. Nobody else can tell you what will make you feel relaxed and contented during the next few months, but whatever it is, go for it.

The proud bulge of the baby not only makes your body a new shape but also brings your partner even closer.

Parents talking about...

different reactions to pregnancy

❝ My sister and I were both pregnant at the same time, but two women couldn't have reacted more differently. My sister went part-time at work, let herself drop (or got her husband to let her drop) lots of minor irritants in her life—like a long drive every Sunday to have lunch with in-laws she didn't get along with, and cooking from scratch every night and twice on weekends—and gave herself little treats like regular hair and nail "do's." I took a course that set me up for promotion at work; built up my relationship with my husband's parents and persuaded him that this was the time to put in a new kitchen and fix up the garden. Her life would have bored me; mine would have stressed her out. Our mom just says it's lucky we didn't marry each other's husbands! ❞

Being happy may not mean having everything you want

Your body is building your baby. In the first three months the fetus shares pretty much everything that affects your body, bad and good. That's why in these early stages, sometimes even before a woman knows she is pregnant, the developing baby is at the highest risk of ill effects from drugs, infections, chemicals, and so forth.

Once the placenta is complete it filters out a lot of potentially harmful substances, but not all. If there's a high level of stress hormones such as cortisol in your bloodstream or a high level of alcohol, cortisol or alcohol will get through to your baby. That's proven. What is not agreed is exactly how much of what, at which stage of pregnancy, is likely to do harm.

Pregnancy health hazards

◆ **Smoking:** All health authorities recommend that pregnant women who smoke (and everyone else) should quit as soon as possible. A baby will be worse affected the more his mother smokes, but there's little discussion about "acceptable levels," partly because all smoking is risky and partly because an addicted smoker is unlikely to report accurately, or stick to, a low consumption. Fathers, or anyone who lives with a pregnant woman, should quit smoking too, because secondhand smoke may affect babies similarly.

Babies of mothers who smoke have an increased risk of being stillborn or born at low birth weight (they average 8 ounces/200 g lighter than the babies of comparable non-smokers). These ill effects are due to smoking acting to constrict blood vessels and therefore reducing the amount of oxygen that crosses the placenta.

◆ **Drinking alcohol:** The official recommendation in the U.S. is that women should not drink any alcohol at all during pregnancy. However, some women may find it difficult to give up a glass of wine with dinner or the occasional cocktail. According to the Surgeon General there is no known safe consumption level for pregnant women. It's a good idea to stop when you're thinking about getting pregnant, since alcohol consumption can make it more difficult to conceive, and because you won't know that you're pregnant in the first

few weeks. Almost half of the babies born in the United States are unplanned, though, so if you learn that you're pregnant but hadn't stopped drinking yet, stop right away.

Alcohol is especially risky to a baby in the womb; when it passes through the placenta into his body, it has to be processed by his liver just as alcohol on your side of the barrier has to be processed by yours. The liver is one of the last organs to mature, and so alcohol-processing in the womb is very inefficient. So the baby is exposed to more alcohol, and for longer, than you are.

The most serious risk to babies of mothers who drink heavily is Fetal Alcohol Syndrome (FAS), which may restrict growth, cause facial abnormalities, and damage sight, hearing, and learning. The most common ill effect is a reduced birth weight. FAS is completely preventable, since its only cause is exposure to alcohol in the womb. Keep your baby safe by avoiding alcohol from conception through birth.

In some countries, such as the UK, some health authorities believe that one or two drinks once or twice a week will do no harm, but in others there is zero tolerance for drinking in pregnancy; in the United States women have even been prosecuted for it on the grounds that their behavior endangers the child. However other authorities are reluctant to impose a ban-by-guilt, especially since an occasional glass is an important part of many women's relaxation and social life. They believe that parents-to-be should make up their own minds on this issue.

◆ **Coffee and other caffeine-containing drinks:** Caffeine—in coffee, tea, cocoa, and some cola drinks—acts as a stimulant to the heart and central nervous system, but potentially damaging effects, such as an increase in blood pressure, are related only to very high levels of consumption. Caffeine certainly passes the placental barrier, but no harmful effects on the fetus from moderate intakes have been found. However, the fact that a substance has not been shown to be harmful does not mean it could not be, and caffeine certainly may increase a pregnant woman's tendency toward palpitations or heartburn. Some research suggests that large amounts of caffeine may contribute to miscarriage, but other studies have conflicting results. The March of Dimes recommends a "safe level" not exceeding 200 mg of caffeine per day during pregnancy. (200 mg means 12 ounces of brewed coffee. Instant coffee has roughly half the amount of caffeine. Tea contains 48 mg per 8-ounce cup. Cocoa contains 8–12 mg. Soda contains 37 mg per 12-ounce can.)

Many foods carry a risk of food poisoning, and while nobody wants food poisoning, some food-borne infections are especially damaging to babies in the womb. Pregnant women are advised to avoid foods that are potential sources.

◆ **Unpasteurized cheeses:** Most dairy products in the United States are made with pasteurized milk, but some are made from raw, unpasteurized milk, including soft cheeses like Mexican-style Queso Fresco, Camembert, and similar soft cheeses, and blue-veined ones such as Stilton (and similar goat's and sheep's milk cheeses). These, as well as pates, including vegetable pates, can carry Listeria. Listeriosis is rare (about 1 in 20,000 pregnancies) but can cause miscarriage, stillbirth, or serious illness in newborns.

Official advice is to avoid these foods altogether and to be very cautious about other foods that may be prone to contamination with Listeria, such as creamy, ready-made dishes like coleslaw or refrigerated smoked seafood.

◆ **Incompletely-washed or undercooked foods:** Vegetables and fruits, raw or undercooked meat, and unpasteurized goat's milk or goats' cheese may carry a parasite that can give you Toxoplasmosis. Careful washing (or re-washing of bagged salads and other "ready-to-serve" items) and thorough cooking is important. Toxoplasmosis can also infect you from cat feces. If you must clean a litter box or do gardening where a cat may have been while you are pregnant, wear gloves and thoroughly wash your hands. Toxoplasmosis is extremely rare (it's estimated that between 400 and 4,000 babies per year are born with it in the United States) but the effects can include miscarriage or stillbirth, or survival with growth, sight, and hearing problems and various types of brain damage.

◆ **Raw or lightly cooked eggs:** Even organic eggs can carry Salmonella, as can seafood and inadequately cooked meat and poultry, especially dishes made from ground beef. All should be cooked thoroughly. Fortunately there are pasteurized alternatives to egg yolks in mayonnaise, or egg whites in meringue, commercially available, though there's no replacement for that soft-boiled egg. Salmonella is relatively common (there are about 40,000 U.S. cases per year), and hormonal changes mean that pregnant women are at an increased risk. The illness is unpleasant, with nausea, vomiting and diarrhea, but it poses no risk to fetuses.

◆ **Large oily fish:** Fresh tuna, trout, mackerel and sardines contain Omega 3 fats and that's good for you and for your baby's developing brain. However, some of these types of fish also contain levels of mercury that make a high intake of them risky to your developing baby's nervous system. Pregnant women are therefore advised to eat two servings of fish each week that are lower in mercury, such as salmon, shrimp, pollock, canned light tuna, and catfish. They should avoid eating shark, swordfish, king mackerel and tilefish, because these fish live for a long time and are therefore especially likely to accumulate risky levels of mercury in their bodies.

Late pregnancy is a great time for socializing, even though you need to be careful what you eat and drink.

Where would you like to have your baby?

Most women in North America opt to have their babies in the hospital, but some women go to birthing centers, and a small percentage choose to have home births.

The choice is an important one because it sets the scene for the kind of birth you are hoping for, and the way your prenatal care is organized and carried out depends on it. If you don't know much about what's available in your area, or about the differences between one kind of setting and another, do research: Search for hospitals and birthing centers on the internet; go visit them. But remember, now and when you make your detailed birth plan, that all through your pregnancy and labor your baby's health and safety and your own are the absolute priority— indeed the only things that really matter. So choose by all means, and make sure everyone involved knows how you'd like the birth to go, but don't get so hooked on your vision that anything different is disappointing. The calmer and more confident you feel during labor, the

Twin tip

If you are carrying twins you will automatically be booked for delivery in a hospital. You may be able to choose which hospital though, so do some local research.

smoother and easier it is likely to be. Labor is a delicately balanced process largely controlled by your hormones. The hormone oxytocin makes your uterus contract, but if you are stressed or anxious you secrete another hormone, adrenaline— an antagonist to oxytocin.

Hospitals, with their uniforms and rules and their sense of being separate from the ordinary world, intimidate some people, but make others feel safe in the hands of experts. The idea of having a baby at home scares some people—fathers as well as mothers—but seems comfortably private and personal to others.

From research

Unassisted birth. Giving birth without medical assistance is the choice of only tens of women a year, but the numbers are (slowly) growing. The American Medical Association and the American College of Obstetricians and Gynecologists oppose home births because of the potential for complications. Some women may be told that deliberately giving birth unassisted is illegal. It may be inadvisable, but it is not illegal. Nor is it illegal for a partner or friend to support a woman who has chosen to deliver without a doctor. Such a person would only be at risk of prosecution if he or she assisted at the birth pretending to be a doctor.

Hospital birth

If you or your coming baby have medical problems, you will need the care of a high-tech unit and be grateful that it is at hand. But many women having normal births do not need high-tech interventions and may sometimes be better off without any, since a small intervention can lead to bigger ones in a vicious circle: A hospital unit may have protocols that say how long the stages of labor should last. If your first stage is slow, then a drip can speed things up. But the drip-speeded contractions become more painful, so you need an epidural. Having an epidural increases the chances of your needing help with the delivery, and that help—forceps or ventouse—means an episiotomy and stitching…

Home birth

In North America, a very small percentage of babies are delivered at home. The American Medical Association and the American College of Obstetricians and Gynecologists oppose home births because of the potential for complications, even with low-risk pregnancies. However, the American College of Nurse-Midwives and the Society of Obstetricians and Gynaecologists of Canada support a woman's decision to have a home birth, if it's appropriate for her situation. Only healthy women with low-risk pregnancies and no pre-existing medical conditions should consider giving birth at home. Because you are in the familiar surroundings of your own home you may feel more in control. The only "aid" you cannot have at home is an epidural, which must be administered by an anesthetist, so are available only in hospital settings. A planned home birth can have a positive outcome, but

experts recommend a hospital birth. That word "planned" is important. Planning for a home birth doesn't necessarily mean that your baby will be born at home. If health problems crop up during your pregnancy or the baby is lying in an awkward position, you may need to change to a hospital birth. And even once labor has started at home, you may be transferred to a hospital if there are difficulties. An emergency transfer during labor is no fun, but studies suggest that women who had planned a home birth but had to be transferred to the hospital still felt that spending part of their labor at home made the experience worthwhile.

Birth center or midwife-run unit

If you are healthy and having a normal pregnancy but home birth isn't an option, or you or your partner don't like the idea, a birth center, or a low-tech hospital unit run by midwives, may be an excellent option. It increases your chances of having a normal labor and birth because intervention rates are much lower than in hospitals.

Warm water can help with relaxation and pain relief. If you're planning a home birth (and your hot water supply is up to it) you can buy or rent a birthing pool.

Prenatal testing

Tests commonly carried out in pregnancy are of two types.
Screening tests assess the chances that your baby is fine—or the
risk that he is not—and diagnostic tests tell you if he does or does
not have a chromosomal abnormality or inherited disorder.

Screening tests

These are a range of ultrasound scans and
blood tests; sometimes the results of the two go
together. Your first ultrasound scan at around 12
weeks not only gives an expected birth date but
also checks for normal growth and development.
A second scan carried out at about 18–22 weeks
is called the "fetal anomaly" (or anatomy) scan,
and looks in detail at your baby's overall growth
and at the shape of his head, his heart, his spine,
his limbs, and the rest of his body.

Increasing maternal age increases the (small)
risk of Down's syndrome and of Spina Bifida.
Women over 35 may be offered an integrated
test consisting of a "nuchal translucency (NT)
scan" measuring the amount of fluid between
two layers of skin at the back of your baby's
neck and, two or three weeks later, a blood test
to measure four pregnancy marker hormones
called "AFP" (alpha-fetoprotein); free B-human
chorionic gonadotrophone; unconjugated oestriol
and inhibin-A. Used together with your age, this
two-stage test has a detection rate of 85–90%.
While usually only older women, at higher risk,

are offered integrated tests by their doctors,
most women are offered a blood test called the
"double-triple-quadruple test" or the "maternal
serum screen." This measures "AFP" (Alpha-
fetoprotein); together with one (the double)
two (the triple) or three (the quadruple) of those
other principal pregnancy hormones. The more
hormones are measured, the more accurate the
test will be. A quadruple test will be about 75%
accurate, a triple 67–73% and a double 66%.

Screening tests are not invasive or unpleasant
and pose no risk to your baby, but they cannot
do what you want, which is to tell you for certain
whether or not your baby has any serious
problem. All they can tell you is the probability:
A 1-in-1000 probability after a particular test
suggests a very low risk; a probability of 1 in 150
is a higher risk, but there are still 149 chances
that your baby is fine. Although it varies from
place to place and hospital to hospital, a risk
greater than one chance in 250 is the cut off
point at which you are likely to be offered
diagnostic tests.

Diagnostic tests

These may be carried out on a sample of tissue
from the placenta (chorionic villus sampling
or CVS), on cells taken from the amniotic fluid
(amniocentesis), or from a blood sample taken
from the fetal vein in the umbilical cord
(cordocentesis). Which of these you are offered
depends not only on your hospital but also on
the stage of your pregnancy when problems
are suspected. CVS can only be carried out
at around 11 weeks; amniocentesis between
14 and 18 weeks and cordocentesis not before
18, but up to 24 weeks.

Parents talking about…

deciding on prenatal tests

❝We're both clear that we want this baby
whatever he is like; this is our baby and neither
of us would dream of Anna having an abortion.
But that leaves me saying "no more testing,
let's just take what we get," but Anna saying
"I want to have the amnio. I'd rather know so
I can prepare myself.❞

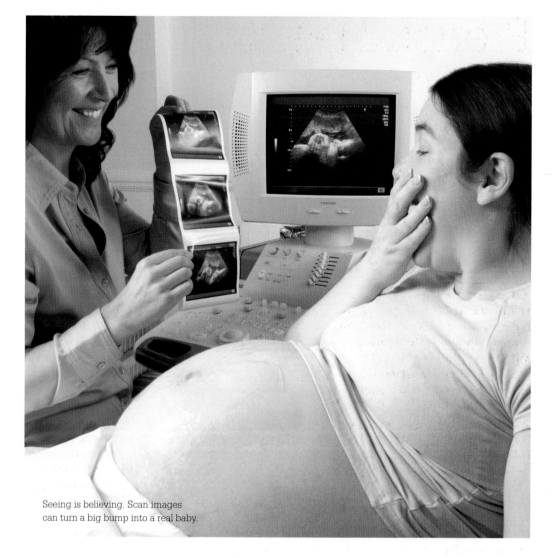

Seeing is believing. Scan images
can turn a big bump into a real baby.

Diagnostic tests are invasive and unpleasant and
they do carry a very small risk of miscarriage—
approximately 1 in 100 in many hospitals. However,
they can tell you almost definitely if your baby has
a chromosome abnormality or inherited disorder.
"Almost" because there is a risk of the diagnostic
test results being wrong, especially if you are very
overweight or underweight, or if you are a diabetic
and taking insulin. About 3 in 100 women who had
a nuchal translucency test and amniocentesis in
2007 and were informed they were carrying Down's
syndrome babies were not. Not everyone who is
offered diagnostic testing such as amniocentesis
goes for it, or should. It's a difficult decision that

the two of you need to make together and in
consultation with health professionals you trust.

An important consideration is what you
would do with any information a diagnostic test
gave you. If, for example, you think you would
want to terminate the pregnancy if Down's
syndrome was diagnosed (as 9 out of 10 women
do), then testing is probably appropriate—and
the sooner the better. But if you would not
consider a termination whatever a test showed,
there may be no point in having one; it may be
better for you to live with the level of risk you've
been told about and hang onto the fact that the
chances of your baby being unaffected are high.

Changing relationships

Since being pregnant changes both of you it will probably change your relationships as well, not only with each other, but also with your families and friends.

Relationships between partners can get off-kilter during pregnancy, which is a shame because the two of you really need to feel close and mutually supportive when it's time for birth and the baby. If there is a problem, now or afterward, it's likely to be related to the biological fact that the baby grows inside you, not him. As the mother, you may sometimes resent having to cope with all the pregnancy, birth, and breast-feeding discomforts while he gets away without any of them. But as the father, whose biological role was over months ago, he may be very vulnerable to feeling left out. You've each got real issues and you both need to talk and share feelings. If patterns set in during pregnancy such that you spend more and more time talking to your mother or your sister (and he either doesn't talk or spends more time with his chosen version of "the boys"), it may be very difficult to change them later. It can easily happen. Getting pregnant means you're going to add a new member to your existing families and that may bring you closer, especially to parents who are going to be grandparents. New closeness is fine—as long as it's with both of you and there are no tugs-of-love going on between your two families, but that's not always the case. New mothers tend to need their own mothers during this new stage in life, and mothers-in-law and the men of both generations are liable to feel excluded. And if you're among the first in your social group to have a baby, you may turn more and more to any available family because you begin to feel less close to friends and work colleagues. Child-free women are often not much interested in pregnancy symptoms or nursery décor, and don't feel so collegiate once they know you're soon going on maternity leave. You may hold on to some of these friends; they will visit you and the baby, gifts in hand, but only a few will keep coming to your house instead of going out on the town.

Building networks

If you're going to continue having a social life, and what's more a social life that involves both of you, even during the early months of parenthood, you need some new stage-specific friends: ideally other pregnant couples. Of course you won't necessarily have much else in common with couples just because they're pregnant. But then you probably didn't have much in common with some of the people you made friends with at school or work, either. You got together with them then because you were all in the same boat at the same time and place. The same applies now—although it's a different boat—and friendships that are short-term and baby-focused can fill the gap left by office acquaintanceships. Some may even still be friends when all the children have left home.

Twin tip

Some parents-to-be are thrilled to hear that they are going to have twins, but others—especially those who had no reason such as family history or IVF to anticipate it—are taken aback; even horrified. Either way, try to find and make friends with other parents of twins. Twin babies are mostly just like singleton babies, but bringing them up, and the details of how best to manage two at a time, are special, and the people who can best give you confidence that you'll be able to cope are people who are already coping.

Get fit and make friends at the same time. In the gym or the pool, this is one time in your life when there's no need to be shy about your figure or your skills.

An easy way to meet other pregnant couples who live locally is to join classes or activities specifically designed for you. If you are not a joining type, the idea may make you shudder. But as well as prenatal classes and parenting courses (which probably won't start until late in pregnancy) there's a range of activities available that are fun, will help you get (or stay) physically fit through your pregnancy, and provide opportunities to make new friends. Some are for women only, so once you meet someone you hit it off with, it will be up to you to bring partners together.

Pregnancy fitness classes: what you can expect

Find out about these "exercise" classes from your local gym or community center, or by searching the internet.

◆ **Pilates:** Especially suitable during pregnancy as it is a gentle form of exercise and helps condition abdominal and pelvic floor muscles. Classes designed for pregnant women will offer exercises adapted to each stage, and teach breathing techniques that may be useful in labor. If you cannot find a pregnancy-specific class, a general one will be fine, although it won't help you get to know other pregnant women. But be sure to tell the instructor you are pregnant.

◆ **Aquarobics:** These classes can be an excellent way to keep fit and supple. As pregnancy advances, the buoyancy and hydrostatic pressure make water-borne exercises feel more comfortable than land-based ones, and being relieved of the weight of your bulge is both relaxing and fun. You don't have to be able to swim, as long as you aren't afraid of the water, but do tell the instructor if you are a non-swimmer so that you aren't taken out of your comfort zone.

◆ **Aerobics:** Aerobic exercise strengthens heart, lungs, and muscles, which is just as good for pregnant women as for everyone else. Find a special pregnancy-aerobics class if you can, though. General classes probably won't have many pregnant members and may include kicks and leaps that aren't suitable for you.

◆ **Yoga:** Many parents-to-be find yoga extremely helpful in pregnancy, helping you to be—and remain—supple, while the breathing techniques help you relax and focus. Some types of yoga, such as Bikram, may not be suitable, though, and you'll get more help with labor from pregnancy-specific yoga.

Birth preparation classes

These are run by hospitals or privately by certified instructors, usually for a small fee. Your doctor will be able to recommend classes for you to attend, and you are encouraged to bring your partner along. Classes will not usually start until you are in your third trimester, but ask your doctor if you need to book early, especially for private classes. Some courses can take place over an eight-week period, while others are one-shot, all-day sessions. You should be able to find something that will mesh well with your schedule. The Lamaze Method and the Bradley Method are two commonly offered types of courses.

Prenatal classes vary, but whatever kind of classes you attend you can be sure of meeting up with other couples, and you may well make real friendships. Having "children" the same age is as much a bond at 30 weeks of pregnancy as it is at the school gate five years later. Relationships with couples whose babies are born within a week or two of yours often turn into informal "postpartum support groups" and people with whom to explore local parent-and-baby activities, from baby massage to moms' movie screenings.

◆ **Hospital-run classes:** The hospital where you plan to give birth will almost certainly offer classes, but some are little more than a couple of sessions and a tour of the maternity unit. Talk to your doctor about additional resources if necessary.

Any course should cover: signs that labor is beginning; stages of labor; options for pain relief; and interventions such as induction, assisted deliveries, and Caesareans. The focus is generally on hospital birth, so you may need to go elsewhere if you're interested in information about home births. Some courses cover baby-care topics and a few also feature breast-feeding workshops. Arrangements for fathers range from a somewhat tokenistic "fathers' session" to full participation.

◆ **Independent courses:** Most of these cover a similar range of topics, but in smaller groups (sometimes, just you and your partner) and in more detail. Course topics vary by the instructors, who may be nurses. The International Childbirth Education Association certifies childbirth educators. To find a certified instructor in your area, visit www.icea.org. Birth partners, whether fathers or not, are welcomed.

Birth partners

Even if the first class is still four months away, having a prenatal course scheduled makes the actual birth seem very real. This might be a good time to talk about who will be with you in the delivery room. You don't have a choice about being there yourself, but you do have a choice about who will be there with you.

Chances are that the two of you will agree that your partner should be with you throughout. Only about 10% of today's fathers don't see their babies born (and some of those miss the moment by mistake). However some of the 90% of fathers are more spectators than birth

---

You may hear...

birthing experts such as Michel Odent say that labor often goes faster and more smoothly when only women are present. While that's a minority view, some midwives think that having a woman birth companion as well as their partner is helpful to a lot of mothers.

that "natural birth" requires particular breathing techniques. If you did hear this it was probably from someone who had a baby in the 1960s. At that time, women in Lamaze classes practiced a certain type of breathing that was intended to help them through labor, but women today learn a variety of methods that can help them feel more comfortable during labor and birth, instead of specific breathing techniques.

Active birth workshops combine pregnancy-specific yoga with practical birth preparations for both parents.

partners, and that may not be the most helpful option for the mother in labor.

A committed birth partner who learned with you through pregnancy can be completely involved emotionally though totally unaffected physically. That means that he can help you make the best possible use of the coping techniques you have been taught, and give you physical support. And, as labor advances and you abandon your normal self to the birth process, you can leave him or her as your alter ego: watching over your interests and the baby's, and communicating your needs to the doctor and nurses. As labor progresses, drawing you deeper and deeper into the vortex of birth, that partner may become your only link with reality. Doctors come and go, checking up, listening in, but as the world becomes a blur of strange effort they vanish into the fog, leaving his the only face you can still see clearly; his words the only ones you can still understand. What finally emerges is a truly mutual baby.

But there will always be some people who do not want it that way. Every pair of people who are going to have to incorporate a child into their partnership must also find a way of incorporating the experience of childbirth into their

relationship, but it certainly does not have to happen in the same way for everyone. Fathers who sit out difficult births in waiting rooms are not necessarily failing their partners, and neither are mothers who prefer all-female support in the delivery room. Feeling together matters far more than being together.

Of course, some women aren't with the father—or any partner—during pregnancy and birth. Whatever your particular situation, you will need a birth companion. If the baby's father is with you but won't be taking that role, it's better for both of you to acknowledge it from the get-go. It doesn't necessarily mean that he can't be there to see his baby born, it just means that he spectates (and is free to go out of the room for some of the tough parts), and you have someone else to participate. If you're on your own the choice of that someone else is even more crucial. It could be a doula (professional birth partner) whom you employ; it could be your mother or your sister or your best friend.

Parents talking about...
fathers as birth partners

❝ She took it for granted that I'd be there and I didn't give it much thought: just went along with it. When it came to the dads' evening at the hospital, though, I was a bit taken aback to find that these guys had been going along to all the classes, practicing breathing for labor, and learning all sorts of massage and stuff. I read some books but I was way behind and the more I read the less confident I felt. We got to the hospital OK, and the first hour or two were fine. She liked holding my hand and she laughed at my jokes. Once labor got going, though, I felt completely useless. I *was* completely useless. Truth is I was shocked. I hated seeing her in pain, didn't know what I could do to help, and eventually got moved out of the way by the nurses. Yes, I was there when River was born but I stayed up at the head end and didn't see her come out. ❞

Making a birth plan

The primary reason to make a birth plan is to help you and your birth companion think about labor and envision how you would like things to go.

If your birth plan is to help you communicate effectively with your doctor, make sure it fits with the setting where you'll have the baby. There's no point stressing that your priority is maximum pain relief if you are planning a home delivery—you won't be able to have an epidural. Or that you want several children present if you'll be booked into a hospital—they will not be allowed in the delivery room. Or setting your mind on a water birth if you've chosen a birth center with no birthing pool.

Once labor gets going the best laid labor plans can change, and a lot of details—music, lotions, and so forth – get forgotten. The planning is still worthwhile, though. Some of the issues that are addressed in a birth plan require you to do some research and talk to your doctor before you write them in.

Issues to think about for your birth plan

◆ **Birthing pool:** Do you want to use a birthing pool? If so, only for pain relief in labor or also to give birth in?

◆ **Caesarean birth:** Would you prefer to be asleep or awake? And if you were awake, would you want to see what was going on?

◆ **Eating and drinking in labor:** Talk to your doctor about what is recommended.

◆ **Episiotomy:** Of course nobody wants an episiotomy, but would you still want to avoid being surgically cut if you were warned that you were at risk of a tear?

◆ **Induction:** If your baby was overdue, would you want to wait as long as possible before being induced?

◆ **Massage:** Do you want massage in labor? Would you like help with this from a doula or your birth partner?

◆ **Monitoring/Mobility:** How important to you is being free to move around in labor? Are you comfortable accepting monitoring that confines you to bed, including continuous electronic monitoring or a fetal scalp electrode, or would you prefer intermittent electronic monitoring, or only a handheld sonicaid device?

◆ **Pain relief:** Do you plan to use only self-help techniques such as breathing, positioning, and massage? Do you want TENS (transcutaneous electrical nerve stimulation)? Would you want to rely on laboring in water for pain relief? Might you consider hypnosis or meditation? Would you like an epidural as soon as active labor is confirmed or would you prefer to do without one?

◆ **Managing the third stage of labor (cutting the umbilical cord and delivery of the placenta):** Active management is designed to reduce the possibility of bleeding (postpartum hemorrhage). It involves giving you (with your permission) an injection of syntometrin (or equivalent drug) as the baby is delivered and clamping and cutting the cord immediately. This encourages the uterus to clamp down quickly; the placenta is usually delivered within 20 minutes. A physiological third stage delays clamping and cutting the cord until it has stopped pulsing

Twin tip

If you're carrying twins you will be booked for hospital delivery and the chance of you having a C-section is roughly twice as high (50–60%) as it would be if you were having a single baby (25–30%). Still, that means that there's an almost 50% chance of you having an entirely normal delivery—so go ahead and make that birth plan.

blood to the baby, and does nothing to hurry delivery of the placenta which may take as much as an hour. Think about what you would prefer.

◆ **Cutting the cord:** Do you want to delay this? Does your partner want to be the one to cut the cord? Do you want the baby delivered directly onto your bare belly and to be helped to nurse within a few minutes?

◆ **Nursing:** Will you want to try breast-feeding your baby for the first time in the labor and delivery room?

◆ **Special Care:** If your baby needed to go to the hospital's neonatal intensive care unit (NICU), would you want your birth companion to accompany the baby or stay with you until you could go too?

Even if your birth plan is forgotten on the day, making it will help you think through your hopes and fears.

Thinking ahead about being parents

After their babies are born, many people say their prenatal classes were too focused on birth and should have included more about life later on.

The real problem, though, is often parents rather than courses. Many pregnant parents find it extraordinarily difficult to think about life after birth, so however much information they are offered they don't take it in. Sometimes parents leave the "newborn" chapters of books until their babies have been born, and then are too busy and exhausted to get around to reading them.

The point of being pregnant isn't having a birth, it's having a baby, and once yours is born someone will have to care for her 24/7 for at least 10 years. Talking about who is going to do that and how it's going to be managed will get you started on thinking about living with a baby, and checking out which ideas and attitudes you do and don't share. You may find some surprises. A lot of parents say they are going to share the baby's care, but mothers and fathers often have different ideas of what "shared care" or "joint parenting" actually is. Does equal sharing mean equal hours, 50/50 down the line, or can it be one parent doing a quarter to the other's three-quarters? A lot of couples build their child's care around one-and-a-half full-time jobs, but which of you will be which? Don't just assume that you'll be the one to work part time. It usually is the mother, but that doesn't mean it should be or has to be.

At the other extreme there are many mothers and fathers who still have a traditional view of family roles, seeing women as children's primary carers whom fathers should assist but not replace, and men as the principal earners, whom women should assist but not replace. In between there are many other approaches to parenthood, and the ones you hold today may well change before your maternity leave is over. What is important right now, in pregnancy, is that each of you should be aware of the other's thinking.

Until a child of your own became an imminent reality one or both of you may have assumed that in an ideal modern partnership (such as yours!) fathers and mothers are indistinguishably "parents." Now, though, you both need to think that through. However far modern parenting encroaches on old established maternal and paternal roles, differences between mothers, fathers, and others are inescapable biological facts. People can't get rid of them by pretending that gender and gene differences do not exist or by ignoring them or keeping quiet about them, and anyway it is not the facts themselves that cause the evils of sexism and elitism, but their traditional social implications. Those are what need changing.

You may hear...

a child brings a couple together. In fact, a first child is a marriage's biggest stressor. A baby puts a biological bomb under the illusions of sexual equality that build up when single, childless men and women share workplaces. Babies ruin sex, that vital relationship-glue, at least for a while. They ruin finances, lifestyles, and careers—especially women's careers. In fact becoming parents clearly puts people at a disadvantage compared with peers who have taken a no-children route. However, most parents say that children also give them a kind of pleasure, a depth of emotional satisfaction, that nothing else brings.

A seldom-mentioned part of the preparation for parenthood: finding out how to manage the baby's equipment.

Before long you are going to be "Mommy" and "Daddy" to a new person. Each of you is a separate individual, and gender is a basic part of who you will be to your child as it is basic to who you are to yourselves and to each other. We are, at last, pruning out stereotypes about who can take care of a baby with colic, create and embroider a bedtime ritual or a quilt, play particular games, or model particular behaviors. We're beginning to uproot the old assumption that no man can take full care of a child and every woman can. But whatever fathers and mothers do with their children, however fully they share their care, those children will always remain aware of differences in the ways they do it, and parts of those differences will always be associated with gender.

Family

Children will always be aware of differences between mothers and fathers and other parent figures or caregivers. In the course of childhood, more and more children experience life in different households where a succession of adults function as family. A divorce, followed by even one lover per parent and one new spouse each, makes five parenting combinations, and each new combination may bring the child new grandparent, aunt, or uncle figures, as well as quasi-adult step- or half-siblings. Adoption, not only of infants within cultures but of older children and across cultures, further complicates family, while egg and sperm donation and surrogacy are beginning to complicate it even further. While everyone should realize that a blood relationship with a child doesn't make a mother or father, nobody should believe that mothering or fathering a child makes him or her into the child's parent. Stepparents and foster parents are substitute mother and father figures; enormously important, sometimes preferable, but never the same. Even adults who adopt infants and are the only parents those children have ever known are still replacements for the parents they had but never knew. People will always want to know about their origins.

You go from being pregnant to being a parent in a flash (or perhaps a yell): no chance to put one behind you before you start on the other. Mostly that doesn't matter: You can ease yourselves into having this baby outside rather than inside during a few days' babymoon. If you've never before been much involved with babies, though, you might be caught unawares by a few issues that you need to act on right away. If you haven't thought about them, or discussed them, you might even find yourselves disagreeing.

Parents talking about...
circumcising their baby

❝ I just never gave it a thought and when I did give it a thought I freaked. Make his poor little penis really sore on purpose? What's that about? No way. And when my mother-in-law said "but of course" and my husband didn't say anything…well, it was a bad scene. **❞**

Circumcision

One such issue may be circumcision. "May be" because it won't be an issue if your baby is a girl or if you are both practicing members of the Jewish faith. In all other circumstances you need to get some talking—and maybe arguing—about circumcision out of the way ahead of time.

The universal ill effect of circumcision is that the procedure causes pain and shock and a very sore penis for several days, which is not a happy start for a new baby. If you plan a non-ritual circumcision of your newborn son, ask for pain relief for him. If a circumcision is carried out after the first few days it should be performed under general anesthetic—which of course carries risks of its own.

Everyday matters

Most of the decisions you'll have to make quickly aren't quite that all-or-nothing. But it's still a good idea to make sure the two of you have roughly the same amount of information (both having some is better than one having lots and the other none) and either a similar viewpoint or a genuinely open mind.

◆ **Feeding:** It's surprising how often first-time parents have different ideas about how the baby will be fed. Of course the final decision on that one will be down to you since you will either breast-feed your baby or you won't. But you still need your partner to have an educated view, and you need to know what his view is. If you plan to breast-feed, his support will play a big part in helping you get started and keep going; on the other hand, any lack of support, dismissiveness, let alone disapproval, will make it more likely that you'll soon be bottle-feeding. If you don't want to breast-feed, though, or you aren't sure that you do, it might be a shock to find that your partner is assuming that you will.

It may be useful and fun to explore each other's views about a few things where there isn't a one-time and immediate decision to be made. Having the baby share your bed or have her bed in your room, for instance.

From research

Changing rates of circumcision. Circumcision is less common in this generation than in the last. Only 65% of newborns were circumcised in 1999, but 79% of adults surveyed between 1999 and 2004 said that they had been circumcised. The American Academy of Pediatrics doesn't routinely recommend the procedure for newborns, due to insufficient data.

Carried out without anesthesia the procedure itself is acutely painful; the administration of local anesthesia is not pain-free, and general anesthesia has its own risks. There are risks to the operation itself, ranging from universal soreness and distress leading to a setback in establishing feeding and weight gain, to infection or hemorrhage, which are very rare—probably less than 1%.

However, research findings suggesting major health benefits of circumcision to populations have been accumulating for a generation, and are now being widely acknowledged. Circumcised men have lower rates of cancer of the penis, and their partners are less likely to have cervical cancer. They also acquire and pass on lower incidences of sexually transmitted diseases, including HIV.

The World Health Organization and UNAIDS now recommend universal male circumcision. The influential Centers for Disease Control and Prevention notes that in African studies, circumcision was associated with a lower risk of HIV infection. Because of this, circumcision may have a role in HIV prevention in the United States; the CDC is developing public health guidelines.

◆ **Sleeping:** Not getting enough sleep, or having sleep constantly disturbed, is a very big issue for many parents. In fact many people whose children are older still say that night-waking was the worst thing about having babies.

It's very difficult to know what you will feel when you come to it, but it's still worth thinking about the approach you hope you'll take if this turns out to be a problem area for you. New babies have to be fed in the night—and not-so-new babies often demand night feedings, too. Some parents decide to have the baby in bed with them so that his feedings are as quick and easy as possible. Other parents are equally sure that they'd rather keep getting up to the baby than lose their privacy to a family bed.

There are pros and cons to both approaches (*see p. 103*). Sharing a bed with your baby is thought by some health authorities to make it very slightly more likely that he will be one of the rare victims of Sudden Infant Death Syndrome (SIDS), but others stress that on a global scale, bed-sharing is normal. There is even some research that suggests that a baby in your bed is actually safer than a baby on his own—unless you have been drinking or taking drugs. A compromise might be to have a co-sleeper, or bedside-bassinet for your baby that attaches to your adult bed. (*see p. 105*)

The opposite approach gives your baby his own separate bed from the beginning (though it's advisable to have him in the same room) and does everything possible to make sure that's where he sleeps. The advantage is that as long as the baby sleeps well you have much more privacy and freedom to conduct your night life as you wish. The disadvantage is that every time he wakes and cries one of you has to get up and go to him, and stay up—or at least be kept awake—until he goes back to sleep.

When the two of you are talking about this, there are three things you need to be aware of. Firstly, that if the choice of sleeping place was left to a baby he would invariably choose a family bed over a crib of his own. Babies love sleeping close to a parent, and once they have done so for a few weeks they make it extraordinarily difficult for parents to change their minds and put them

to sleep alone. Secondly the "third way," leaving your baby to cry himself to sleep, isn't really an option now that we know what damaging effects being left to cry unanswered can have on babies' brains. Thirdly, your baby's sleep and waking patterns won't stop being an issue just because he stops needing to be fed in the night. Many babies go on waking every night. Some have phases when they wake with some kind of nightmare, and all wake a great deal when they are cutting a tooth or have a cold or a sore bottom. So one way or another, your baby will wake, and when he wakes he will want you.

◆ **Diapers:** Yes, it's even worth talking about diapers. It's not going to matter to the baby what kind you use, but when the time comes, discovering that you disagree about fundamentals, like "cloth or disposable, and bio or not?" may make it more difficult to sort out who changes the diapers and who does the laundry.

The contemporary choice is a lot more complicated than it used to be, although you still have to decide between disposable and washable. There are eco-friendly disposables made of biodegradable materials, and there are pre-shaped cloth diapers with separate waterproof covers—almost as easy to put on as disposables and made of quick-drying (usually bamboo-based) material. Both of these options are more environmentally friendly and more expensive than supermarket disposables and basic cloth diapers. In a few years, using cheaper disposables may become "green" as new recycling options develop, extracting the methane to generate new energy and turning the diapers into plant pots.

Twin tip

Don't let the fact that you are going to have twins overwhelm everything else. Talk about how you both feel about, say, family beds or breast-feeding in principle. Only when you know what approach you'd like to take to a particular issue is it time to talk about managing it times two.

Practical planning

In addition to thinking about what it will feel like to be parents, it's a good idea to give some thought to this new lifestyle. For a start, you need to know how much maternity or parental leave you are entitled to and how much you'll be paid.

Maternity rights and regulations are extremely complex. It's never too early in pregnancy to start finding out about them, because getting what you are entitled to from your employer or from state benefits, or what your employer will give you under the terms of its own plan, may depend on giving advance notice. (Leave and benefits options differ in Canada. Contact your human resources department and your provincial or territorial government for details.)

◆ **Pregnant employees:** If you're eligible to be covered by the U.S. Family and Medical Leave Act (FMLA), you can take up to 12 weeks off when you have your baby and still retain your right to go back to the same or an equivalent position at your company. You'll need to have worked for your company for at least 12 months, including at least 1,250 hours during the previous year, and the company must employ at least 50 people. To take advantage of the coverage, employees are required to tell their employers 30 days before they plan to begin taking leave. Employers are required to continue your health insurance coverage during your absence. FMLA is unpaid, but a small percentage of companies (9%) offer paid maternity leave to employees. (About half of the companies that offer paid leave pay for six weeks or less, according to a recent report from the Institute for Women's Policy Research.) Every company has its own policies, which a human resources representative can explain. Some companies allow their employees to use sick or vacation time toward maternity leave. A handful

Get organized while you've still got time on hand. Shopping that's fun now may be impossible later.

of states offer new mothers paid maternity leave, and other states may follow suit.

◆ **Paternity leave:** Very few new fathers in the United States receive paid paternity leave. If you want to take time off when your baby is born, you may need to rely on sick days, vacation time, or FMLA leave.

Plan carefully

Not everyone takes as much maternity leave as they can get, and you may need to work out the household's finances before you can plan yours. Don't assume that you will wait until the baby is born to start you leave, though. Many women used to work right up until the first sign of labor in order to save every precious day of maternity leave to spend with their baby. But some women opt to begin maternity leave a bit early, taking time off to rest and play for a few days or weeks before the birth; some research suggests that this may be good for the baby as well as for you. If there is an older child or children in the family, this may be an especially valuable time to strengthen your bonds and get excited together.

If there are things you want or need to do to your home before the baby is born (other than making a nursery, which is more a project for you than a necessity for the baby), don't leave it until the last minute so that it's touch and go whether the new baby or the new boiler arrive first.

From research

Health benefits of aid maternity leave.
Every 10 weeks reduces infant mortality and morbidity (ill health) rates by 5% according to international research. The obvious reason for this is that the longer the leave, the easier it is for women to breast-feed. Another explanation is thought to be that knowing they have a long leave available to them makes it easier for many women to give up work well before their due date rather than working right up until the birth to maximize the time they will have at home with the baby.

Twin tip

Figure out how you will handle "twinness."
Whether they are biologically identical or not, and whether they are both boys, both girls, or one of each if they are fraternal, your two babies may or may not look alike. A difference in birth weight can mean that identical twins look very different, while a strong family resemblance can mean that your fraternal twin girls are hard for a stranger to tell apart. In these next months you'll need to establish a family policy about how much their twin status is emphasized by their clothes and possessions.

The best policy is probably "as little as possible." Your babies are never, for one minute, going to forget that they are twins, and neither are family members. So why emphasize it in outward ways? Better, surely, to emphasize what may sometimes be forgotten: that they are two members of the family who happen to be the same age.

Twin babies dressed alike look cute and attract attention (sisters dressed alike do, too) but that's not a good enough reason to buy them identical clothing. Later on they may prefer to dress alike or wear the same outfits in different colors, but until or unless they make that choice it's probably better to dress them individually. That doesn't mean they can't both wear blue pants if that's what's clean, but it does mean that you don't go out of your way to make a point of it. As to toys and equipment: They will often have the same stuff because it's age-appropriate, available, and affordable, but don't insist on color-matching or assign each child a particular color so that red cups and toothbrushes always belong to X and blue ones to Y.

If they do grow to look very similar, it's important to make it easy for grandparents, teachers, and neighbors to tell them apart so that they don't fall back on saying "Hello, twins." If different haircuts don't do it, try name tags or bracelets. Whatever you think up, though, mischievous three-year-olds will have fun swapping....

Planning a "babymoon"

Honeymoons to give newly married couples peaceful time to get to know each other are taken for granted, but babymoons are not. That's a pity because most contemporary brides and bridegrooms already know each other a very great deal better than parents know a new baby.

If ever you need time, privacy, and permission to gaze into someone's eyes, talk endless nonsense, and cuddle her a lot, it will be after your baby is born.

If this is your first baby and you and her father are living together you can probably arrange to have a few days to concentrate on her and on each other just by getting organized in advance. You may want an answering machine to make it easier to space out (and select) visitors, and your home will probably need some attention after those hours of early labor, to make your bed, bedroom, and bathroom luxurious places to spend time. Other than that all it takes is easy and delicious meals in the freezer and favorite snacks and drinks in the fridge. If you're living on your own, though, you will need somebody to stay with you at least for a few days: somebody who will concentrate on your comfort while you concentrate on your baby.

Parents talking about...

"babymoons"

❝ The first time around we really did have a babymoon, even though it wasn't one baby but two! Second time, though, with twin two-year-olds waiting for us, it wasn't so easy. I did spend a lot of time in our bed with the baby, though, which meant it was safe for the twins to hold him and I was pretty boring so they soon wandered off. Their father spent a lot of time with them but didn't feel he was entirely missing out on Charlie because every time a grandparent said "what can I do to help?" we'd say "take the twins out to the playground" and the minute he'd seen them off he'd run for the bedroom. ❞

Visitors and helpers

Too many visitors can be exhausting, especially if they come with little or no notice and seem to think that a bunch of flowers or some tiny pajamas entitles them to drinks (leaving you cups to wash) and more cuddles than your baby is up for. The best visitors call first, come when invited, think your baby is the most scrumptious ever and want to hear every detail of the labor and delivery from each of your points of view (not the baby's perhaps). If you have lots of relatives who feel (and perhaps are) entitled to see and greet this baby early on, and especially if you are going to have twins (which fascinate everyone), you might consider having them all to lunch at once. Get each couple or person to bring a dish for everyone (if they compete with each other you'll probably have lots of delicious food) and enlist the most reliable of them to clear up afterward.

If there's going to be a roomful of excited people, you might want to leave the baby next door when she's sleeping, just taking people in to peep at her. When you bring her in to feed, you don't have to let everyone hold her. "Grandparents only," or "the pediatrician says to guard against colds" work well.

The right helper can make a huge difference to these first couple of weeks after birth. The right person is someone you both love who will happily take care of everything but the baby; keeping the household running just well enough for you not to get frantic while you concentrate on your newborn. It's great if she's a mother herself (yours or his maybe) and can give you her opinion when you ask for it, even show you the easiest way to do something, but it's not so great if her efficiency makes you feel inefficient or if she has strong views that make your toes curl. Don't invite somebody who always irritates or upsets one of you, even if she seems ideal in every other way, unless you are having not just a baby but twins.

The first few weeks with two newborn babies is more than any one person ought to have to cope with, and a big challenge for two. What's more, most mothers of twins feel anxious about being on their own with the babies for hours at a time, so you will continue needing someone to help once your partner is back at work, even if it's not the person you'd have chosen.

You probably won't enjoy having somebody living in your home whom you don't feel very warmly toward, even though you're grateful to her for helping out, so as soon as you feel more confident about coping, consider getting some domestic help sessions through an agency, leaving relations and friends to be welcome visitors.

Twin tip

It's not enough to decide how you two think about "twinness": You also need to think about how your families may feel, because if you intend to highlight the babies' individuality rather than their similarities, you may need to be clear and assertive with your relatives from the beginning, since their expectations may differ.

The arrival of twins in the family is still the cause for much excitement, and most people expect twins to look identical—or at least look very similar. Some of your relatives may actually be disappointed if the babies "don't look like twins."

Quiet, alert and looking: It's never too soon for you and your new baby to get to know each other.

When will your pregnancy end?

Nobody can give you an exact answer to that question unless you're having a Caesarean. You've known your Expected Date of Delivery since the pregnancy was confirmed, or since a dating scan at the end of the first trimester, but babies are seldom born on the expected day—less than half in the expected week.

A pregnancy is said to be of normal length if it lasts between 37 and 41 weeks. The average length of a twin pregnancy is 37 rather than 40 weeks. Any baby born before 37 weeks gestation is said to be premature, a baby born after 42 weeks is post-mature.

Under ideal circumstances, babies instigate their own births. When they are ready to be born (usually at somewhere around 40 weeks) their adrenal glands release a hormone (known as DHEA) which travels to the placenta triggering the production of estrogen and eventually the onset of contractions.

Occasionally labor begins before the optimum time, or, if the baby or the mother is thought to be at risk, labor may be induced early. Since it is still difficult to be sure exactly how "old" a baby in the womb is, any induction carries at least some risk that a baby who was thought to be at term will turn out to be pre-term, or that a baby known to be pre-term will be "younger" than expected. How important the prematurity is depends on its extent. A baby born at 36 weeks may have no problems. A baby born at 33 weeks will have less serious problems than she would have had if she had been born at 30 weeks.

Sometimes a baby is induced because labor fails to start at the end of a normal-length pregnancy. The potential problems of post-maturity are not as widely recognized as those of prematurity but are just as real. If baby and mother are both doing well, pregnancy will usually be allowed to overrun by a week or more. Sometimes when labor shows no signs

of beginning by week 42 it's because the pregnancy hasn't actually been going on quite that long. There may have been a miscalculation of the date of conception, the mother's menstrual cycle may be extra-long, or she may have conceived unusually late in it. Under any of those circumstances a 42 week pregnancy may actually have lasted 41 weeks.

It's a pity to induce a baby if she was almost but not quite ready to instigate her own birth, but it's risky to wait for long, because by the end of pregnancy the placenta is reaching the end of its useful life. Labor's failure to begin may be caused by placental insufficiency or may lead to it and if placental function is failing or begins to fail, the baby is at risk. This is why once your due date has come and gone your baby's wellbeing will be very carefully monitored.

Small-for-dates babies

Decisions about whether it is better for a baby if the mother's pregnancy continues, or if she is induced are always difficult and never more so than when the baby is thought to be "small for gestational age" (SGA) or small-for-dates.

There's nothing wrong with a baby being small if that is the size her genetic inheritance meant her to be. You may hear her referred to as "constitutionally small," and the likelihood is that you and your husband, and perhaps your own parents and siblings, are smaller than average. However some babies are not just unusually small but smaller than they should be for their gestational age because they are suffering from

Whose birthday first,
yours, or your baby's?

"intra-uterine growth restriction" (IUGR). This
may be because they have health problems or
because they are not receiving everything they
need through the placenta. Distinguishing
between a constitutionally small baby and one
suffering from growth restriction is important.
The earlier the distinction can be made the
better, and the longer the pregnancy continues
the more crucial it becomes. A constitutionally
small baby should be allowed to go to full term
like any other baby, but a baby suffering from
growth restriction is at increasing risk of
complications, including stillbirth, as the
pregnancy nears its end and especially if she
becomes post-mature. Despite her small size,
and the risks associated with prematurity, a
baby who is not growing as she should may
need rescuing before she reaches full term.

From research

Fetal size. If there are concerns about a fetus'
size, detailed measurements will be calculated
from sophisticated scans and a customized
prenatal growth chart known as GROW
(Gestation Related Optimal Weight) may be
used to track infant growth. GROW chart
software calculates an individualized weight
standard for the stage in pregnancy and
expected date of delivery, adjusted for details
of parity, maternal height, weight early in
pregnancy, and ethnic group. The charts can
be used to plot estimated fetal measurements
and weight against the individually predicted
and standard growth points.

Birth

After long months of waiting, talking, and wondering, going into labor can feel like a climax. It isn't of course. It's not birth you've been waiting for, but the person who will be born.

It's his or her arrival in your shared world that will be the real climax of your pregnancy, and from the moment you become parents you will have to act as parents. Of course labor matters, and birth is a personal drama, but don't expect too much of yourselves and each other during those hours. It's fine to have read and thought and planned for the birth, but neither your body nor your baby was in on all that, and between the two, things may turn out quite differently. Try to hang on to the fact that the only point of labor is bringing the baby from inside you to outside. The only criterion of a "good birth" is getting the baby out with both of you in the best possible shape. Doing that is what matters, not how you do it. Try not to let yourself get so set on a home birth or a water birth that having your baby in a hospital feels disappointing. Don't be so determined to be the best birth partner ever that having your massage rejected and your wet cloths and ice cubes batted away hurts your feelings. Above all do make sure that you both feel able to be flexible about pain relief. It's a mistake to let yourselves get so carried away by plans for a "natural birth" that you discount even the possibility of medical help. If a time comes when you feel you need pain relief you should have it—and your partner should know better than to argue with you ("but honey, you said not to let them give you anything…"). On the other hand it's a mistake to avoid thinking about pain in labor because you are assuming that you'll have an immediate epidural. You might not be in established labor; the anesthetist might be too busy to come right away; when she does come your labor might be too far advanced. You need to feel confident in your own resources; ready to cope with whatever it takes to get this baby out, and clear that doing that is all that matters. Few

things are sadder than a woman who has just given birth to a healthy baby feeling like a failure because things didn't go as planned, or angry because nobody listened to her.

We know a lot about what birth is like for mothers but very little about what it is like for babies. People have likened the baby's experience to squeezing through an impossibly narrow cave, but all we actually know, from babies' rapid changes of heart rate, and from shock reactions, is that the experience is physically dramatic.

It is the shock of being forced out of the warm, dark, liquid environment of the womb into cool air and light, noise, and texture, that triggers your baby's first efforts to breathe for himself. The blood pulsing in the umbilical cord is still giving him oxygen, but the placenta,

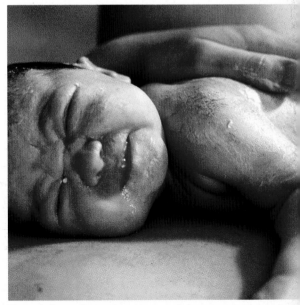

The real climax of your pregnancy: your baby.

which carried oxygen from your bloodstream to his, is no longer functioning so he must breathe.

Your new baby cannot do this easily until his nose and mouth are clear of amniotic fluid and mucus, so unless he does breathe spontaneously, the midwife will use gentle suction to clear those passageways. Once he is safely breathing, he needs time to rest, muster new resources and

discover the different comfort of being on your soft belly instead of inside it. Now that he is safely delivered there's no more need for bright lights and bustle. His new surroundings can be low-key: kind to senses bombarded for the first time with unfiltered light, unmuffled sound.

If everything in his new world is toned down, and your baby is left in peace on you instead

Your options for childbirth

During an office visit early in your pregnancy, your doctor should explain to you the type of care that you'll receive at the hospital when you deliver your baby. If you or your birth partner have any questions, don't hesitate to ask.

◆ Every aspect of your care should be explained to you and should take account of your needs and preferences, whether these are religious, ethnic, cultural, or due to additional factors such as physical or learning disabilities, or difficulties with understanding or speaking English. An interpreter should be provided for you if necessary.
◆ You can ask any questions and can change your mind at any time.
◆ Wherever you have your baby, the following forms of pain relief may be available from your partner, midwife, nurse, or doctor: breathing and relaxation techniques; being in water (not every hospital offers a bathtub or birthing pool for labor or delivery; find out in advance if it's important to you); massage by your birth partner; analgesic drugs given by injection. Epidurals though, have to be administered by anesthetists and are therefore only available in a hospital.
◆ If you do have an epidural, a low-dose version should be available so that you can continue to move around. Once started, the epidural should be continued until the placenta has been delivered and any necessary stitches put in.
◆ Once you are in labor you should not be left on your own unless you choose to be. As well as encouraging your birth partner to support you, the nurse assigned to you should offer you one-to-one care.

◆ A nurse will check your baby's heartbeat every 15 minutes, or more frequently, using a handheld device. You should only be connected to a monitoring machine (even for a short period) if there is concern about your baby's well-being and this has been explained to you.
◆ You should be encouraged to move around and take any position that you find comfortable. You should not be expected to lie on your back and should be discouraged from doing so when pushing in the second stage. The only time when it is acceptable in a normal labor to ask you to use stirrups is if you need stitches inserted after the delivery. Standing, kneeling, sitting, or semi-squatting, well propped and supported—or even fully squatting if this is comfortable for you—may all help the progress of second-stage labor and reduce pain.
◆ As soon as your baby is born he should be helped up to you to hold, naked, skin to skin, with a towel or blanket over both of you to keep him warm. You should be helped to put him to the breast as soon as you wish.
◆ Active management of the third stage of labor, designed to reduce the possibility of bleeding (postpartum hemorrhage), may be offered, but if you are at low risk of bleeding you should be able to opt for a physiological third stage which leaves the cord attached to the placenta until it has stopped pulsing blood to the baby, and allows your body to deliver the placenta in its own time.
◆ Once the third stage is completed, you should have at least an hour with your baby before the midwife takes him out of your arms to weigh and measure and dress him.

Left in peace, your baby begins to discover comfort on your belly rather than in it.

of in you, he will begin to relax. You may see his face smoothing itself out; his breathing steadying, his head lifting. He may even move his limbs against you as if he is crawling up to find a breast. Helped to find a nipple, he will soon nuzzle and may soon suck for the first time, discovering new togetherness.

That togetherness matters more, right now, than any of the weighing and washing, eye drops and cord-stump dressings, clothing and wrapping that are scheduled for him, and more than the cleaning up and washing and changing and drink of water that is scheduled for you. It all has to be done, but none of it has to be done immediately. Your baby is born. It's time for the three of you to meet face to face and skin to skin.

From research

APGAR scores. The doctor will assess your baby's condition one minute after delivery and again after five minutes, using the checklist devised by Dr. Virginia Apgar, whose name is an acronym for what is tested: Appearance (color); Pulse (heartbeat), Grimace (in response to stimulation) Activity (muscle tone), Respiration (breathing). The maximum possible score is 10. Babies with a score of 7 or above are usually doing fine; scores between 4 and 6 may suggest that a baby needs help with breathing—airways may be cleared and oxygen given. Scores below 4 may suggest the baby needs special care.

Is this bonding?

That first meeting and greeting is important to all of you, and being your new baby's first experience of physical comfort outside the womb puts you exactly where a mother ought to be: At the very center of the baby's new life.

But important isn't the same as essential. Those first post-birth minutes can't be like that for every baby and mother because physical safety must come first, and ensuring it sometimes gets in the way. If your baby is taken away from you immediately after delivery because he needs professional care for a while, don't decide that you've missed your best shot at bonding or failed to give him the best possible start in life. That peaceful time together would have been a joyous start, but doing without it won't leave a permanent weakness in your bonds. Try to believe it. If you can't, look back a couple of generations and remind yourself that while many women were anesthetized for the delivery and most fathers were pacing waiting rooms, parents and babies still bonded as securely then as they do now.

Mothers and doctors have always known that while bonding may happen in a flash of

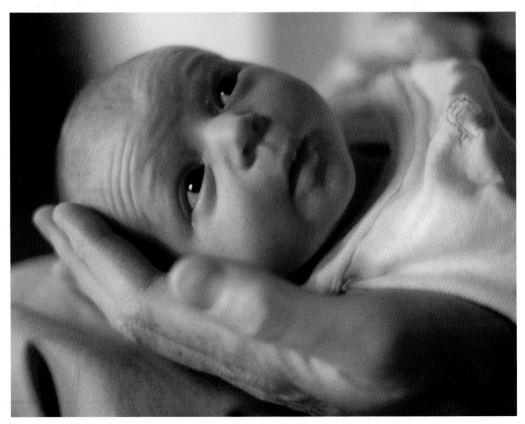

Your bond with your baby may not be instantaneous but her bond with you is not in question.

welcoming recognition at the moment of delivery, ("Hello, baby, I didn't realize it was you") the bonds between mother and baby more usually evolve over hours or days and may not build up to full strength for several weeks. So while any contact between mother and newborn baby is better than none, writing it into delivery-room rules is not a recipe for instant bonding, and the more emphasis we place on them and it, the more women feel that they have failed if that first meeting is delayed or they find themselves underwhelmed by it. The truth is that some mothers feel something closer to panic than joy ("what have I done?") while many mothers' first reaction to their babies is kept so low-key by exhaustion or feelings of relief at the birth being over that bonding doesn't seem to come into it.

Your newborn baby's bond with you is not in question. He is not only bonded to you but also still almost as much part of you now as when he was inside. We talk carelessly of "independent life," but although he now breathes and sucks and excretes for himself, he is still physiologically dependent on your body to regulate his: to feed him, to lend him immunity from infection and keep him warm, to regulate his heart rate and blood pressure to control his growth hormone levels, disperse his stress hormones, and regulate his muscular activity by your touch.

But for you it is different. Now that you no longer have the baby inside your body, feeling that he is part of you and you of him depends on you taking him inside you on an emotional level. That may take hours or days to begin and weeks to reach full power when the baby's early communications—eye contact, sounds, and first smiles—transform one-way responsibility into something that feels like reciprocated love. Clearly, then, mothers and newly delivered babies need time to be close and get to know each other, not only in the first hour after birth but in the first weeks. You will know when you have bonded with your baby because you will scarcely be able to distinguish his needs from your own, your main need being to meet his.

Many men find the symbiosis that comes to bind women and their new babies difficult to understand and therefore worrying and sometimes

Parents talking about...
going out without the baby

Emily didn't want to go out and her husband Max asked her if she felt anxious about the babysitter. Emily said no, she knew the baby would be safe with this particular woman. Max asked her whether in that case she was perhaps, being over-anxious about the baby, but again Emily said no. She assured him that she wasn't anxious about him at all; she knew he was doing fine.

Puzzled, Max suggested that perhaps she simply didn't feel like going to a party: Maybe she was tired and using the baby as an excuse to stay at home, but yet again Emily said no. In fact, she said, if it were not for the baby (or if she could take the baby along too) she'd really love to go.

Getting a bit irritated now, Max suggested that if that was so she was being unnecessarily self-sacrificing, but Emily said she was not being self-sacrificing at all, and tried to explain that she was not staying home for the baby's sake but for her own. She felt so interlocked with him that knowing that if he woke he would be happier if she was there, meant that she would be happier to be there…

unwelcome. They do not exactly share their partners' feelings for their babies, and therefore those feelings seem to mock their intentions and their attempts to share parenting. Unfortunately it is very difficult for women to explain what they feel. The couple described above tried very hard to understand each other when four weeks after their baby's birth, the mother found herself unable to leave him to go to a planned party, and her husband found himself disappointed and hurt. The mother was not taking her stand for the baby or for herself, but for a temporarily two-part self that was both her and him. This is the kind of occasion when men and women need to face and come to terms with the fact that although both are parents, a mother and a father seldom feel exactly the same.

Obstacles to bonding

For many, perhaps for most parents, bonding is partly a matter of adapting to being this baby's parent. It often takes time, and external circumstances can help or hinder, but only to a small extent. If a mother has real difficulty establishing a bond with her baby, it is never because of practicalities, always because of feelings. Barriers between people are erected on feelings, and only finding the courage to look at those feelings and work through them can pull those barriers down. Being born is tough for babies, and even if the labor was normal the physical shock of being delivered and then of expanding unused lungs to take first breaths leaves a baby urgently in need of comforting and welcoming. But giving birth is tough for mothers too, and if you lose sight of the fact that producing a living, breathing baby is a triumph however it is done, and instead have a sense of failure because you did not "do it" as you planned—drug-free and joyous, perhaps—but needed intervention and obstetric help, it may be difficult for you to see past the birth and focus on the baby.

Sometimes mothers start off unable to give their babies the comfort they need because labor and delivery have shocked them to a point where they urgently need sympathy and tender loving care themselves. If you are such a mother you may have no sympathy to spare for the baby right now and nothing left to give. You need care and comfort and a listening ear and you need them urgently. Left long without them it may come to seem to you as if it is your *baby* who has caused your acute distress. You may even come to see him as your enemy rather than your well-earned reward.

Other mothers have difficulty recognizing their real live babies as the babies they have been dreaming of, often because there is something shocking about a baby's appearance or physical condition: a cleft lip, perhaps; a spinal lesion as in Spina Bifida; even a large birthmark on the face. If you should be in such a situation, it is vital that both parents are carefully and immediately told the facts about any such condition and its likely treatment, and are told

again as the shock gradually wears off and rejection makes way for protection. Finally, of course, when a baby needs emergency care, parents may feel completely impotent. It seems that they can do nothing to help the baby, that he belongs to the only people who can keep him alive: specialist staff with high-tech machines.

Feelings like these are rare but nevertheless they are normal, so don't add to the distress that led to those feelings by being shocked by the feelings themselves. Of course you expected to feel nothing but love for your new baby, and that will come. But it will come sooner if instead of smothering what you are really feeling in silent shame, and leaving your partner to do the same, you talk to each other. New mothers almost all need to talk about their labor and delivery, and the more difficult the experience has been, the greater the need. You may find it easiest to talk to your doctor, to your birth companion, to your mother, or to friends with babies, perhaps including others from your prenatal classes. You may talk to them all.

Don't be surprised if you become a "birth bore," telling the story again and again to any and all who will listen. You will need to talk about it. All newly delivered women do. In a few weeks it will probably be you who is listening and someone else from your prenatal group who is talking. In the meantime, talking about it will help you understand what happened, get it into perspective, and, eventually, put it comfortably away in the back of your mind, leaving the forefront of your mind free for your baby and your mothering and for your new relationship with his father, your co-parent.

What's your baby like? (And is he OK?)

Most of the gorgeous "new" babies in magazine and television advertisements are at least a week and often a month old. That's new in lifetime terms, but it's not new to someone who's just had a baby. Brand new is crumpled and mottled often with tight-closed eyes and vernix-greasy hair (if any). In fact, brand new is not conventionally pretty at all, and while you will probably think yours the most beautiful

Whether the birth was traumatic or joyous or a little of each, talking about what happened will help you come to terms with it and move on.

baby in the world, early visitors, including older children, may be quite taken aback.

The doctor gets a good look at your baby during the delivery and as she lifts him onto your belly. Your baby's sex is usually the first thing she'll tell you, and that he's fine.

When it's time for washing and dressing and all that, the doctor or nurse will weigh your baby. Since there's a very wide range of sizes and shapes that are normal for newborns, it may seem odd that everyone cares so much exactly what he weighed. The point is not that a few ounces more or less would have been preferable but that your baby's weight, whatever it may be, is the starting point for his growth.

Average weight babies

Babies' average birth weight, with many variations scattered around it, is just over 7 lbs 8 oz (3.4 kg). 95% of newborns weigh between 5 lbs 8 oz and 10 lbs (2.5 kg and 4.5 kg). Boys tend to weigh a little more than girls, and first

babies usually weigh a little less than later borns. Babies who have had to share the resources of the womb—twins or more—are usually lighter than singletons. There's also a large genetic component in babies' size at birth, with bigger parents tending to have bigger babies.

Heavier babies

If you deliver a baby who weighs 9–10 lbs (4–4.5 kg) you will probably be proud of yourself for succeeding in getting him out, and proud of him because his extra covering of fat makes him look more beautiful than most of the other babies. Your pediatrician may not be quite so delighted with his extra weight though. Extra-large doesn't mean extra-healthy. In fact a few very large newborns have put on extra weight because their mothers have diabetes or pre-diabetes, which of course affects the amount of sugar that crosses the placenta. Such babies tend to have metabolic problems in the early days, so don't be surprised if the doctor keeps a special eye on your baby to be sure that he is just a well-grown large baby.

Lighter babies

If your baby weighs 5.8 lbs (2.5 kg) or more he will be treated like an average birth weight baby, though he may be encouraged to feed frequently. If the baby weighs less than that—perhaps 5–5.8 lbs (2.3–2.5 kg) he may be taken to the NICU even if he seems entirely healthy. Try not to panic. This may well be no more than a precaution. Some lighter babies aren't efficient at breathing, keeping themselves warm, or sucking. So to be on the safe side, all babies who are under 5.8 lbs (2.5 kg) may be closely monitored so that any problems can be spotted early. If no problems appear, he will probably be returned to your bedside within a few hours.

Lighter babies used to be kept in the hospital until they had started to gain over their birth weights or until they had reached a particular weight. Today's decisions about when babies can go home are usually based more on how they are doing, and especially how well they are feeding, than on what the scales say. Babies who weigh less than 5 lbs (2.3 kg)

Born at 37 weeks, both babies are flourishing, but one clearly got less than his share of nourishment in the womb.

probably are lighter than nature intended them to be. The lower your baby's birth weight, the more special the care he will need, although the exact type of care will of course depend on the reasons for his low weight.

Pre-term babies

Most very small babies are small because they have been born too soon—before they have had the usual 40 weeks in the womb. Time missed in the womb is not only missed growing time but also missed development time. The more time he's missed, the less ready he will be for independent life, and the more difficulties he is likely to face in the newborn period. A baby born at 36–38 weeks has missed 2–4 weeks gestation and will probably only need a little help, such as extra warmth, extra oxygen, and frequent, tiny feeds of breast milk. A baby born sooner than that is likely to need much more help. He may not be ready for aspects of independent life. For instance, he might not be able to breathe for himself and need help from a respirator, and he might not be able to suck, needing to be fed through a tube passed down his nose into his stomach.

Small-for-dates babies

Babies are referred to as "small-for-dates" when they are smaller at birth than was expected from their time in the womb. Such babies have "Intra Uterine Growth Retardation" (IUGR) (see p. 37). An IUGR baby may be born very small although he spent the full 40 weeks inside you. Or he may be born early, but even smaller than he ought to have been by that time.

Although very small newborns will be treated similarly whether they are pre-term or small-for-dates, it is important to know which is which.

Small-for-dates babies—the ones who have had intra-uterine growth retardation—have usually been short of nourishment in the womb, perhaps because of problems with the placenta or perhaps because two or more babies were sharing. An IUGR baby's small size does not predict later problems with development; indeed it is thought that the slower growth results from a reduced demand for calories and is a protective mechanism allowing a baby to develop fully when nourishment is scarce. If you can discover why nourishment was scarce in your womb for this baby, you may be able to provide an easier environment for any later babies.

Special care

The special care that's now available to babies who are in trouble, either before birth, or afterward in the neonatal intensive care unit (NICU), is so sophisticated that many do amazingly well.

If labor seems to be starting weeks too early for example, it can sometimes be stopped and can often be delayed with drugs, giving hospital staff time to assess the baby's condition and perhaps act to improve his chances. Very pre-term babies' lungs are often immature, and RDS (respiratory distress syndrome) is a common newborn problem. Hormones administered while the baby is still in the womb may speed up the lungs' maturation and increase the baby's chances of breathing for himself after birth.

Once your baby has been delivered, and your body can no longer help his to function, an incubator (or isolette) serves as a buffer between the total physical dependence of a fetus and the physical "independence" of a newborn. In the incubator the baby can be given whatever help he seems to need, from simple warmth, controlled humidity, and perhaps some

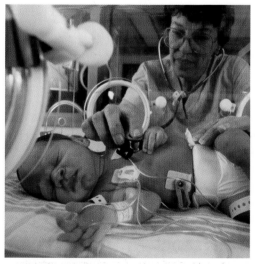

If your baby is not quite ready to cope outside your body, the neonatal intensive care unit (NICU) is the very safest place for her to be.

> ## Parents talking about...
> ### neonatal intensive care
> 66 Watching them rush her away to the NICU was one of the worst moments of my whole life. And even later on, although we both knew we should be grateful for all that technology and expertise, we sort of hated the whole place as if it had kidnapped our baby. 99

oxygen, to help with all his body systems, including a respirator to breathe for him. All that sophisticated machinery is dedicated to monitoring your baby's condition and will set off visual and auditory alarms to summon attention when he needs help. And as long as he remains in the NICU, that attention will be from highly trained specialist nursing and medical staff. The incubator is the safest possible place for him to be.

You and the NICU

Having a baby in the NICU is horrible, and the more worrying your baby's condition, the worse it will be. If you also have another child—maybe an older sibling, maybe the twin of this one—it may seem impossible to provide enough attention for both. If you also had a C-section or assisted delivery you may really wonder how to get through these first days postpartum. You will, of course, but this is a time when two parents aren't enough. Is there a grandparent able and available?

It's really important that you both spend as much time with the new baby as you possibly can though. He's not ready to live without special care, but that does not mean that he isn't ready to be in loving contact with you. On the contrary. After months of being warmly, safely inside you, he's outside, which is a lonely place to be. He needs to be close to you; don't abandon him to the professionals, vital though they are.

Twin tip

Will your two babies be in one bassinet?
Hospitals vary in their policy concerning keeping twin babies in the same bassinet or crib. If you would like them to share at your bedside and in the nursery, that will probably be arranged—provided the ward has large enough bassinets. In the NICU, though, although they may share your feeling that being together will comfort the babies, the staff will probably prefer to put them separately to insure against any confusion over medication; any chance of one baby getting more oxygen or warmth than he needs, and any risk of the babies pulling on each other's tubing.

From research

"Kangaroo care." Evolved in South America to cope with a shortage of incubators and a high infant mortality rate, babies dressed only in diapers and warm hats were placed between their mothers' breasts, face to face and skin to skin, and then covered with blankets. The South American babies who were nursed like this did as well as the few for whom there were incubators. Now increasing numbers of European hospitals are introducing this kind of care but as an extra to, rather than a substitute for, incubators. Some studies have shown that even a small amount of kangaroo care—perhaps an hour a day—leads to more rapid weight gain; an earlier readiness to suckle and often to an earlier-than-expected discharge home. Kangaroo care doesn't only help babies, of course, it also helps to protect parents from the horrible helplessness of watching a baby fight for life and being unable to help him or her.

The NICU staff will do their best to help you feel involved with your new baby's care—part of the team rather than onlookers. Both their training and their experience makes them experts in helping parents as well as nursing sick or pre-term babies. They will be especially eager to explain not only details of your baby's condition but also the gadgetry that surrounds him, because the more you understand what's going on, the more the baby will feel like yours rather than the hospital's.

Your baby still belongs to you

The nurses will encourage you to touch your baby through the glove-holes of the incubator from the beginning, unless he is extremely fragile. Later they may show you how to stroke and massage him, and maybe help with his physical care in the incubator. Touching your baby is just as important to him as it is to you. How long it is before you are allowed to get him out of the incubator and hold him depends on the hospital as well as on his condition. Even if he is tiny and festooned with tubes, you may be encouraged to nurse him in your arms, using a system known as "Kangaroo Care" that treats a mother's body as a sort of human incubator. It's the closest we have yet come to putting a baby who wasn't ready to be born back inside.

This baby doesn't belong to the hospital, he belongs to you. You can prove that to yourself by doing for him the one vitally important thing that nobody else in the world can do: building up your milk supply. Like all very small or ill babies, yours will really need to have breast milk as soon as he is ready for any milk at all. When he is ready for the milk he may still not be strong enough to nurse, so the milk may be given by tube or dropper. But even if your baby is not ready for milk by any means, it is still worth getting your supply established because he will need to be breast-fed when he is stronger. The hospital will have super-efficient breast pumps that are much easier to use than manual ones, let alone expressing by hand. A nurse will show you how to use one, and even if you eventually have to go home, leaving the baby in the NICU, it will be worthwhile to keep pumping. He could perhaps have breast milk from the milk-bank while he remains in

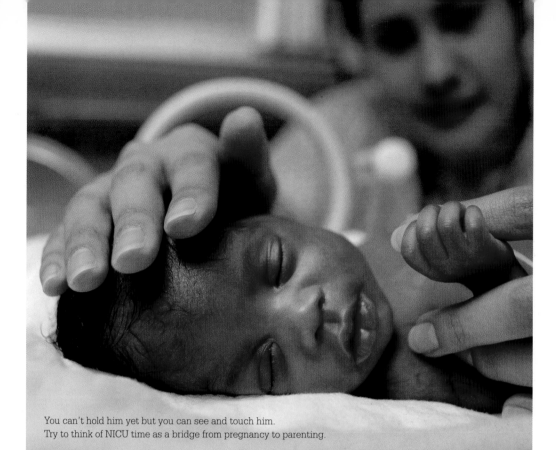

You can't hold him yet but you can see and touch him.
Try to think of NICU time as a bridge from pregnancy to parenting.

special care, but only regular expressing can ensure that you have a good supply for him in the future when he joins you at home.

Try to see the time your baby spends in the NICU as if it was an extension of your pregnancy during which you can actually see your baby. He will grow and develop during the weeks between his actual birth and the date you had expected him, but not quite as he would have done inside you: Incubators are not artificial wombs, and it will be important to allow for his premature birth in comparison with other babies of the "same" age. Like any other child, his birthday is and always will be the day he was born, but although that means that he is three months old three months later, he will not be nearly as mature as three-month-old babies who were born at full term, and won't be comparable with them until at least three months after his EDD (expected delivery date). Keep your pre-term baby's gestational or "corrected" age in mind through at least the first two years. The weeks between his actual birth

Parents talking about...

neonatal intensive care

❝ Our baby was six weeks premature, and we both felt that the first week of intensive care was by far the worst. It was such a shock, such a miserable sense of disappointment and anticlimax not to have her with us. After that, though, we did manage to treat this time like an extra bit of pregnancy: a sort of hiatus between having the baby invisible inside and fully part of our lives outside. ❞

date and expected birth date will make less and less difference as he gets older though, the significance of those lost weeks gradually diminishing. The vast difference between your niece who is two months old and your baby whose corrected age is only two *weeks* will almost vanish by the time they are both two years old.

Making sure the baby is all right

Soon after birth your baby should be thoroughly checked over by a pediatrician. This examination will be the first of many doctor appointments throughout your baby's life. The checkup will likely set your mind at ease.

This examination is well worth waiting for because it is the pediatrician's opportunity not only to assure herself that all is well with your baby but also to demonstrate and explain that it is. The baby will probably be weighed and measured (again). Average weight is 7 lbs 8 oz (3.4 kg); 95% of newborns weigh between 5 lbs 8 oz and 10 lbs (3.3–4.5 kg). Average length is 20 in (50 cm); 95% of newborns measure between 18 and 22 in (45–55 cm). Average head circumference is 13.8 in (35 cm); normal range is 12.9–14.7 in (32–37 cm).

The pediatrician's first check

Starting from the top, the doctor will check the fontanelles—the areas of the skull where the bones have not yet fused (so that the skull could be compressed a little during birth)—and feel inside your baby's mouth to make sure that there is no cleft in her palate.

She'll listen with a stethoscope to your baby's heart sounds and respiration. If she should mention a heart murmur, don't jump to the conclusion that your baby has heart trouble. These murmurs are common in newborns and seldom indicate a problem. With one hand on your baby's tummy and the other behind, the doctor will check the size and position of the kidneys, liver, and spleen. She will also feel for the pulses in your baby's groins. The doctor will check that your baby's genitals are normal and that a boy's testes are either descended or can be persuaded to descend.

She will check your baby's arms and legs, making sure that each pair is the same length with the right number of fingers and toes, and that legs and feet are properly aligned.

She will check the baby's hip joints (which babies do not enjoy) looking for any sign of dislocation or instability that might lead to dislocation.

Peace will probably be restored when she completes her examination by holding the baby face down along her forearm while she runs her thumb all the way down her spine, checking that the vertebrae are in place along it.

Your baby's first medical check up should be the ideal opportunity to ask questions, but it often is not. Your baby may howl; the doctor may be in a hurry, and neither parent may yet be capable of formulating a sensible question or taking in the answer. If you are in the hospital, there will always be someone to ask, and once you are at home, you'll visit the pediatrician often and you will have a telephone number you can use in between. But that "in between" can seem like a lot of hours, full of things to worry about.

It takes several days for a new baby's body to adapt to life outside the womb and begin to function efficiently. In the meantime, her physiology is not at all the same as an older baby's, and the newborn may produce all kinds of color changes, spots, blotches, swellings, and secretions, some of which look very peculiar. Most of them would indeed be peculiar if they occurred in an older person, but are normal, or at least insignificant, when they occur in the first two weeks of life. The list that follows describes some of the commonest of these phenomena and tells you why they happen and what they mean. If you need direct reassurance, or if you notice one of them after your baby is two or three weeks old, consult your doctor.

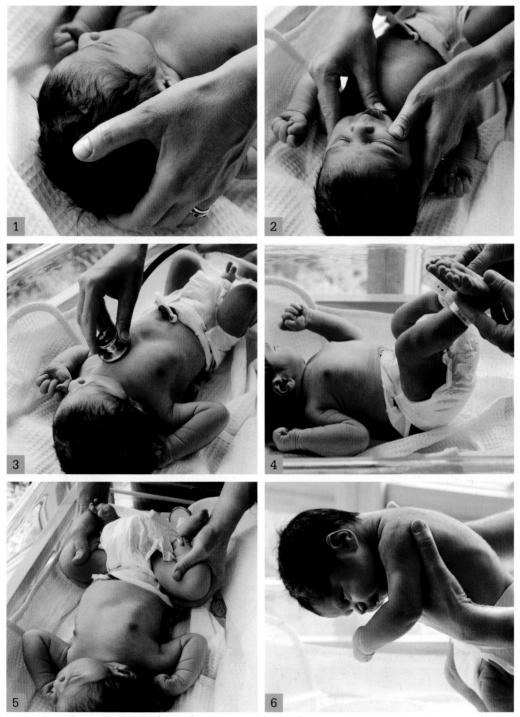

(1) The doctor checks the fontanelles where the skull is not yet fused. (2) Makes sure the mouth and palate have fused so there's no cleft. (3) Uses a stethoscope to make sure the heart and lungs sound normal. (4) Checks that the pairs of limbs are of equal length with 10 each of fingers and toes. (5) Examines the hip joints for any dislocation or instability. (6) Inspects the spine to be sure it is straight with all the vertebrae in place.

Your newborn baby's body at first sight

◆ **Hair:** Your baby may have no hair or lots. Any amount of hair on the head is normal. Whatever it is like at birth, most of the newborn hair will gradually fall out and be replaced, possibly by hair of a completely different color.

◆ **Body hair:** In the womb babies are covered with a fine fuzz of hair called lanugo. Some, especially babies born prematurely, still have traces, usually across the shoulder blades and down the spine, but it will rub off in the first week or two.

◆ **Head shape:** Her head may look odd— especially if there is little hair covering it. Babies' skulls are designed to "give" a little to help their mothers get them through the birth canal. If you had an unassisted labor, the enormous pressure of the second stage may have squeezed your baby's head into an elongated shape. Forceps sometimes leave bruises or actual (temporary) depressions, while the suction of a ventouse may have raised a ring-doughnut-shaped swelling on the top of the baby's head. These signs that your baby had a hard time being born can be very distressing, but they don't mean that she is actually damaged or deformed.

◆ **Fontanelles:** These are the areas where the bones of the skull have not yet fused together. The most noticeable one lies toward the back of the top of the baby's head. The spaces between the bones are covered by an extremely tough membrane that will withstand all normal handling (even a toddler's caresses!). If your baby doesn't have much hair it's normal to be able to see her pulse beating under the fontanelle. If the fontanelle ever looks sunken, though, she may be dehydrated (perhaps from very hot weather or fever or both) and should be offered a feeding at once. A tight fontanelle that bulges outward even when the baby is not crying is often a sign of illness; the baby should be seen by a doctor as an emergency.

◆ **Puffy eyes:** Her eyes may be swollen, puffy, or red-streaked, from pressure during birth. Swelling may make it difficult for your baby to open her eyes at first, but will soon subside.

◆ **Squinting:** Your baby may look as if she has a squint when her eyes are perfectly normal. Often it is the marked folds of skin in the inner corners of their eyes that give this misleading impression. Until the muscles have strengthened, though, and the baby has learned to control them she may have difficulty holding both eyes in line so that they both focus steadily on one object. As she looks at you, you may suddenly notice that one eye has drifted out of focus. A "wandering eye" almost always rights itself by the time the baby is six months old. But point it out to the doctor so that its progress can be checked. In a true squint the baby's eyes never both focus together on the same object but are permanently out of alignment with each other. If you are the first to notice that your baby has a "fixed squint," you should report it at once to the doctor. Early treatment is both essential and highly successful.

◆ **Ears:** Your baby's ears may seem to stick out a great deal, but that doesn't necessarily mean that they are set in a sticking-out position. Newborn ears are soft and malleable and also look very different once the head takes on a more mature shape and more hair grows.

◆ **Skin color:** Her skin may seem odd-colored and blotchy; it's so thin that it is an overall pinky-red color to begin with no matter what color it will be eventually, and because her circulation is not fully efficient, blood may pool in the lower half of her body when she has been still for a long time, so that it looks half red and half pale. Sometimes when she's asleep her hands and feet may look bluish because they are not receiving their full quota of blood. As soon as you pick the baby up or turn her over, the skin color will even out.

◆ **Birthmarks:** There are many kinds of birthmark; only a doctor can say whether the mark that worries you is a birthmark and if so whether it is a kind that will vanish on its own. Do remember, though, that red marks on the skin, especially on the face, are often due to pressure during delivery and that these will disappear within a week or two.

When you first look carefully at your baby with no clothes on

◆ **Swollen breasts:** You may notice swollen breasts in the first three to five days after birth. That's because hormones that flooded through you just before the birth and were intended only

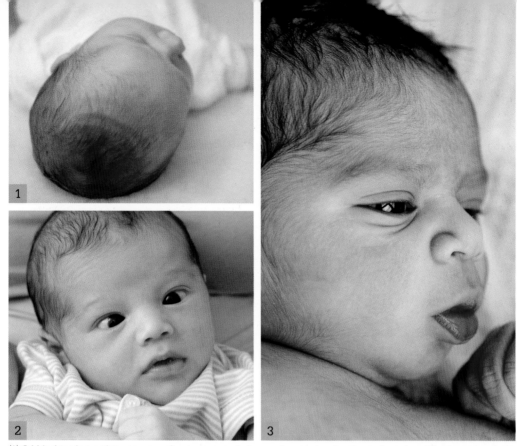

(1) Odd-looking but nothing to worry about; your new baby may have a ring-doughnut-shaped swelling from a ventouse (suction cap); (2) eyes that look as if they are squinting; (3) puffy eyes, and soft hair (lanugo) on the face and body.

for you, reached your baby too. Leave the breasts alone. Even if they contain tiny amounts of liquid, attempts to squeeze it out might introduce infection. The swelling will die down in a few days as the baby's body rids itself of the hormones.

◆ **Genitals:** These often look surprisingly large. In both boys and girls genitals are larger, in proportion to the rest of their bodies, at birth than at any other time before puberty. During the first few days after birth they may look even larger than normal, and the scrotum or the vulva may look red and inflamed. Again the cause is those maternal hormones entering the baby's bloodstream. The baby's sexual parts may look conspicuous and peculiar, but don't worry. The doctor or midwife who delivered the baby will have checked that all is normal; the inflammation and swelling will rapidly subside and he or she will soon "grow into" those apparently over-large organs.

◆ **The cord stump:** This may look strange to you, but your doctor will tell you how to clean

and dress it to make sure that your baby's navel heals cleanly. There's nothing to worry about unless you see any signs of infection—redness or discharge—which should be reported to your pediatrician immediately.

◆ **Umbilical hernia:** A small swelling close to the navel, which sticks out more when the baby cries, is an umbilical hernia. Although it cannot actually be called "normal," it is very common. It is caused by a slight weakness of the muscles in the wall of the abdomen that allows the contents to bulge forward. Almost all such hernias right themselves completely by one year, and most doctors believe they heal more quickly if they are not strapped up. Very few ever require surgery.

◆ **Undescended testes:** Your baby boy's testes develop in the abdomen and usually descend into the scrotum just before a full-term birth. But if the doctor cannot feel them during her examination of the newborn, it may be that they are "retractile," meaning that they have descended, but can still go up again into the abdomen and do so in reaction to the touch of cold hands. Provided that they can be "milked" down, they will eventually come down and stay down on their own. An undescended testicle is one which cannot be persuaded into the scrotum after a full-term birth or by the time a premature baby reaches his expected date of birth. If you cannot ever see or feel both your son's testes in the scrotum, mention it to the doctor who checks him at around six weeks of age.

In the first few days

You may notice any, some or all of the following: they are not all strictly "normal" but they aren't worrying either.

Skin

◆ **Spots:** Newborn skin is fragile and easily damaged—diaper rash is not the only common kind of chafing. Spots are common because the pores do not yet work efficiently. Common kinds are "neonatal urticaria"—a rash of red blotchy spots with tiny red centers, which come and go, often in a few hours, on different parts of the body; "Milia" (often called "milk spots")—tiny white spots, usually on the nose and cheeks, that may last for several weeks; and the grimly named but harmless "toxic erythema"—irregular red blotches with pale middles that look like a collection of insect bites. None of these looks pretty, but they are all harmless.

◆ **Blue patches:** Small and temporary accumulations of pigment under the skin are called "Mongolian blue spots." They are more usual in babies of African or Mongolian descent but can also be seen in any baby whose skin is going to be fairly dark. They have nothing to do with bruising or with any disorder of the blood.

◆ **Peeling:** Most new babies' skin peels a little in the first few days. It is often most noticeable on the palms of the hands and soles of the feet. Post-mature babies may have extra-dry skin, and babies of Afro-Caribbean or Asian descent often have both skin and hair that is very dry compared to babies of European descent.

◆ **Scurf on the scalp:** This is as normal as skin peeling elsewhere; it is nothing to do with dandruff and does not suggest a lack of hygiene.

"Cradle cap"—a really thick cap-shaped layer of brownish scales—is harmless to the baby, but doesn't look very nice to parents. It sometimes spreads to the baby's eyebrows and behind the ears. Your doctor may suggest that you try a special shampoo, ointment, or oil.

Mouth

◆ **"Tongue-tie":** If you think (or someone suggests to you) that your baby is "tongue-tied," it's probably because new babies' tongues are anchored along a much greater proportion of their length than the tongues of older people. In some babies the anchoring fold of skin is so long that the baby has almost no tongue that is free and mobile. In the past it was thought that unless the anchoring skin was cut, the baby would not be able to suck properly or learn to talk. Now we know that a true tongue-tie (one that will not right itself with normal growth) is exceedingly rare. Most of the growth of a baby's tongue during the first year of life is in the tip, so by the first birthday, the tongue is fully mobile. In the meantime, its close anchorage has no ill effects.

◆ **Blisters on the upper lip:** Babies make "sucking blisters" themselves with their suction. They can occur at any time while the baby is milk fed. They may (or may not) vanish between feeds. They are unimportant.

◆ **White tongue:** While they are being fed only on milk, babies' tongues are often white all over. This is absolutely normal. Infection or illness produces patches of white on an otherwise pink tongue.

◆ **Fluid-filled papules on the gum:** These are harmless (and common) cysts. The yellowish-white spots that might suddenly become visible on the roof of your baby's mouth when she yawns widely may look worrying but are equally harmless. Both will clear without treatment well before a first tooth is likely.

Penis

◆ **Tight foreskin (phimosis):** This is a problem your new baby boy cannot have, because the penis and foreskin develop from a single bud in the fetus, are still fused at birth, and only gradually separate in the first years of a boy's life. Don't try to retract or wash under his foreskin because it is not made to retract yet.

Secretions and bodily fluids

♦ **Yellowish discharge/crusting on eyelids and lashes:** This suggests a common, mild infection, resulting from contact with blood during delivery, and known as "sticky eye." It is not serious, but the baby should be seen by a doctor, who may recommend drops or a solution for bathing the eyes.

♦ **Discharge from ears:** The only normal discharge from your baby's ears is wax, which is an antiseptic protection for the ear canal. If you see a substance coming from your baby's ear and you are not sure that it is wax, consult your pediatrician. If it is wax, she will be only too pleased to reassure you. If by any chance it is pus, treatment is urgently needed.

♦ **Diaper contents:** Feeding, digesting food, and excreting waste are processes that are established gradually over several days. If you have only ever changed diapers for older babies, the contents of these first ones may surprise you. First stools consist mostly of meconium, a greenish-black, sticky substance that filled your baby's intestines in the womb and has to be evacuated before ordinary digestion can take place. Almost all babies pass meconium in the first 24 hours. If you don't have much diaper-changing experience, ask a nurse for assistance with a meconium-filled diaper, since you won't encounter this sticky, messy substance again.

♦ **Blood in stools:** Very occasionally blood is noticed in the stools in the first day or two. It is usually blood from the mother, swallowed during the delivery and passed through the baby, unchanged. But to be certain, keep the diaper to show to your doctor.

♦ **Reddish urine:** Very early urine often contains a harmless substance called "urates" which appears red on the diaper. It is harmless, but since it looks like blood you may prefer to keep the diaper to show your pediatrician.

♦ **Vaginal bleeding:** A minute amount of vaginal bleeding—a smear on the diaper—is common and insignificant in girls in the first week of life. It is due to maternal estrogen passing into the baby just before birth. A clear or whitish discharge from the vagina is also quite normal. It will stop in a very few days.

♦ **Frequent urination:** Once the urine flow is established, it's normal for your baby to wet as often as 30 times in the 24 hours. On the other hand, a baby who stays dry for four to six hours at this stage should be seen by a doctor. She might have become seriously dehydrated, or even have some obstruction to the flow of urine.

♦ **Nasal discharge:** Your baby may accumulate enough mucus in her nose to cause sniffles or some visible "runniness," but in these first few days of life it's unlikely to mean that she already has a cold.

♦ **Tears:** Most babies cry without tears until they are four to six weeks old. A few shed tears from the beginning. It does not matter either way.

♦ **Watery eye:** If your baby sheds tears when she is not crying, it is likely that the tear ducts have not fully opened to allow tears to drain away via the nose. Such tear ducts usually open by the end of the first year.

♦ **Sweating:** New babies' heads are so large in relation to the rest of their bodies that they readily gain and lose heat from them. Many babies sweat a great deal around the head and neck even when their heads are not covered. This has no importance unless the baby shows other signs of being feverish or unwell. It is a good reason, though, for rinsing the head and hair frequently, since the salty sweat may irritate the skin in the folds of the neck.

♦ **Vomiting:** Spitting up a little after feeding, especially when the baby is bounced around to encourage her to burp, is normal. Mixed with saliva and spread over your shoulder, the quantity lost tends to look much greater than it is. Two types of vomiting merit an immediate appointment with a doctor: greenish or yellow vomit during the first 10 days may indicate a bowel obstruction; vomiting with such force that it shoots across the room ("projectile vomiting") means that conditions such as pyloric stenosis need to be ruled out.

New baby,
new parents

Meeting your new baby

Many new parents expect the first few days after their baby's birth to be a time of joy and celebration. Some of it will be, but probably not all of it. For most couples this is a confusing time of high emotion—negativè as well as positive—and for mothers, a time of exhaustion.

Labor is called labor for good reason. For the first few days after birthing your baby you may feel more tired than you can ever remember feeling in your life before. In fact everything you feel is likely to be over the top: exhaustion and elation; joy and pain; pride and panic.... Of course there are lots of physiological reasons for feeling as you do—your hormone balance is totally out of whack, your breasts are all set to provide milk that is not fully in, your cervix is not yet closed, and stitches or no stitches, peeing stings—but don't look for reasons to use as excuses because you don't need any. All newly delivered mothers feel extraordinary—even if they don't tell you about it—and so do a lot of new fathers, because even if their bodies don't have to give birth, having a baby is a big experience.

Once your baby is born nothing in your lives as individuals or as a couple will ever be the same again, and that can be a very scary thought—perhaps especially for the increasing numbers of people who wait until they are settled and reasonably successful in their adult lives and careers before trying for a baby, and really don't want to change. Some new parents start out by refusing to acknowledge that anything especially earth-shattering has happened to them. If they can deny that they have any reason to be disturbed or upset, the disturbance itself is easier to ignore; if it is

Everything you feel is over the top: A new baby is just amazing.

Who wants
anything ever to
be the same again?

ignored, perhaps it will go away. "Birth is a natural thing, after all," they say, and, "almost everyone has a baby sooner or later, we'll be back to normal soon." But the disturbance isn't the baby's birth; the disturbance is the baby, and the baby is not going to go away. Try not to sell yourselves on the idea that if you can just get through the first extraordinary days and restore old routines, you'll feel "like yourselves" again, because you won't.

Moving on to a new normality

"Getting back to normal" means different things to different people. Unfortunately for new parents' relationships it often means different things to a new father and a new mother. To a lot of men, "normal life" is so clearly defined by their jobs that "getting back to normal" mostly means getting back to work. Whether a new father takes days or weeks of time off from work, most do of course have to go back to work eventually. He is aware, from the beginning, that by doing so he may be able to distance himself from the extraordinary business of having become a father; able to swap the supercharged emotional atmosphere of his home and bed for the reassuringly impersonal sameness of his workplace. He will be at home in the evenings and on weekends, of course, but even then the fact that he is back at work may excuse him from immersing himself in what is going on there. He is tired after his day's work, after all, so not very much can be expected of him. He has to get up early, so he needs his sleep (ostrich-like, head under the pillow). And even at the weekend, there will be plenty of chores to do that are certainly helpful in the practical sense, but which also protect him from too much feeling

Don't let "back to normal" mean managing to fit your baby into your work.

or talking about feelings…. Most of the new fathers who behave like this are not uncaring and sexist but caring and overwhelmed.

A new mother may of course have been just as involved in outside work as her partner, but unlike him it offers her no escape now. She cannot "get back to normal" by reverting to her pre-pregnancy life because that has been over for months, certainly since she became unable to sleep on her stomach or see her feet when standing up. She cannot get back into pregnancy (blissful though parts of that time may have been) because, as she can now see, a lot of that way of life had birth rather than a baby as its focus. In truth she cannot get back to normal in any way at all because the baby's arrival has shattered her life so that like a dropped jigsaw puzzle, its picture is in a thousand pieces. Her only escape from present chaos is not back but forward: on to a time when it feels normal to think of herself as a woman who is a mother (as well as whoever else she is), and when mothering her baby feels like a (large) chunk of ordinary life.

That time will come for you, there's no doubt about that, but it will come sooner if you can go with the flow of this strange part of your life rather than trying to force all the pieces to make a picture just like the old one. Some women cannot bear the timeless confusion of life with a new baby: days that slip by with beds unmade until afternoon, meals ordered in at the last minute, and nothing more useful accomplished than a shower. Surely it must be a temporary aberration, excusable perhaps by the physical discomforts of stitches that are still sore or breasts that are overfull, but something that they will "get over," like an illness, rather than something that they will "get through" into a different kind of peace. Such a woman may talk as if she will only be at home "until I feel better," and pass the early days after her baby's birth planning and replanning an imminent return to her job, a summer camping trip, or any project that would require her to be fit, free, and babyless. Ask who is to care for the baby while she is at work, or how she will cope with baby care on a mountainside, and she will look at you with blank anxiety. Her plans are freedom-fantasies, not to be clothed in everyday practicality.

Your baby has changed everything: You need to move forward to a time when being his mother *is* normal.

Parents who behave like this are not allowing themselves to behave as they feel, because they are trying not to feel so as not to have to cope with what they feel. But if parents hold a baby at arm's length and try not to let her change them (because they cannot face their feelings), they will have to try to change her, irrespective of her feelings. If they and their lives are not to adapt to her needs, she must be adapted to fit in with theirs. Hardly surprisingly, the fit is usually appalling and all three feel the pinch.

At the very best, this kind of defensiveness is a waste of time. You have your baby, but you cannot really begin to enjoy her until you can accept the feelings she has brought with her and begin to approve of yourselves in your new roles as her parents. But defensiveness may be far worse than a waste of time because now, as

in pregnancy, squashed down feelings often pop up as depression. Postpartum depression (PPD) or postpartum illness (PPI), which covers a wider spectrum of symptoms, is usually described as a female condition starting soon after birth, but baby-related depression is not exclusive to mothers nor to the first days after birth. Both women and men can suffer from it and when they do, their babies suffer, too. Depression closes people off from warm spontaneous contact with others. Babies need this kind of contact with parents almost as much as they need food and physical care. Without it they cannot make the uniquely personal two-way relationships on which their successful development as human beings, and their parents' ultimate pleasure in parenting, both depend.

If you come off the high of birth and keep on going down, you need and deserve help now.

When adjusting to your new roles is difficult

More than half of all new mothers come down from the high of birth and keep on going down—into a pit of exhaustion, self-doubt, and hormonal chaos that is usually called "baby blues." Sad and scary though they can be, baby blues usually last no more than a few days; in fact women often find that their mood is related to their milk supply, lifting as the milk comes in and the baby settles to breast-feeding, or as the supply gradually ceases if the baby is being bottle-fed.

Postpartum depression

Postpartum depression is quite different. Affecting between 10 and 13 in every 100 women in the days (or sometimes weeks) after delivery, it is a potentially serious illness that, unless it is recognized and treated early, can last for months.

Some men, especially medical men, like to refer to all postpartum depression as "hormonal": part of the myth of menstrual moon-madness men use to excuse themselves the effort of understanding why women get weepy. Of course there are hormonal upheavals in the bodies of newly delivered women, but that is not the whole story. This particular life event is an obvious trigger for depression in a woman who is vulnerable to it. Once the brief drama of delivery is over and the baby declared healthy, most of the care and concern that has surrounded her will melt away, leaving her with her old life and identity in an unraveled tangle in the baby's innocent fists, and no clear-cut way of reknitting it to accommodate them both. No wonder a sense of anxious anticlimax is common and depression far from rare.

In more child-oriented societies, postpartum depression (even "baby blues") is so rare that the very concept is hard to communicate, as this puzzled West African response shows: "Has this unhappy woman you tell me of not got her child?" Well, maybe yes, but also maybe no. The mother no longer has the baby inside her body, but she may, or may not, have taken her inside herself on an emotional level so that she feels that the baby is part of her. Until she does, until she is so bonded with the baby that she suffers when the baby suffers and finds her own pleasure

channeled through her ("Love me, love my baby"); the baby is an outsider. She may even be experienced as an intruder into the mother's personal space, her life, her sexual partnership.

If you are depressed, your world will be gray and you will be turned in on yourself in spirals of anxiety. You will probably manage to take care of your baby somehow, or to arrange for someone else to do so, but depression will dampen your pleasure in her and therefore deprive her of being your joy. If you think you are suffering from depression rather than the blues, do look for help—medical, emotional, and practical. It matters to your baby as well as to you.

You may not manage it though, if asking for help is all up to you. When you are feeling utterly worthless, you'll probably feel unworthy of your doctor's time. If getting dressed in the morning is almost more than you can manage, making an appointment to see your doctor to tell her what you are feeling will probably be beyond you. You need someone else to seek help on your behalf. Partners, grandmothers, and friends should all be alert to the possibility of postpartum depression. If they find themselves about to say "pull yourself together," they should bite their tongues and suggest calling the doctor instead. Girlfriends may be especially important. Postpartum depression and the kind of help that women find useful are widely variable, but almost every sufferer finds supportive friendships with other mothers invaluable.

From research

Postpartum depression. There are several symptoms suggesting depression, and the sufferer may have any combination. Their effect is overwhelming and incapacitating.
◆ Tearfulness
◆ Despair
◆ Anxiety and panic attacks
◆ Low self-esteem
◆ Sleeplessness
◆ Headaches
◆ Irritability
About one third of mothers with PPD will have difficulty bonding with the baby.

You may have to fight for the time and space you need to be a father.

A new shape to life

Somehow you have to accept what your new baby's existence makes you feel. You have to accept what she needs from you, find pleasure in giving it, and delight in being a new person's other half. Above all, you have to be open to change, in yourselves and in your lives, because this is probably the biggest change you have made or will ever make.

Once your baby is outside your body she cannot, and should not be ignored. Everything and everybody else who is important to you, including each other, will have to move over to make space for her. She is not a toy; something you can stow away when you are tired of playing with it or need to do something else. Bringing up a baby is not a hobby, either. You cannot fit it in around the edges of an already full and fulfilling life. Your baby's care will be central.

Society will do little to help the two of you make room for your baby at the center of your lives. It's rare for parents to be offered the time and space, the support and money they need, and many people will resent you for taking it. As a father you may almost be forced to pretend that your baby *is* a toy and that being a parent *is* your new hobby. Far from offering you flex-time or a bonus, your employer may offer overtime

"now that you've got another mouth to feed." As a mother you cannot go on living as you did before and should not even have to pretend to do so, to outsiders, to your partner, your family, your friends, or to yourself. For a while—perhaps for three months, perhaps for two or three times longer—you will find that deep down inside you, nothing matters as much as your baby, and nothing that is unimportant to your baby can be very important to you. Accustomed as you are to living with a cult of individualism and demands to "take care of yourself," you will not really be able to tell where "you" end and "the baby" begins, because you will feel as if you and she were still part of each other. Even when you are physically away from her, leaving her minute-by-minute care to her father or to somebody else, invisible elastic threads will seem to join you together, preventing you from going too far. You are not just your baby's protector, champion, and playmate, you are her other half; she is not designed to live without you in these first months. You know it, even when you don't dare say it and even when nobody else acknowledges it.

Many first-time mothers are amazed at the strength of their own feelings, and if outsiders suggest that the feelings are inappropriate, that amazement is tinged with alarm and dismay. Instead of saying "It's all right. You are meant to feel like this for a bit; your baby needs you to feel like this. Relax, accept it, revel in it," people suggest the very opposite. A nurse on the maternity floor says, "Now you have a nice nap. Take advantage of being here. We'll look after baby." "Baby" is your baby and she is one hour old. You have only just got her. The very last thing you want is to have her taken away again so that a separate "you" can rest. Your mother says, "I hope you're not going to go on having her in the bedroom all night. She'd be much better off in her own room next door…" She is six days old and she used to be inside you. If your now separated bodies are to be cut off from each other in sleep, you want to trail your hand over the edge of her basket and know that her waking sounds are only two feet from your ear.

Sooner or later somebody will probably tell you that you are too focussed on breast-feeding, that you are "overprotective" or a "fussy mother." Try not to listen. Isn't offering milk from your body to the baby that body made being a mother rather than obsessing? You will stop wanting to feed and comfort her in that particular way as and when she grows out of wanting you to. How could you be overprotective of a baby who is completely helpless and for whom you know you would kill or die? As for being "fussy," if that means trying to make your baby's new way of life as easy, comfortable, and perfect as you can, including calling doctors at midnight if necessary and asking 47 questions at check-ups, go for it. Nobody will fuss over your baby if you do not.

If you can believe that reveling in your baby is a highly desirable way to spend the next few months, you will be able to treat this period of your life as the unique experience it really is. Just have confidence that it will pass. However deeply you submerge yourself, you will not drown in babies and be lost to the adult world forever. Give yourselves a few months for each child you plan to have, and give yourselves freely and without rationing. It is very little time to take out of a whole adult life; whatever you lose by it, the gain to all of you will be infinitely greater.

You are your baby's completing half; nobody will fuss over her if you do not.

Meeting your new baby's needs

A new baby's physiological needs are few, simple, and repetitive. She needs only food, warmth, tactile comfort, and a modicum of cleanliness. But she needs them given with what many parents find it hardest to provide: calm.

The fulfilment of every single one of these needs constitutes a novel experience for a brand new nervous system. You may tremble because you have never bathed a new baby before, but your baby has never known water since she started to breathe for herself. Everything needs to be done for her as gently, as calmly and as slowly as possible. She needs no extra stimulation from adults, she has all she can cope with in the myriad new sensations of being outside the womb. She will feel changes of temperature on her skin, detect light and darkness; feel fullness and emptiness, wetness, dryness; feel herself moved through the air, held, put down, moved around. She will hear noises; she must suck for food and water; she will feel her own limbs move, experience different textures against her skin, different tastes in her mouth. She is very busy, in these first weeks, just being alive and staying that way in what from her point of view is a new world. Although she has reflexes and working senses to help her she has no understanding of the new sensations that bombard her. She is programmed to pay attention to you, look at your faces, listen to your voices, but she does not know that you and she are separate; that she is herself and you are her parents. She is programmed for survival, not yet for acquiring knowledge.

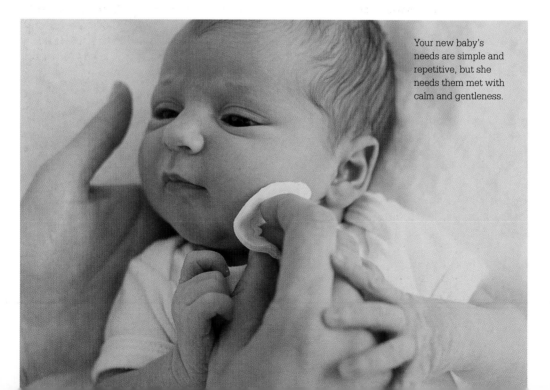

Your new baby's needs are simple and repetitive, but she needs them met with calm and gentleness.

From research

Newborn brain cells. A baby in the womb develops billions of cells in her upper brain but it is only after birth that they start to connect into functioning neurons. Those connections will be responsible for much of her intelligence, especially her social intelligence, and it is her upbringing and relationships with parents and others that will shape them.

Living with unpredictability

Newborn behavior has no patterns so it cannot be predicted. Your baby may loudly announce that she is hungry twice an hour for six hours and then sleep without a murmur or a suck for another six hours. Her "hunger" is still formless and shapeless, her digestion is still unsettled, and hunger sensations are not clearly recognizable. Much the same is true of her sleep. The fact that she has slept only in 20-minute snatches all night does not mean that she is certain to sleep a long stretch in the day. She may—there's no harm in hoping—but don't count on it. As for her crying: all you can be certain of is that there will be some, but why she starts when she starts, and what makes her stop at this precise moment may well be a mystery.

This unpredictability puts people who care for brand new babies—parents, substitute-parents or professionals—at a serious disadvantage because they have no baselines against which to measure the baby's behavior or their own caregiving. You may know a great deal about babies in general, but you don't know anything about this one in particular. How can you be sure whether she is ill or unhappy when you have no baselines of how she looks and behaves when she is well and cheerful? Since she hasn't been around long enough for anything to be usual, how can you know if today's crying or feeding or sleeping is unusual? And if you don't know that, how can you judge whether today's crying suggests that something is wrong, or whether her feeding or her sleeping is sufficient? Your baby's well-being is in your hands though, so somehow you have to make assessments of how she is, and risk making judgments as to what you should do, while your baby gradually settles into life outside the womb and you settle into being her parents.

Love?

In the meantime, don't be surprised or shocked if you don't actually love her. Bonding with a baby may (or may not) be an instantaneous bolt-from-the-blue business, but love is different. There are many different definitions of the word "love," but whichever one you choose it is certain to include two people getting to know each other better and wanting to be closer. You don't know your baby as a person yet and she certainly doesn't know you. What's more she isn't lovable yet because she hasn't had time to develop the characteristics that will make her a unique individual. Perhaps you love her because she is the baby you have been wanting, the fulfilment of dreams of being parents, but you can't instantly love her as one person loves another, because she will not be fully a person until she has settled into life outside you.

Biochemistry is on the side of love developing. If you are the baby's birth mother your body will start loving her if you will let it, even before she is settled enough to be a person. Your mind may still be full of doubts about parenting, but your body is ready and waiting for the baby. As you hold her, your skin seems to greet hers. Her little body fits

Twin tip

Some parents worry that they'll love one baby more than the other. Some parents say they *do*. That's most likely to happen when a parent always spends time with both babies together—a bigger, jollier, prettier one and a smaller, spottier, more fretful one. The bond each parent has with each child almost always evens out over a few weeks, but it will do so faster if you both spend time one to one with each baby so you're learning (and learning to love) Josh, spots and all, without being distracted by Jarvis' smiling.

Your baby's happiness is in your hands.

From research

Newborn behavior. Your baby's behavior may be affected by her birth. Labors and births that are classified as "normal" nevertheless put varying amounts of stress on babies as well as on their mothers. If your baby's condition led to an assisted delivery or her APGAR score was low, that additional stress may show itself in extra crying, in being irritable, or being difficult to comfort during the first few weeks.

The "quiet-alert" state. New babies spend most of their time sleeping or feeding or crying or fussing, but in between there is a "quiet alert" state which provides windows for early sociability and learning. Many babies have a relatively long quiet-alert period very soon after birth and will gaze intently at a parent and even imitate facial expressions such as sticking out the tongue.

against you, kneading your belly, nestling to your breast, fitting a surprisingly hard and hot little head into the curve of your neck and shoulder. Having latched on immediately after birth she will soon be sucking for pleasure and colostrum, and once you start to produce milk, the physical pleasure of nursing, and the link it makes between you, is startlingly strong.

Love doesn't require biology though. Even if you are not the birth mother or biological father, reveling in the feel of the baby in your arms, the perfect miniature hand in yours, the cheek you find yourself rubbing against like a cat, speeds up the time when she can join in this essential business of loving. If you keep her close, she will not just lie there passively, leaving it to you to make all the effort. Her survival depends on your love so she will make advances to you too.

So don't assume that mixed feelings toward your baby today mean that you aren't going to love her in the future. Yes, you can be suddenly irritated by her crying, but you can also be overwhelmed with tenderness as her hand closes around your finger. You can welcome visitors, glowing with pride at showing them that you are a parent, but then be suddenly overcome with a sense that parenthood has trapped you so that you will never again be a separate individual person but forever committed to this baby. It's true that becoming a parent has changed things for you forever, but it's also true that when your feelings stop swinging so wildly from one extreme to the other, that thought won't panic you. So don't panic. And don't even play with the idea of making an early break back to the workplace even if it feels to you as if that's exactly what your partner is doing. You need time to adapt to your new role and to form a real relationship with your baby before you pull yourself away from her and go back to work, as though pretending that nothing very momentous or lasting has happened to you. Something momentous has happened, and when you do go back to work it should be as the parent you've become not as someone who's on the run from parenthood.

In these first days when you don't really know your not-yet-knowable baby or the new life of being a parent, you may turn to child

Keep your baby close and she'll play her part in ensuring that you love each other.

rearing plans and policies, looking for rules to follow that will bring some order out of chaos. But plans and policies are no use to you yet because they can only be judged by their consistent results, and nothing you (or anyone else) can think up will get consistency from a newborn. Your best guides to handling her are her physical needs, reflexes and reactions. Handle her so that the change from womb to world is minimized.

Keep things simple

There's nothing complicated about your new baby's needs, but they do roll rapidly around, and when she needs something, she needs it *now*.

◆ Milk, her food and water.

◆ Soft, light clothing and bedding, for warmth and comfort in cuddling arms, or a small, safe bed.

◆ Skin kept just clean enough that it does not get sore.

◆ Protection, not only from danger but also from fear and frustration.

The enchanting clothes, exciting toys, ingenious equipment and endless toiletries that tempt you in every baby department may be fun for you to buy. But right now she doesn't need most of them and is better off without. A new baby only needs soft warm wrappings. Don't dress her up—she'll hate the dressing business and not notice the clothes. Dress and wrap her for comfort. Don't even try to take her out in that stroller—the bumps will terrify her and she doesn't need "fresh air." Hold her closely, move with her slowly, and put her down gently. Otherwise all she needs you to do is feed her if she even might be hungry, wash the parts of her that are dirty, and put your face within a foot of hers and talk to her when she looks at you. Unless she is actually ill and under medical care, you don't have to do anything that startles or upsets her. If your handling makes her relaxed and content you've got it right; if it distresses her, you don't. If you can let her responses guide you, the baby will gradually come to realize that she gets what she needs when she needs it. That means that by the time she is a settled baby she will experience this world outside the womb as a good place—and that's the best possible start for any child.

Taking charge of your new baby

Even if you are one of the majority of women who give birth in a hospital, you and your partner are very likely to be at home and in sole charge of your baby about two days after the delivery. You may have seen how the nurses lifted and dressed

---

Parents talking about...

taking their baby home

❝ The worst thing about our first full day as parents was not being able to install the car seat. We had bought one, but we'd had this romantic vision of me carrying the baby home in the car, all wrapped up in the lovely shawl my mom gave us so it was only when the hospital pointed out that it would be illegal to take the baby in the car without a car seat, that my husband (who hadn't had any sleep either) started reading the instructions.... **❞**

From research

Infant carriers/car seats. All newborn seats are rear-facing. Your baby should never travel in the car facing forward before she turns one and weighs 20 pounds (9 kg). Up to that time a quarter of her whole weight is in her head, so an accident when she is facing forward means potentially disastrous whiplash. Don't install your baby's seat in the front passenger seat of your car if it has an air bag.

In the event of a collision, the more upright your baby is the better. But for normal everyday life lying flat is ideal. Most car seats compromise by holding babies at about 45°. This means that your baby should not spend more than two hours at a time in a car seat; longer than that risks breathing problems; some babies who have spent long periods in car seats have even been found to have low levels of oxygen in their blood.

Most infant carriers can be attached to the frame of a stroller. Of course it's nice to be able to take your sleeping baby out of the car in her seat, put her into her stroller and go shopping or meet friends. But don't let that convenience mean that your baby spends half the day in the carrier, even if it allows a nearly flat position when used with a stroller. Flat means flat, not almost.

You don't need a "getting started" CD, you just need the baby.

her. You may have been shown how to bathe her and how to make sure she is well latched onto the breast. But you may not get even as much teaching as that, and you're unlikely to get much more. Unless you're one of the lucky minority with babies to practice on among your family or friendship group, most of the rest will be hands-on learning by doing.

Babies don't come with a "getting started" CD, and there are things about handling them when they're brand new that it's helpful to be shown or told about, especially with twins. If you don't have a beloved grandmother or dextrous doula waiting for you at home, though, don't worry. Provided you have peaceful time to spend holding and watching and just being with her, you can learn almost all you need to know about handling your baby from her physical reactions.

Whether you've planned these first days as a "babymoon" or not, the best way to start learning about your baby is to have her with you on your big bed so that as well as putting her to the

Twin tip

Two babies need two adults. Picking up or putting down two new, wobbly-headed babies together is really difficult; some parents never get the knack. Right now your two babies need both their parents, and any doubt about their father's equal involvement evaporates. At home, arrange safe places to put one baby while you hold or do something with the other: A changing mat you can put one on while you settle the other in her crib or bouncy seat; somewhere in the car where you can lay both babies before you buckle each in turn into the car seats.

breast whenever she seems interested, you can watch her, stroke her, and hold her without worrying about dropping her as you lift her from a crib or bumping her head on a doorframe as you move around the house.

Your new baby's reflexes

One of the first things you'll probably notice is that your baby is very scrunched-up looking. She never lies flat or straight; whatever position you lie her in, she curls inward around a head that is so big and heavy, it acts as a pivot for the rest of her.

That large head acts as an anchor too, restricting her voluntary movements. She can lift that head a little and she will always try to turn it to avoid smothering, but movements of her arms and legs are limited by her curled position, and having her head always turned to one side prevents her from seeing things—such as your faces—directly above her. Don't try to straighten her out. If you want her to see something, put it in her eyeline.

Why it matters...

that you understand newborn reflexes.
Watching your newborn baby's reflex behaviors can help you understand how she wants to be handled, and whether or not you're getting it right.

The "Moro response" and "Reflex grasping" were probably vitally important to our prehistoric ancestors, whose infants clung to their mothers. Contemporary human babies cannot cling on to an adult as baby monkeys do, but they seem to want to. Almost all new babies are happiest being carried belly-to-belly with the adult with a hand supporting their wobbly necks. Slightly older babies like to have their arms around the adult neck, or their fingers twined in the hair or hanging onto the nearest ear.

When new babies are not being carried, many are calmest and happiest when they are "held" by tight swaddling. Many seem to feel exposed when they are partially or completely naked.

You'll be able to see your baby's muscle-control developing from day one, starting from the top and moving downward. By the time she's about a month old she'll have enough control over her neck muscles to be able to support her head upright for a few seconds, but right now she can't. If you go to pick her up with your hands under her knees and shoulders, her head will drop back. When you hold her face to face with you against your shoulder, she rests her head against you, but if you hold her away from you without your hand behind her neck, her head will flop.

◆ **The "Moro response":** If you don't support your baby's head, or if you (or her three-year-old brother) handle her roughly so that she feels that she's going to be dropped, or if you put her down carelessly so that your hands start to release her before she feels the firm security of the mattress, you'll probably see the primitive reflex attempt to save herself that is called the "Moro response." As her head goes back her arms will snatch up at yours and her legs will curve convulsively upwards as if seeking a body around which to clasp themselves. She will probably cry out in fear. The Moro response is a reflex you want to see as seldom as possible: It's a clear message to be more careful.

Some of the other reflex behaviors you'll see have a different message for you: Don't be fooled. During the first week of life, this baby, whose muscles are still so incompetent she can't even balance her head, may look as if she is going to crawl or even walk within weeks. She isn't though. Reflex behaviors don't lead to voluntary ones; indeed they have to die out to make room for further development.

◆ **Reflex "crawling":** If you put her on her tummy, the baby's curled-up position means that she flexes her legs and arms, even "scrabbling" so that she looks as if she's trying to crawl off. That will stop when she becomes able to uncurl herself and lie flat.

◆ **Reflex "walking":** If you hold your baby in a standing position, supporting all her weight with the soles of her feet just touching a firm surface such as your thigh, she will take quite deliberate "steps," placing one foot after another. This behavior will also drop out of her repertoire very soon. Held in that position in a week or so she will simply sag.

◆ **Reflex "grasping":** Your baby will grasp anything that touches the palm of her hand—such as your finger—with such strength that according to some reports you could actually hang her up by her hands and she would not fall. Don't try this at home, though. The grip weakens within a couple of days.

Unlike crawling or walking reflexes, the grasp reflex is not something which your baby has to unlearn and then learn all over again. Although it quickly loses its extraordinary strength, this reflex reaction leaves useful traces that eventually merge with manual development.

Her hand will grip around anything she can hold, such as your finger or a toy that touches her palm. If you try to remove it, her fist will grip it more tightly in a reflex attempt to hang on. This reaction will continue through all the weeks to come before your baby is ready to take hold of objects on purpose.

(1) Reflex walking drops out after a week or so. (2) This crawling reflex only lasts until she begins to lie flat. (3) Reflex grasping is so strong it can take her weight. But take care—it will weaken a few days after the baby's birth. (4) This is the reflex that you don't want to see: The Moro response means "I'm scared of being dropped."

Your new baby's senses

A baby is born with all five senses in working order, and from the moment she emerges from her mother's body they are bombarded with sights and sounds, and sensations.

She does not have to learn how to see, to hear, to sense touch through the skin, or even to smell or taste, but she does have to learn what those sensory messages mean. She can see your face but she has no knowledge or experience to tell her that an object that looks like this *is* a face.

Your baby is learning about the world through her senses from the very beginning. If you watch her you can soon see what sights, sounds, and sensations your baby does and doesn't like.

Touching and being touched

We've already seen that touch elicits some newborn reflexes. Babies react to the feel of an object in their fists by gripping onto it, to a stroking touch on the cheek by rooting, and to a solid surface under the soles of their feet when they are held upright by making stepping movements.

Touch is also enormously important in its own right. Babies enjoy touch, but more than that, they *need* it. Skin-to-skin contact comforts and relaxes newborns and makes them breathe more deeply so that they get more oxygen.

The skin of a newborn baby has never-before-known changes in texture, moisture, pressure, or temperature, so it is acutely sensitive. It really matters to your baby that her clothing is soft, diapers are not fastened too tightly, and the water with which you wash her face is neither cold nor hot.

From the first day of life onward, your baby may feel exposed and unhappy when her clothes are taken off—even if the room is really warm. Laying a textured fabric such as a towel, a diaper, or your soft sweater over her bare tummy will usually soothe her.

Both new and older babies are calmed and pleased by warm, soft, firm pressure, especially up the front surface of their bodies. In fact that's something that doesn't change. We all enjoy hugs.

Smelling and tasting

Eons ago, smell and taste gave our distant ancestors crucial guidance as to which plants or berries were edible and which might be poisonous.

From research

How we know what babies feel or think.
A lot of research ingenuity has been devoted to studying the feelings of babies too young to cooperate or communicate, and to finding ways of measuring their responses so that one baby can be compared with another. Given a choice, babies will always look first or for longer at the sight they find most interesting; that's how we know that babies prefer drawings of faces to colorful abstracts.

Similarly, we know that a brand new baby can recognize his mother's voice and prefers it to any other, because given a headset and two recorded voices linked to a pacifier and two different rates of sucking, babies as young as two days old learn to suck at the rate that will let them hear their mother's voice rather than the stranger's. We know that babies can recognize the smell of their own mother's milk, too, because if a breast pad used by her mother is put to one side of the baby's head and a breast pad from another mother is put to the other side, the baby will turn her head toward the mother-smell in 75% of trials.

That is probably why today's new babies share a lot of adult reactions to smells and tastes, turning disgusted faces away from the smell of rotten eggs and recoiling, even crying, in response to a sour or bitter taste. At the beginning, though, your baby is even more sensitive to slight differences in smell and taste than you are. She can tell the difference between the smell of your milk and anyone else's, and differentiate accurately between plain, slightly sweetened, and very sweet water, sucking bottles containing any of these but sucking longer and harder as the sweetness increases.

Hearing, listening, and making sounds

Babies can hear from before birth and react with soothed pleasure after birth to recordings of sounds with which they have lived before it. Loud, sudden sounds—such as your phone ringing close to her ear—will make your baby jump. Very loud but dull sounds, such as thunder overhead, will not bother her nearly as much as a sharp, sudden noise like a tray of silverware being dropped. She will enjoy real, melodic music, but she may enjoy the "music" of rhythmically pounding domestic machinery, such as a spinning clothes dryer, just as much.

Your baby can hear all these sounds and many others, but her favorite sounds—the ones she listens to with obvious concentration— are human voices: people talking. Her interest in voices is pre-programmed because her survival depends on adult people.

Your baby's interest in your voices may not always be obvious because in these first weeks her listening and looking are separate systems, so she listens to you without looking at you. Watch carefully, though, and you will see that she often reacts to your voice before she can see you. If she is crying and you talk as you go to her, she will often stop crying before you get there. If she is lying still on her playmat when you start talking to her, she will begin to move, looking excited. If she has been waving her arms around when she first hears your voice, she will probably stop and freeze to attention. When she hears your voice, she listens, and when you talk directly to her, her heart beats faster.

Skin-to-skin and face-to-face: Your baby loves this kind of cuddling, and it's good for her, too.

You may hear...

that very young babies don't actually feel pain. It is said that their reactions to painful procedures, like having a heel pricked to get blood for testing, are just a matter of reflex. Research disproved this brutal fallacy more than 20 years ago. It concluded that newborn responses to pain are similar to adults' but often greater, so if you know that a procedure would hurt you, it will undoubtedly hurt your baby too.

The eyes have it. She's scanned the face from hairline to chin and she's ended up, as she always does, gazing into your eyes.

Your baby cannot understand your words, of course—that's months ahead. But even as a newborn she detects and reacts to the tones she hears in your voice. She reacts with pleasure to gentle affectionate chatter, but louder, rougher talk alarms her, and if you speak sharply to someone else, or perhaps to the family dog, while you are holding your baby, she may cry.

A baby's only deliberate sounds during these early days are cries. Because babies' crying sounds very different on different occasions, people have worked hard at trying to establish a "language of cries" that would enable parents to understand what their baby is crying about— or crying for. However most of the variation you'll hear in your baby's crying is in its volume, its pitch and its intensity. Of course you'll be able to tell the difference between frantic or panicky crying and grumbling. But does the grumbly crying really have a different meaning or is it simply the earliest stages of crying that will become frantic if it is not answered? Listening to your baby when she cries will certainly teach you to recognize a lot of differences in her mood and state, but while that is useful in itself, it doesn't help you to answer the crucial question: *"Why is she crying again (or still)?"*

You may hear...

of "The Secret Language of Babies" coined by an Australian mother in 2007 and given wide exposure on the Oprah Winfrey show. It suggests a "crying vocabulary" including: "Eh" (I need to burp); "Neh" (I'm hungry); and "Owh" (I'm sleepy). More recently a baby monitoring device called "WhyCry" has claimed to convert cries into digital sound waves and identify them as caused by "stress," "annoyance," "boredom," "sleepiness," or "hunger". It's impossible to predict technological progress, but right now it still seems more important to watch and listen to your actual baby than even the niftiest device.

Looking

It used to be thought that new babies could see very little, but that's because although they *can* focus their eyes to see things at different distances, it is difficult for them until the muscles that control the eyes strengthen, so they often don't bother. The focusing distance that is easy for a new baby is about 8–10 in (20–25 cm) from the bridge of the nose. She can see things clearly at that precise distance, but objects that are farther away are blurred. If she's lying on your bed and there's nothing particular for her to look at within her focal distance, she'll gaze at the window or a blowing curtain. As every short-sighted adult knows, movement and brightness are always easy to see.

Faces are the most important things for a new baby to look at, just as voices are the most important things for her to listen to, and for the same reason. She is programmed to study a face whenever she gets the opportunity, and it cannot be chance that her ideal focusing range is exactly the distance from which she sees your face when she is breast-feeding. That ensures that she gets lots of opportunities. Perhaps the blurring out of things that are farther away from her is actually useful in survival terms, helping her to concentrate on the vital face of a caring adult.

Your baby does not study your face because it is you, of course; she studies your face because it is a face. She'll give her concentrated attention to any face that comes into her visual range and if there's no real face available to look at she'll focus on anything that looks like one.

From research

Looking at "faces." Many studies have been made of what features make things "face-like" for babies. Those features are a hairline, eyes, a mouth, and a chin-line. If a picture, or the merest sketch, has all those, your baby will behave as if it is a real face. Watch her eyes and you'll see that she starts at the top by scanning the hairline, then scans slowly down to the chin-line, finishing by gazing at the eyes.

Newborn crying

However comfortably you are settled together on your babymoon bed, it won't be long before your baby cries. Babies are genetically programmed to cry for someone to make them feel better whenever they are uncomfortable or distressed, and in their first weeks outside the womb, that is often.

Your new baby's crying may be triggered by hunger or tiredness or cold, or by something that shocks or scares her, such as a sharp sound, a bright light, a rough fabric, or a sudden movement. But you may never know the reason for a particular crying session because, at this early stage, there may not be a specific definable cause. Some newborn crying that cannot be

You may hear...

that babies cry for nothing, cry to exercise their lungs, or cry to manipulate you.
That's all nonsense at this age. Babies cry because they are uncomfortable or unhappy and they need an adult to restore their equilibrium so they feel better again. Lungs get all the exercise they can use in a lifetime of nonstop breathing, and being manipulative requires sophisticated thinking that depends on a brain chemical called "glutamate" working in the frontal lobes (or neo-cortex). That glutamate system is not established in a new baby's brain so she isn't capable of thinking much about anything—let alone how to control you.

From research

All baby mammals cry. It's not only human babies who are genetically programmed to cry for help. Separate a puppy or a kitten from its littermates and mother, and if nobody offers alternative comfort, it will cry for hours.

more specifically identified is referred to as "developmental," meaning that it's related to the internal turmoil babies experience while they are settling into life outside the womb. Attributing a baby's distress to her development is somewhat like putting adult distress down to "The Human Condition." Still, if the explanation is not directly helpful to parents, it does at least make it clear that the crying is not their fault. Whatever the reason, it is clear that your baby experiences everything from overall comfort and contentment to overwhelming discomfort and distress, but she has neither the brain development nor the experience to understand or manage these feelings for herself. She can detect potential threats: The area in her lower brain (the amygdala) that is responsible for that is fully functional from birth. But she cannot interpret those alarm signals. When the bed rocks because her loving father has sat down on the edge, she may react as her prehistoric ancestor might have reacted to a saber-toothed tiger or the beginning of an earthquake.

If your brand-new baby begins to cry as she wakes, so that there has been no incident, no "reason" for the crying, it's likely that her discomfort is internal: She may be hungry (though she doesn't yet know that sensation as a desire to feed), she may have a bubble of gas to burp up, she may have been woken by the novel sensation of making a poop. It really doesn't matter if you don't actually know why she's crying, because what she needs from you is that you take charge of making her feel comfortable again. That may mean that you try all the kinds of comfort you have at your disposal: picking her up, holding her closely, offering the breast, checking her diaper.

If your baby never cried, you'd never be sure she was OK.

Staying safe

Parents want to keep new babies happy and protect them from all harm, but that isn't always as obvious and easy as it sounds. If their baby never seems happy, mothers and fathers can feel like failures at parenting when it's barely begun. And when a baby keeps crying for no obvious reason and no matter what the parents do, the noise, designed by nature to alert adults to babies' needs, may be hard to bear. If you feel your stress levels rising, you need to protect that beloved baby from yourself. Irritation could make you handle him roughly or even shake him, which could have tragic consequences (*see p. 274*). Pass him to someone else, or if there's nobody, put him in his crib and leave him for a short time while you take a break and get a grip.

Newborn feeding

Sucking for food is not only essential to your baby's survival, but also his principal pleasure in life outside the womb. For you too, it can be a source of satisfaction and, eventually, delight.

Breast-feeding is definitely, measurably, unarguably better for your baby than bottle-feeding. The advantages start on day one and last for years, probably for life. Breast-feeding is seriously better for you, too. Of course it's up to you whether you breast-feed or not and for how long—it's your body and your baby after all—but making an informed choice depends on having all the available information. And once all that information is set out, it's clear that the way you feed your baby isn't a lifestyle choice, a matter of convenience or of what's expected and accepted among your relatives and friends. If you can breast-feed your baby, that's the best way to go. Your partner's not off the hook because he can't do it: Nothing will help breast-feeding more than his unwavering support.

Decisions, decisions…

Unless there is a physical reason why you can't breast-feed or you can't even cope with the thought of it, there's really no decision to be made at this early stage.

Why? Because even if you're very unsure about being a breast-feeding mother, it's sensible to start out that way in order to keep your options open for the long term while doing your baby good in the meantime. Should you find it impossible to enjoy, manage, or even tolerate nursing, you can always wean the baby (gently) from breast to bottle. But if you start off with a bottle it will soon be too late to change your mind. Unless you've been expressing milk regularly (as you might if your baby is pre-term and has difficulty suckling in the first days), you cannot switch from bottle to breast because there won't be any milk.

Almost all breasts are capable of nursing provided their owner is willing, and that includes small breasts, breasts with flat or inverted nipples, breasts with pierced nipples, and, usually, breasts with cosmetic implants.

There are so many scientifically proven advantages to breast-feeding that when you see them listed it's surprising that not everybody who can breast-feed does. Your breast milk is tailored to your baby—to what he needs this morning, next month, and next year. It passes

You may hear...

that bottle-feeding is better for modern families because the father can share the joy of feeding his baby and the mother can sleep while he does some night feeds. Oh please! Every parent knows that feeding is the baby's basic need and has to come before father's joy or even mother's sleep. Anyway once mother and baby have had a month or so to learn breast-feeding, father can give as many bottles as he likes—of expressed breast milk.

Parents talking about...

breast versus bottle

❝When we were pregnant friends told us that breast-feeding was such a hassle that we'd never be able to get out or have any fun. We've found the opposite: Bottle-feeding friends are tied to making up formula and carrying enough bottles that are kept safely cold. They can't spontaneously decide to stay overnight after a party, and if a plane's delayed by six hours they're in a panic. All our baby needs is me.❞

The decision is yours, but breast-feeding keeps your options open.

From research

Contraindications to breast-feeding. There are a few medical conditions and treatments that make breast-feeding inadvisable, such as: Untreated active tuberculosis (TB), adult T-cell leukemia and lymphoma, active herpes lesions on the breast, chemotherapy, and various specialized drugs such as lithium.

Breast milk can transmit HIV, but the risk is small. HIV-positive mothers with access to safe formula should bottle-feed, but for those without, breast-feeding may be a lesser risk than poor hygiene and a lack of clean water. Drug dependent mothers who breast-feed risk inducing narcotic dependency in their babies. Babies with a rare genetic metabolic disorder called Galactosemia must not have breast milk.

antibodies from you to him, protecting against or modifying many infections. It contains beneficial bacteria which help keep his digestive tract healthy and high levels of essential fats. In fact breast milk is said to contain at least 400 nutrients that aren't available in any formula.

Benefits of breast-feeding

Proven benefits to babies:

◆ Breast milk (yours, remember, not just anybody's) is uniquely right for your baby, adjusting itself to his age and stage and to conditions, too. So if the weather is particularly warm and he needs extra water, your breast milk will adjust to the situation and provide it.

◆ Breast milk changes within each feeding to accommodate your baby's appetite. That not only means more contentment, but also less risk of obesity. The first milk your baby gets from each breast, the foremilk, is low in calories so your baby can suck for thirst and pleasure without feeling too full. It's when he empties the breast that he gets the high-nutrient hindmilk.

◆ Breast-fed babies have fewer or less-severe respiratory infections and long-lasting colds, and fewer episodes of wheeziness and glue ear than bottle-fed babies.

◆ They suffer fewer urinary tract infections, gastrointestinal infections and bouts of diarrhea.

◆ Breast-fed babies are less likely to develop juvenile diabetes.

◆ They are less likely to become obese in childhood.

◆ Breast-fed infants' immune systems are more effective, which reduces the risk of disorders such as asthma and eczema, even where there is a family history of them.

◆ Breast-feeding reduces the small chance of Sudden Infant Death Syndrome even further.

Probable benefits to babies:

◆ Research suggests that breast-fed babies turn out to be more intelligent. Recent large studies found that six-year-olds who had been exclusively breast-fed as babies scored an extra 5.9 points in a battery of IQ and performance tests.

◆ The risk of childhood leukemia is less.

Twin tip

If two babies demand milk from you, your breasts will supply it just as they would for one, and with the same provisos: that both babies are allowed to nurse when and for as long as they want to. Once you have gotten breast-feeding established, nursing twins is not much different from nursing a single baby, provided you can feed them both at the same time (which means persuading them both to accept the same routine). You may need to feed first one and then the other at the very beginning while they are learning to latch on, but that really will mean that you spend most of your time breast-feeding. Once both babies are competent at latching on, get someone who has nursed twins, or helped other twin mothers, to show you how to position the babies so that you can nurse both together. One in the conventional nursing position and the other in the "football hold" under the other arm is an option that works for many mothers.

A double football hold with plenty of pillows can work well when feeding twins.

Proven benefits to mothers' health:

◆ Breast-feeding women tend to get back to their pre-pregnancy weight more rapidly.

◆ The hormones released in nursing help to relax mothers and combat stress. After night feeds it is those hormones that will make it easier for you to get back to sleep.

◆ The uterus returns to its pre-pregnancy state much faster.

◆ Women who breast-feed are less likely to develop breast or ovarian cancer before they reach menopause.

◆ They are less likely to suffer osteoporosis and therefore fractures in later life.

◆ The risk of type 2 diabetes is less.

◆ Postpartum depression is less likely.

◆ Breast-feeding will usually relieve PMS (pre-menstrual syndrome) in the long term as well as menstruation in the short term. Do remember though, that even if your periods have not returned, you cannot assume that breast-feeding will reliably prevent pregnancy.

Probable benefits to your relationship:

◆ Did anyone ever tell you that for many women established nursing feels wonderful, not just emotionally, because it brings you and the baby close and you know it's the best way to feed her, but also physically? Try it.

◆ Breast milk, and getting it by nursing at the breast, is what your baby most wants and most enjoys, and you are the one and only person who can provide it. When breast-feeding goes smoothly it's wonderful; when it doesn't, it's not. The first couple of weeks can be, well, challenging—but persistence pays off and it's worth every effort.

◆ Breast-feeding makes those frequent night feedings much easier.

◆ Breast-feeding makes sure that you spend quite a lot of time sitting or lying down, which means that you'll be resting.

◆ Once breast-feeding is established and you both take it for granted, your baby need never be kept waiting for a feeding, and you can go anywhere and do almost anything without worrying about being delayed or otherwise stuck out without a bottle.

Go as and where you please and don't worry about delays: your breasts always have everything your baby needs.

From research

Breast-feeding and SIDS. Recent large-scale research work has shown that not only exclusive, but also partial breast-feeding may reduce the risk of SIDS.

The beginning of breast-feeding

Breast-feeding for most of a year is ideal, but if you can only breast-feed for a couple of months it is still worthwhile for your baby. And even one single week ensures that he gets that precious colostrum.

From your point of view, nursing for as little as two or three weeks isn't ideal as it will probably give you more of the worst breast-feeding has to offer, than of the blissful best. It will certainly give you some physical advantages, though.

But if breast-feeding briefly is better for both of you than not at all, breast-feeding half-heartedly may not work well. Nursing is most likely to be a pleasure if you ignore anyone who suggests that it won't be—that you'll get too tired or that you won't make enough milk. Those dire warnings easily turn into self-fulfilling prophecies, especially in the first days after birth when they have kernels of truth. Trust yourself (and surround yourself with people who trust you) to provide, and your baby to take, everything he needs. Don't even buy bottles or formula or pacifiers.

Don't expect getting started with breast-feeding to be easy, though. And don't be discouraged if you have friends who breast-feed anywhere, anytime, and can feed their babies one handed while doing something else with the other, while you concentrate one hundred percent and still struggle. It's because people don't realize that it's not unusual for a lot of first-time mothers to find the early days of nursing worrying, strange, and uncomfortable—even painful—that so many give it up instead of getting through to the good time ahead. To assure yourself that there is a good time ahead, with milk available like magic whenever the baby wants it and wherever you want it to be, look at mothers who have breast-fed one baby and now are having another. Whatever difficulties they may have in the first few weeks they hardly ever give up because they know from experience that keeping it up will be worthwhile.

Using your baby's rooting and sucking reflexes

Your baby is too young and immature to know that the discomfort he feels is hunger; that food will make him comfortable again or that sucking the breast or a bottle is the way to get food. He learns all this from you and from experience, building on his rooting and sucking reflexes.

Your baby's rooting reflex makes him respond to any gentle breast-like touch or stroking on his cheek by turning his face toward it to search for the nipple and pursing his lips ready to suck. If those pursed lips touch something nipple-like, he opens his mouth widely, ready to latch on.

Writing it out makes it all sound far more complicated than it is. In fact if breast-feeding goes smoothly from the beginning, you can just go for it without worrying about what is reflex and

From research

Sucking reflexes. These develop later than rooting reflexes and in brand new babies, especially pre-term babies, they have to compete with the babies' gag reflexes. It's far more urgent for your new baby to get mucus out of her airways than food into her tummy, so don't be surprised or feel rejected if a mouthful of breast simply makes her gag and spit up rather than suck and swallow.

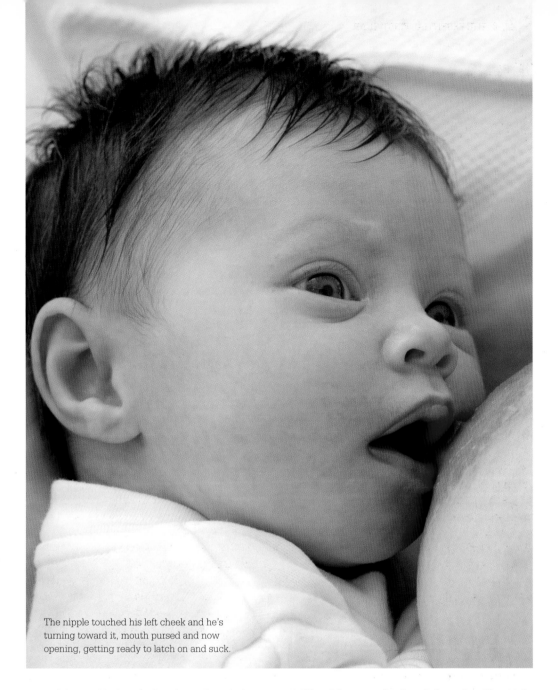

The nipple touched his left cheek and he's turning toward it, mouth pursed and now opening, getting ready to latch on and suck.

what is learned behavior. It's if your baby's first feedings don't go smoothly that it will probably be helpful to have a clear picture of the processes so that you can at least avoid working against them:

◆ **Avoid contradictory cues:** Your baby will turn his head towards a touch on his cheek so if you touch both cheeks at once he won't know which way to turn. And if you try to turn his head by holding both cheeks he will probably fight you.

◆ **Give him cues in the right order:** He needs to be rooting for the nipple before you present it, so don't start a feed by touching it to his lips.

◆ **Get the timing right:** If your nipple is still in your bra when your baby's mouth opens for it, you probably won't be able to latch him on without starting again.

◆ **Let your baby set the pace:** You cannot force your baby to suck, and it is better not to try.

The right circumstances for early feedings

Get comfortable; there are many different positions for nursing, so do experiment. Your baby needs to learn a vital lesson: Sucking = milk = comfort.

It will help him to learn and to get enthusiastic about the whole nursing business if feedings are kept comfortable and peaceful, and the more enthusiastic he becomes, the more comfortable and peaceful you will feel.

Your own comfort while nursing mostly depends on getting the baby fully latched on (see p. 88) but temporary discomforts caused by the hormone oxytocin flooding through your body during very early feeds may take you aback. Oxytocin is the hormone that stimulates labor contractions, so it's not surprising that it also stimulates the contractions that gradually reduce your womb to its pre-pregnant size. You may feel these as "after-pains"—something like severe menstrual cramps—at any time, but especially when oxytocin is released in response to your baby's sucking. Less uncomfortable but equally surprising is the oxytocin-stimulated "let-down" reflex, which feels like a warm tingling in your breasts and releases milk to the baby from the breast he is sucking, and sometimes a leak from the other.

◆ **Don't try to feed a baby who is really upset and screaming.** He is overwhelmed by his feelings and will not latch on well enough to discover that he can suck himself comfortable. It will be better for both of you if he is offered a feed before he ever reaches that point, but if your baby has been kept waiting and is upset, he

---

Twin tip

Whatever nursing position you are using, surround yourself with cushions or pillows so that if one of the babies isn't ready to latch on or needs a rest, you can gently roll him off the breast and beside you without disturbing the other baby. You've then got one free hand to stroke and pat.

Why it matters...

how the baby latches on. A breast-fed baby should not ever suck your nipples. If he does, he will get little or no milk and you will probably get extremely sore.

The baby gets the milk by squeezing the edges of the areola between his gums and his tongue and squirting it through the nipple. That means that he needs to have most of the lower half of the areola in his mouth, with his tongue beneath it and the nipple pointing toward the roof of his mouth.

---

needs comforting before you attempt to persuade him to suck. You might try rocking him, walking around with him, or simply swaddling him.

◆ **If your baby seems to be distracted from sucking by noise and movement, try to feed him on your own for a few days.** At least try to position yourself so that your body is between your baby and the room, and your face is directly above his. If you can get him to focus on you, other things will be less distracting. A constant stream of talk from you may also blanket out other sounds.

◆ **If your baby is too sleepy to keep sucking, don't try to force him to stay awake.** It really doesn't matter if he goes to sleep after a few sucks because if he needs a few more later on, he will ask for them. Try to protect him from people who think he should be bounced around or have his feet flicked to keep him awake for a "good feed." He won't nurse well right now if he is upset, and you don't want him ever to associate feeding with stress.

Starting nursing can be difficult for your baby as well as for you. If your breast is not yet full of milk, but only has some colostrum in it, it may be soft enough to block his nose when he tries to suck, and then he may panic. You can either move his bottom a little bit closer to your body so that his forehead moves fractionally away, or you can use the fingers of your free hand to make a breathing-space depression in the breast, just above the areola.

Different positions may be comfortable for you and help your baby latch on. (1) Sitting up, use pillows to lift her nose level with your nipple, whether you hold her across your body or under your arm (2) in a "football hold". (3) Nursing lying down can be bliss for you both but bring the baby to the breast, not the breast to the baby.

Getting your baby latched on to the breast

A good start with breast-feeding is largely a question of position, position, position. Getting your baby properly latched onto your breast is all-important, both for his feeding and for your comfort, especially the prevention of sore nipples.

During the three to five days after the birth, before your milk comes in, your breasts are still soft; this is the ideal time for your baby to practice feeding as well as getting that all-important colostrum. Put him to the breast often—that practice is important—because once your milk comes in, your newborn will find your larger, harder, breasts more difficult to cope with.

Whatever position you are feeding in, make sure your baby's head and body are in a straight line so he can swallow easily, and that you are supporting his back, shoulders, and neck.

Hold your baby close to you, face to face, with his nose (not his mouth) level with your nipple. That way he can take a big mouthful of breast from underneath the nipple.

Wait until he opens his mouth really wide, as if he was yawning, with his tongue down. You can encourage him to do that by stroking his upper lip.

As soon as his mouth opens wide, bring him even closer into your breast; he will tilt his head back and approach it chin first so that the lower part of the areola goes into his mouth and your nipple points toward the roof of his mouth.

You'll know his position is good if his chin is touching your breast and if any dark skin of your areola that's visible shows more above his top lip than below his bottom lip.

Giving those first feeds

When the milk comes in, it may (but may not) bring some problems with it: minor, short-lived, but definitely uncomfortable and sometimes really painful ones. None of them suggest any failure in your capacity for breast-feeding, but your body may have to learn how to nurse just as your baby does.

After the birth, hormones that control your production of milk (prolactin) and your "let-down" reflex (oxytocin) largely take over from the progesterone and estrogen your placenta has been producing throughout your pregnancy. At first your breasts may respond too emphatically to these chemical messages so that your breasts suddenly swell, not only with milk but with an increased blood supply.

Engorgement

If your breasts become huge and hard, hot, and painful, with even the areolae around the nipples distended, a temporary hormonal imbalance has led to them becoming engorged.

The simplest way to relieve the painful tension in your breasts is have your baby nurse and take some of the excess milk. But if the areolae as well as the breasts are swollen and hard, your baby is unlikely to be able to latch on, and any attempt will be painful for you and fruitless for him. You need to get rid of some of that excess yourself by soaking in a hot bath, or laying warm wet washcloths across your breasts and then very gently stroking your hand down your breast toward your nipple to express some milk before offering him another try.

Engorgement is a temporary problem but it is exceedingly uncomfortable. Cold compresses between feedings may help the swelling and pain to subside by constricting the blood vessels. If you don't have any commercial cold packs available, a packet of frozen peas works well. Divide the peas into two plastic bags so that they are loosely enough packed to fit to the shape of your breasts. If you don't have frozen peas either, or they won't do because you're going out and need to wear a bra (and not defrost in public) you could even try suitably shaped cabbage leaves pre-cooled in the fridge. They don't stay usefully cold for very long though.

Cold packs in your nursing bra feel a great deal better than they look.

Sore nipples

If your baby often sucks your nipples they are very likely to get sore—not because they aren't accustomed to nursing yet, but because they are not designed to be sucked in nursing. The old idea that nipples got sore because of unaccustomed (rather than incorrect) use caused a lot of misery. Misery for mothers, because they got sore nipples, and misery for babies because their sucking time was rationed. Indirectly that idea was also responsible for a lot of breast-feeding "failures" because soreness affected the milk supply and rationing affected the demand. Nipples are not for sucking on, and should only be put into the baby's mouth when it is wide open.

A few other precautions:

◆ **Don't wash your nipples with soap.** In late pregnancy and during breast-feeding they have built-in lubrication from tiny glands ("Montgomery's tubercles") around the areola; better lubrication than any nipple cream.

◆ **Don't scrub your nipples or do anything to harden them.** They are purpose-made for nursing and the more elastic they are, the better.

◆ **Never pull a sucking baby off the nipple.** Wait until he pauses for breath or break the suction with a finger in the corner of his mouth.

◆ **Use a drop of hindmilk to cover your nipples and areolae at the end of each feeding.** If part of the areola ever feels bruised where your baby's gums have worked on it, remember to adjust your position for the next feeding so the main stress falls on a different part.

When you want him to stop nursing, don't pull him off the nipple: Break the suction with a gentle finger in the corner of his mouth.

Taking those first feedings

Minute quantities of colostrum give newborn babies everything they need in the first days of life. Because your baby doesn't need and won't take much food, he will probably lose weight for four or five days and then gain it back over the next four or five when your milk has come in. As a rough rule of thumb, a baby is expected to weigh the same at 10 days as he weighed at birth.

Real breast milk looks bluish and watery compared with thick yellowy colostrum, or the creamy-looking formula you see bottle-fed babies drinking. Breast milk is meant to look like that. Don't decide that it is no good. It is perfect.

Some babies are so ready to suck that they learn the sucking = food = comfort equation quickly and easily. Some of them may have been practicing sucking their fingers in the womb and when they come out they suck anything that's offered—including, of course, their mother's breasts.

Other babies take a while to make the connection. Although they are crying with hunger, putting a nipple in their mouths doesn't help because they don't know they need to suck. Even a taste of colostrum on your finger doesn't help because that taste has not yet come to mean comfort. Your baby will make those connections though. Even if first feeds are a struggle, you can be quite sure that your baby has a set of functional sucking reflexes. The more you can work with those reflexes (rather than trying to plug his yelling mouth with your nipple) the sooner he will suck, discover the food-comfort that sucking brings, and start looking for it.

(Left) Colostrum on the left, foremilk in the centre and rich hindmilk on the right.

(Below) She had the colostrum from her mother's soft breasts; now they're both making a smooth transition to real milk from full breasts.

Why it matters...

that your baby should be exclusively breast-fed.

◆ Breast-feeding is a demand-and-supply system. Your baby demands; your breasts supply.

◆ The more often your baby latches on and sucks, the more often your breasts get hormonal messages to make more milk.

◆ The more milk the baby takes the more your breasts will produce.

◆ If he's already had some formula, he'll take a little bit less breast milk.

◆ Because he takes less your breasts will make less, and because they make less there'll be less for him and he'll take more formula.

◆ Getting attached to a pacifier also means he'll demand less often.

If your baby can find his thumb and get pleasure from it although it's so small, it's better for him than a pacifier.

While he's learning

Unless your baby is pre-term or ill and under special care, don't let health professionals or anxious grandparents persuade you into giving your baby a bottle or a pacifier. You want your baby to get established at the breast so he becomes passionate about nursing for food and comfort. Latex substitutes certainly won't help and may even hinder that process. What's more, if he gets food and drink, or even just sucking comfort, from a bottle or pacifier, your baby's next demand for breast-feeding will be just a bit less urgent and his nursing may be less enthusiastic. Since your milk production depends on the urgency and enthusiasm of his feeding, and on the amount he takes from you, that's the last situation you want.

Breast-feeding is a beautiful supply-and-demand system, but it will work best if you confidently expect it to. So try to believe these truths: You can produce all the food and fluid your newborn baby needs, just as you did when he was in your womb. Colostrum is perfect for your baby now and the milk you make tomorrow will be perfect for him then, and will keep on adjusting itself to be perfect for him in the months to come.

Pacifiers

Don't take it for granted that your baby will use pacifiers. Somehow pacifiers have stopped being viewed as extra help for unhappy babies and become something many parents regard as part of necessary baby equipment and buy ahead of time. There are advantages and disadvantages to pacifiers for different babies and in different circumstances *(see p. 146)* but it's better not to use one for a brand-new baby, especially if you are breast-feeding. There is very strong evidence that babies who are given pacifiers are weaned from the breast earlier than other babies. Using a pacifier every day is linked to a shorter period of exclusive breast-feeding and to scarcity of milk when babies are one month old. Nobody knows whether this is because the women who give new babies pacifiers are already having problems with breast-feeding, because babies find it difficult to switch back and forth between sucking the breast and sucking a pacifier ("nipple confusion"), or because babies who suck a pacifier suck less at the breast and therefore give it less stimulation to produce the milk-producing hormone, prolactin.

Breast-feeding plans

Like birth plans, breast-feeding plans are excellent in principle but very liable to change in practice. If your plans don't work for you and your baby, have no qualms about letting them go.

Parents talking about...

rethinking breast-feeding plans

❝I meant to breast-feed during maternity leave and then use bottles of formula. Lucy foiled that plan because she wouldn't take a bottle at that stage no matter what I did. Good excuse to take a little more time off.❞

❝ It was almost the opposite for me. I thought I'd love nursing and go on for most of the year, but I actually found it really difficult, didn't get much help, and switched to a bottle before three months.❞

Many fathers wish they could feed their babies, but most know that's not a good enough reason to opt for bottle-feeding.

Make bottle-feeding as blissful for
your baby as nursing from the breast.

Thinking about bottle-feeding

Almost all mothers can make enough perfect breast milk, and almost every baby can take it. But "almost" still leaves a few mothers who cannot breast-feed and who have every reason to be thankful for formula and bottles.

Bottles and formula have only been around for a couple of centuries. Before that—and even today in parts of the developing world, the only alternative to a mother's nursing was another woman's. Breast milk is perfect for most babies, but if you have to take prescription drugs that would reach the milk and be damaging to your baby, he will thrive on formula. If he needs your milk but cannot nurse because he is prevented by a cleft lip and palate, or is ill or too premature, then expressed breast milk is the answer and when he first begins to suck he may find bottles easier than the breast. And if you and your baby cannot work out demand and supply to his satisfaction and your comfort, it does not matter how avoidable or reversible the problems may be, it will not be long before the advantages of bottles of formula become obvious to both of you. It's fine to be "pro–breast-feeding" but it's ridiculous to be "anti–bottle-feeding."

Think carefully before you make the change from breast to bottle

If you were really determined to breast-feed, do take your time about giving up because you're finding it difficult. If your breasts are engorged or your nipples are sore, bottle-feeding may look wonderful in comparison, but that may be not because bottle-feeding is wonderful but because breast-feeding is taking a long time to become so. Establishing breast-feeding demands an intense (and sometimes uncomfortable) physical and emotional involvement with your baby. Bottle-feeding formula from the beginning will get you out of that, save you from worrying about whether your body can nourish your baby's (because almost anyone can give him bottles), and let your body belong to you again. Being able to feed the baby from the beginning may mean that his father's bond with him is closer than it would have been if he was exclusively breast-fed. On the other hand the fact that he doesn't get all his feeds from you may make your bond with him feel less tight.

Concerns you might want to raise with a consultant

◆ **The adequacy of your milk supply:** How much milk you produce depends on how often and how efficiently the baby nurses. If you don't think your baby is getting enough—perhaps because he feeds very often and for long periods—the answer is to encourage him, because sucking at the breast is what will build the supply, whereas giving him formula from a bottle will reduce his demands and therefore the amount available.

◆ **Judging whether the baby needs a bottle top-up:** That's unlikely provided he is encouraged to suck when he wants and for as long as he wants, and he is given time on the first breast to ensure that he gets not only the foremilk that's waiting for him in the breast, but also the richer hindmilk that follows it. Indicators that he is getting enough include having at least six thoroughly wet diapers each day and a couple of soiled ones, and regaining his birth weight by two weeks and then continuing to gain.

◆ **Frequent feeds:** Babies vary, and each baby varies from day to day, but many new babies nurse at least 12 times in 24 hours and have a period each day when they want to suck on and off for a couple of hours. Yes, for the moment, breast-feeding is your major activity. Don't try to limit or space out early feeds: They'll get fewer when your supply is balanced against your baby's needs.

◆ **Lengthy feeds:** Again, babies vary in how vigorously and continually they suck, and breasts vary in the rate of flow they produce. As both baby and breasts settle into nursing, feeds may speed up a little, but not all babies ever achieve the oft-quoted 20 minutes.

If you do opt for bottle-feeding

It is usually easier to get a baby started on a bottle than it is on the breast, and since your own comfort is not involved, you can concentrate solely on his.

◆ Settle him close to you and with his head and back in a straight line so he can swallow easily.

◆ As his cheek brushes against you he will probably start rooting, and as his mouth opens you can slip the nipple in.

◆ Keep the bottle tilted so that the nipple is always full and the baby sucks milk not air.

◆ Let him have as much formula as he wants. He may need a break and a burp halfway through, just as he would between breasts.

Bottle hygiene

The first time you use nipples or bottles, you'll need to sterilize them in boiling water for five minutes. After that, sterilization probably isn't necessary; cleaning the parts in hot, soapy water or running them through a dishwasher is fine.

From research

Choosing formula. There is a wide choice of formula on the market: a cow's (rather than goat's or soy) milk formula with whey-based rather than casein-based protein is the best to start with. Nutritionally there is not much difference between these, but convenience and price do vary. Ready-mixed formula is convenient but a lot more expensive and bulkier to store than standard powder.

Some medical authorities believe that household hygiene has been taken too far, and that removing as many germs as possible from babies' environments may confuse their immune systems into reacting against "harmless" substances—foods and so on—producing allergic reactions. Still, it's important to wash all parts thoroughly after every use. Be sure to rinse well, too. If not cleaned properly, they can transmit bacteria.

Everyone agrees that warm or room-temperature milk is a dangerous breeding ground for bacteria, so formula that is mixed ahead of time (or ready-mixed formula once opened) must be refrigerated and only warmed when the baby is ready for it. Any milk left in a bottle must be thrown away, never offered again half an hour later.

Whatever powdered formula you use, make it up exactly according to the manufacturer's instructions on the packet or can. Don't ever add less (or more) water to a given amount of formula, or the feed will be too concentrated (which can be dangerous) or too dilute. And don't ever add anything extra such as sugar or cereal. Making up bottle feeds is science, not creative cooking.

You can buy bottles in an array of colors, shapes, and sizes. Wide-necked bottles are easier to fill than narrow-necked ones, and the small sizes really may not be worth buying, since within a few weeks your baby will need larger feeds than they will hold. Nipples come with different numbers and sizes of holes in a variety of shapes. Some are supposed to reduce the amount of air your baby swallows. A nipple with too small a hole may frustrate your baby so that instead of an easy reward for his sucking he has to work for every sip, and in these early days he may easily give up. If you invert the bottle, the milk should drip out of the nipple at a rate of several drops per second. If it is coming through more slowly than that you need a faster-flowing nipple.

Burping

Babies swallow some air when they're just breathing, more when they are crying, and more still when they are sucking milk. One way or another, then, there is always air in your baby's stomach. It's only a problem when he swallows so much air during a feeding that his tummy gets uncomfortably distended before he's had enough milk.

If that happens to your baby, he will need a half-time burp to make room for the rest of his feeding. When he needs to burp he'll stop sucking, come off the nipple, and probably fuss or cry. Hold him upright for a minute or two and he will burp and then happily return to sucking. Don't remove the nipple from your baby's mouth if he is contentedly sucking, just in case he has too much air in his stomach. He wouldn't still be feeding if he was uncomfortably full; let him suck in peace.

A full feed will leave any baby's minute stomach full to overflowing with milk and air. But while some babies have sucked themselves into sound sleep and stay that way, others are

You may hear...

that soy milk is good for babies who are (or even might be) liable to allergies.
In fact babies may be allergic to the proteins in soy milk itself, and it contains compounds that mimic female hormones and may affect the future fertility of baby boys. If your baby has a medically diagnosed allergy to cow's milk (which will mean he is also allergic to goat's milk) he should have a hypoallergenic formula.

loudly uncomfortable until they can relieve the pressure by burping. If you're fortunate, your baby will be one who burps easily, only needing to be held upright for a minute or two. But some babies need more time and maternal ingenuity before they produce a relieving burp, and even

The ideal position for a cuddly burp (but you might want a cloth....)

If your baby is one who brings up milk as well as air, that burp cloth isn't something you'll want to forget.

then may need another. A cuddle after feeding is nice for both of you, so even if your fully-fed baby is comfortably asleep and obviously not needing a burp right now, it's worth putting him against your shoulder and gently rubbing or patting his back as a precaution against him needing a burp a later. You don't have to go on and on until he does burp though. Maybe he didn't swallow much air this time.

There are babies who seem really uncomfortable until they have burped, even though they don't do it easily. If your baby is one of those, you'll probably try burping him in many different ways and positions. It's fine to experiment with what works for your particular baby, but do keep anatomy in mind. For instance, a sitting position is often advised, but a small baby held sitting may easily have his stomach folded over so that any air is trapped and can't rise above the milk level and escape. Likewise, lying flat, even in the face down position across your lap that your baby may find very soothing, isn't good for burping because it encourages milk and air to mix so that one cannot come up without the other. You want air to rise to the top of the stomach and escape, leaving all the milk behind—that means holding your baby upright.

Spitting up

However careful you are about burping positions, and avoiding energetic bouncing around and over-enthusiastic back-patting, your baby will probably bring up some milk along with the air sometimes. Almost all babies do. Some babies bring up some of their milk at every feeding— sometimes more than once. Mixed with saliva and spread over the shoulder of your clean shirt, it may look like a lot, but it probably isn't. If you are anxious that your baby is losing more milk from his feedings than he can afford, try deliberately spilling a teaspoonful (5 ml) of milk on the other shoulder (the shirt already needs to be washed, after all) to give you a standard of comparison. You'll probably find that your baby is bringing up even less than that.

Common reasons for spitting up milk:

◆ The baby may have sucked more than his stomach can hold. He is simply bringing back the surplus.

◆ Feeding him lying flat meant that the air couldn't rise above the milk. Try holding him more upright next time.

◆ Bouncing him around soon after a feed mixed air and milk together so they could only come up together. Try to handle him gently right after feeding.

◆ He cried a lot because he was kept waiting for the feeding or because he was taken off the nipple mid-feed to burp, but he really just wanted to go on sucking. Crying put a lot of extra air into his stomach, which was then followed by the rest of his milk.

◆ If he is bottle-fed, the bottle may have been held too flat so the entrance to the nipple was not always covered with milk. The baby had sucks of air between sucks of milk, and it is all mixed up together in his stomach.

◆ If he is bottle-fed, the hole in the nipple may have been too small. Having to suck very hard

makes a baby liable to swallow extra air. Make sure that when you turn his bottle upside down, milk drips out of the nipple at several drops per second. (Don't try this using water instead of milk—water is thinner and will come out faster than milk.)

Vomiting

Milk that a baby brings up an hour or more after feeding will be curdled by digestive juices and will probably have a nasty smell. This kind of vomiting may only be due to air that had been trapped in your baby's stomach coming up, bringing partially digested milk with it. However it may suggest a digestive upset or even the beginning of an illness. If your baby has any diarrhea or fever, consult your doctor or clinic.

Projectile vomiting

A baby with projectile vomiting—more common in boys than in girls—doesn't just bring up a little milk when he burps or vomit an hour or so later. Toward the end of each feed he spurts milk out with such force that it may hit the floor or a wall as much as a few feet away. Projectile vomiting does deprive a baby of more of his milk than he can spare, so consult your doctor without delay. She may want to observe a feeding so that she can see the vomiting for herself.

The most likely (though not the only possible) explanation for "projectile vomiting" is a not-uncommon condition called pyloric stenosis. This is a fault in the muscles of the stomach outlet. It is easily and permanently corrected by a small operation.

Staying safe

If there's any reason at all to think that a new baby is unwell, don't wait and see. Medical advice should be sought immediately, even if it is Sunday or the middle of the night. If she seems perfectly well, assume that she is. Feed her as usual whenever she's hungry, but keep an eye open for any symptoms.

Newborn sleep

A small baby's sleeping and waking cycles are a very uncomfortable fit with adults'. For many parents coming to terms with, or surviving, their baby's nights is the most difficult aspect of caring for him.

The more realistic your expectations of your baby's (and therefore your own) sleep in the first weeks, the better. Knowing to expect the worst may not help you cope, but it will help you to be tolerant of each other's difficulties in coping. Don't be misled by the statement that a new baby may sleep as much as 16 to 18 hours of every 24. The information is accurate, but it doesn't mean what it sounds like it means. Eighteen hours a day sounds like the baby is going to be asleep for hours and hours, certainly long enough for you to get adequate sleep yourself. In fact, those hours are the total of many mini-sleeps. In the first weeks your baby will

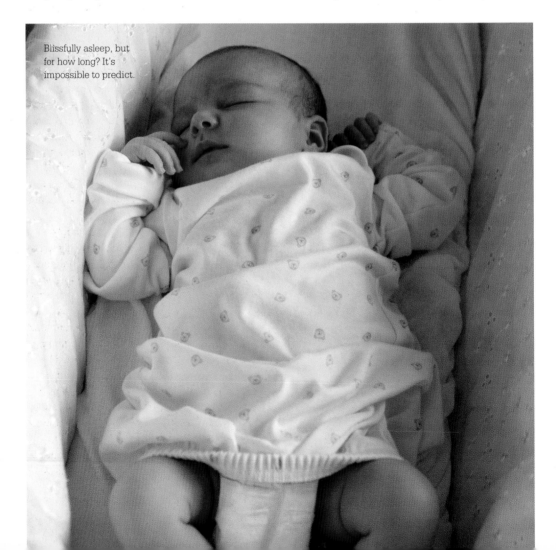

Blissfully asleep, but for how long? It's impossible to predict.

rarely sleep for more than two hours at a time, and will often sleep for as little as half an hour. It takes at least 6–8 weeks for a baby to distinguish night from day well enough to begin to develop a circadian rhythm. In the meantime, he may have his longest sleep from 9–11.30 am and his longest period awake between 1 and 3 am.

You have no way of knowing how long any particular sleep is going to last, and therefore whether it's worth your while to go to bed or embark on a bath. On the other hand once your baby has woken up, you do have some idea how long he will stay awake. In these first weeks most babies can't cope with being awake for more than an hour at a stretch. Being kept awake when he's sleepy won't mean that he'll then sleep for longer though. He may get overtired and find it difficult to settle. Babies vary in how they behave when they are beginning to tire. It's useful to be able to tell when your baby has had enough wakeful time, so watch him carefully. He may be one of the babies who starts to look away or turn his head away from your face or the mobile or toy you were showing him; he may suddenly start to fuss and get irritable; or he may go on looking at his surroundings but get more and more drowsy.

The amount your new baby sleeps is exactly the total amount that his personal physiology tells him to sleep. You are powerless to make him sleep more, and there is nothing that the baby can do to

Twin tip

Twins aren't just two babies, they are two different babies—but if they're willing to accept similar routines, everything will take only one and a half times rather than twice as long. Try all the suggestions for single babies; you've got nothing to lose. If one baby is bigger or stronger than the other though, or one stayed extra time in the hospital (where night is as light as day), it will be weeks before you can even hope that they will eat and sleep and wake at similar times.

make himself sleep less. But if your power over his actual hours of sleep is very limited, your influence over their timing will soon be considerable.

Separating sleep from wakefulness

Brand-new babies often spend a lot of time drifting gradually from wakefulness to sleep and back again, so that it is difficult to be sure which state they are in at any particular moment. Your baby will often start a feeding wide awake and sucking hard, then fall into a trance that would look like sleep if it were not for his occasional bursts of sucking, and soon drop into sleep so sound that even being burped does not wake him.

Moving gradually in and out of sleep is perfectly all right for your baby (he is simply doing what he needs to do when he needs to do it) but it is not ideal for you. If you encourage him gently toward being either awake (and therefore certain to need attention and company) or asleep (and therefore unlikely to need anything at all for a while) it will be much easier for you to organize your life later on. So, even at the very beginning it's probably a good idea to "put him to bed" when he needs to sleep and to "get him up" when he is awake, rather than letting him drift and doze on somebody's lap. If he is always put into his stroller or crib when he is really sleepy, he will soon come to associate those places with being asleep. If he is always taken into whatever company is available when he is awake, he will make that association too.

From research

Your baby's sleep cycles. These probably don't fit with yours. The average sleep cycle of a new baby lasts about 50 minutes, from light sleep to deep sleep and back to light sleep again. The average sleep cycle of an adult is almost twice as long: 90 minutes. Babies are therefore certain to wake far more often than adults do. It also takes a new baby as much as 20 minutes to get from light sleep—during which almost anything (including being put down from your arms into his crib) may rouse him, into deep sleep.

Separating night from day

Although it will be a couple of months before your baby even begins to be a diurnal creature, you may be able to speed up the process a little by making differences between nighttime sleep and daytime naps from the beginning. "Bedtime" routines such as washing him, changing him into nightclothes, and then feeding him in the room where he's going to sleep can be helpful later on, but at this early stage he will probably spend the evening with you so that his night starts at your bedtime.

Swaddling your baby up is intended to give him tactile comfort—and perhaps a reminder of his previous life in the womb—by surrounding him with a warm, soft, gentle holding layer of material. Unlike old-fashioned swaddling, it's not intended to "keep his back straight" or anything of that kind. In fact, it's important to wrap the baby in his natural position with his arms bent at the elbow and his legs flexed. Wrap him like this, making no attempt to straighten him out before you start. Above all, leave his hands where he can suck them if he wants and is able to do so. Efficient wrapping holds the baby's arms and legs in their preferred position so that, when they move, the whole baby moves as one complete bundle rather than feeling himself moving within the shawl. It is magically soothing to most babies.

The swaddle must obviously not be too tight, but if it is too loose it may bother rather than relax the baby. Choose a swaddling blanket that is light and slightly stretchy so that it molds itself a little to his body and "gives" with him. A shawl or small cellular blanket will do in winter. In summer a soft cotton sheet will be comfortably warm to feel without being too hot to wear. In extremely hot weather, a baby who enjoys the comfort of being wrapped but is too hot, will be happy if a soft gauze material is used.

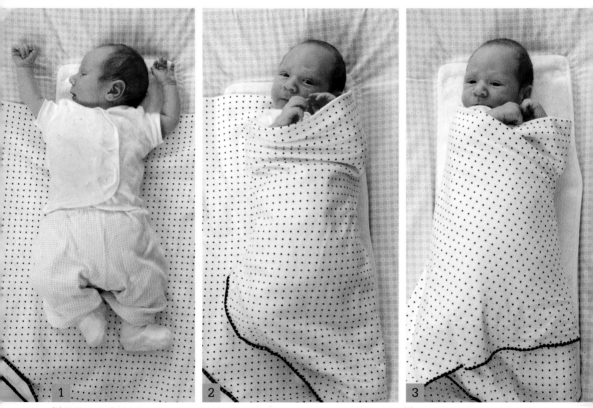

(1) Fold your blanket into a triangle and lie the baby with his head on the long side; (2) bring the left side of the fabric over his left shoulder and tuck it firmly under his body, then (3) do the same with the right.

At night, darken the room a little so that it seems different from daytime, and so that when your baby opens his eyes (as all babies do from time to time during the night) there is nothing brightly lit or clearly visible to catch his eye. But don't make his room so dark that you will have to switch on a light to attend to him.

Night feeds are essential; your baby cannot—and should not—go more than six hours without food and drink. But keep them as sleepy and as brief as possible. The less completely he awakens, the better. If he hasn't pooped you may even be able to skip changing his diaper and feed him still wrapped up.

When he begins to cry, respond immediately so that he has no time to get into a wakeful misery. Don't play and talk while you feed him though, concentrate on soothing cuddles instead. Daytime feeds are social playtimes, but night feeds are for sustenance (physical and emotional) only.

You may hear...

that family beds are dangerous to babies.
In the United States, bed-sharing with infants is highly controversial. Breast-feeding and mother–child bonding may be helped by co-sleeping, but there have been instances of accidental suffocation due to unknown causes when adults and babies share beds. The National Institutes of Health and the March of Dimes advise:

◆ Place your baby on his back to sleep every time he sleeps, including naptime.

◆ Both parents should quit smoking, and no one should smoke in the same room as your baby.

◆ Don't let your baby get too hot. Don't put him to sleep with soft items such as pillows or comforters. Dress him in light sleep clothing and keep the room at a temperature that's comfortable for adults.

◆ Babies shouldn't sleep in bed with adults, but they can be in the same room. If you breast-feed your baby in your bed, place him back in his bassinet or co-sleeper when you're done.

◆ Do not share a bed with your baby if you have been drinking alcohol, take drugs, or smoke.

Twin tip

There is now a bedside bed designed for twins to share. It takes up less room than two bassinets and allows you to rub one baby or move her across for feeding without disturbing the other.

Sleeping arrangements

Some cultures, including post-industrial ones such as Japan, value closeness to babies more than they value infant independence, and take it for granted that babies sleep with parents. Other cultures, including most of the UK and the United States, put a high value on marital privacy and aim to have babies sleeping on their own within a few months of birth. Both approaches seem self-evidently right to the parents who choose them, but whether or not you eventually end up in a family bed may mostly depend on how much difference physical contact with you makes to your baby's sleeping.

Co-sleeping—or a family bed—has many advantages for babies and mothers, especially more peaceful nights and more sleep. Your baby scarcely has to demand to breast-feed and you scarcely have to wake to nurse. And even if he should have an exceptionally wakeful night, you don't have to get up to him and he doesn't have to wait for a comforting cuddle.

Some authorities believe that provided parents are ordinarily well and alert, co-sleeping is safe and may actually protect babies against SIDS. Video studies have shown that sleeping parents unconsciously monitor their baby's position and temperature and make adjustments to the covers to ensure that he breathes properly and does not overheat.

Apart from safety considerations, there are some practical disadvantages, in addition to the obvious ones concerning adult privacy. If your baby is to sleep with you in your bed, how is he to be kept safe when you have to get up, perhaps to go to another child or to the bathroom, and where is he to sleep in the evenings that are part of his night but not of yours? And if he spends

Using a co-sleeper: All the benefits of bed-sharing with none of the risks or snags.

his evenings with you, dozing rather than being put to bed, how is a babysitter to manage when it's time for you to have a night out?

If you have sufficient space in your bedroom and your budget, a "bedside bed" or co-sleeper is a compromise that answers all these concerns about bed-sharing. The baby's bed adjusts to the height of your bed and fastens to it so that there is no gap between your mattress and the baby's. The fourth side slots away at night, but when it is pulled up the baby is as safely contained as he would be in a standard dropside crib.

Night feedings

Feeding a new baby in the night is just as inevitable as feeding him during the day. By all means assume that it's necessary (it is) but try not to assume that it's a necessary evil that you must dread. Although many parents find having their own sleep interrupted exhausting, most of those whose babies are allowed to spontaneously adopt their own routine do soon adapt, and some actually come to enjoy that peaceful middle-of-the-night intimacy.

Decide if both parents are going to wake for feedings. Once the night feeds of the babymoon are over, there is not really much point in both of you waking every time. If you are breast-feeding, you may prefer to forego a snack and a chat in favor of having a partner who is not as short of sleep as you are. If you are bottle-feeding, you may want to try sharing, with one of you doing one night and the other the next. But unless you're prepared to sleep in separate beds, or even rooms, sharing may not work. Mothers tend to find that they wake up anyway—far more easily than fathers do—and can't go back to sleep until they know the baby is settled again.

Plan for your own comfort in the early hours. If you do not want to breast-feed in bed (because you don't intend to bed-share and don't want to find yourself doing it by mistake) make sure you have a comfortable nursing chair and warm enough robe ready. If you are bottle-feeding, leave bottles ready in the refrigerator so you only need to stand them in hot water to warm them or, even better, use ready-mixed formula. Because unopened cans don't have to be

> ## From research
>
> **Warming bottles.** Many authorities say that it's not necessary to warm bottles: Babies can drink them cold, even straight from the fridge. However most parents warm bottles all the same, either because they want formula to be as much like breast milk as possible or because their babies take warm milk more eagerly. It may be that babies quickly become accustomed to milk at a particular temperature and reject the unfamiliar.

> ## Twin tip
>
> **It probably is worthwhile for both of you to wake up if there are two babies to be fed in the middle of the night.** Whether you are breast-feeding or bottle-feeding, a second person to warm and carry and a second pair of hands to hold and burp and swaddle makes feeding two much quicker and easier.

refrigerated, you can bring them with you when you go to bed. Since the formula hasn't been refrigerated, you probably won't feel you need to warm it. Some babies dislike fridge-cold milk, but most readily accept room-temperature.

Feed the baby as soon as crying begins. The less he has to wake up the better. At this age, don't even bother wondering if he might settle down again if you left him. He wants food, and even if he did drop off to sleep again without any he wouldn't stay asleep for long enough to do you any good.

Train yourself to settle back to sleep as soon as you've put the baby down. You'll probably find that easier if you are breast-feeding, since the hormones released in nursing encourage relaxation. If you are bottle-feeding, though, it is easy to put your baby down and then lie awake wondering if he is going to need another burp. If he does, he will tell you; if he doesn't, waiting for him to cry will lose you yet another chunk of precious sleeping time.

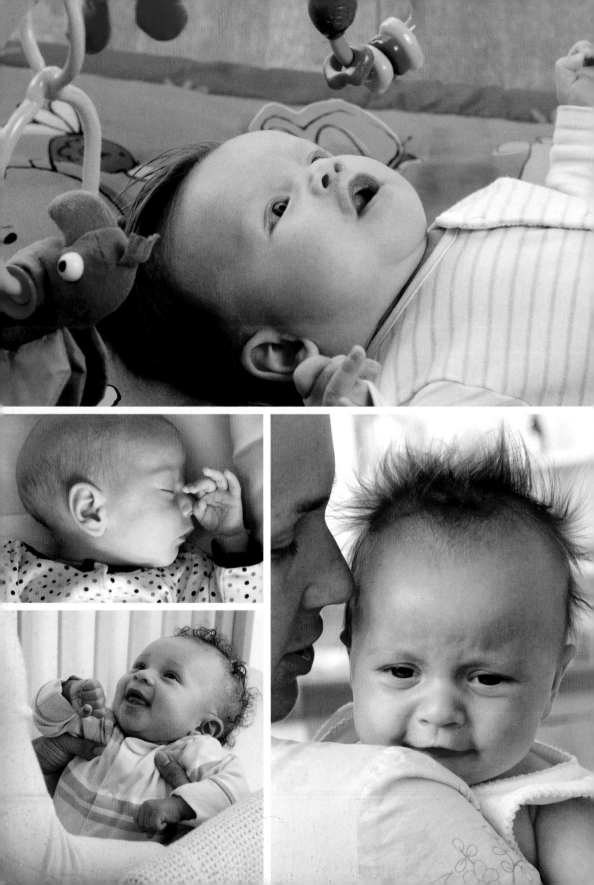

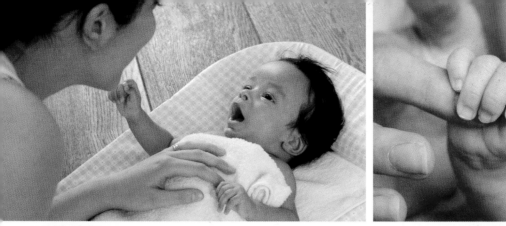

Settling in and moving forward

Settling in together

One day you'll realize that your baby has somehow moved on from being a "newborn" and become a "settled baby." She may be two weeks or two months old when that realization strikes you, and from her point of view it doesn't matter in the least whether it is sooner or later.

It will matter to you, though. The sooner the better. Your baby's day (and night) so far has mostly been taken up with feeding and sleeping, often with crying sandwiched in between, and that won't suddenly change. What will change, though, is the timing and above all the regularity with which those behaviors roll around. Where a newborn baby may feed four times in six hours on Monday morning but only once in the same period on Tuesday, a settled baby will probably consistently adopt one pattern or the other or something in between. So it isn't that your baby will suddenly need to eat less often, sleep for longer stretches or cry much less, but that you'll begin to be able to "guesstimate" her behavior and needs today, from your experience yesterday.

It's getting past the unpredictability that makes a settled baby. It doesn't mean that taking care of her is suddenly easy, but it does mean that you know what to expect from her, even if it's not always what you'd choose; know when she'll want to nurse, even if that's almost all the time; know what frightens her, even if it is almost everything; and know when she's happy, even if that's rare. So once your baby is settled, you'll know what you are up against. The days of just trying to survive are over and you can begin to work and plan for reasonable compromises between her needs and those of everyone else—especially yourself. You may soon find you're beginning to think of her as a person with tastes, preferences, and characteristics of her own, rather than as "the baby."

The more you can have him around with you while you do what has to be done, the better for both of you…

…But when there's dust in the air, he's better off playing somewhere else.

Now your baby is very much a person,
with his own tastes and preferences and
what looks like a dawning sense of humor.

Watch the baby not the clock

The process of getting settled comes from inside your baby not from outside, and it can't be hurried. She will gradually adopt feeding, sleeping, and crying patterns of her own.

In the meantime, trying to impose your timetables on her behavior won't help. You are never going to be an adults-only household again, so striving to arrange to live as if you are, despite the baby, is not a good way forward for any of you. Don't try to minimize the baby's effects on you; just try not to let them distress you. Once you get used to it, life as a family of three is richer and, in some new and different ways, more fun than life as a couple.

It does take some getting used to though. The more uncertain you are of yourself as a mother, and the less you feel able to trust your own feelings, the more likely you are to look for ways of controlling the baby's behavior and limiting the demands she makes on you. Some people advise micromanaging every aspect of babies' lives from the beginning, and if your reading and your friends convince you that adopting such a system will be good for your baby as well as making her care easier for you, it may seem the obvious way to go. The suggestions may include organizing every aspect of the baby's day and night by the clock:

From research

Scheduling. Recent findings suggest that "baby-centered" parenting (feeding on demand and picking babies up as soon as they cry) in the first weeks of life reduces the amount of time babies spend crying by as much as 50% compared with babies whose parents scheduled their routine and delayed response to crying.

Parents talking about...
being told what to do.

❝ The biggest relief is knowing exactly what to do without having to try and think, which I can't do when the baby's crying, or to choose between what my mom says, what the doctor says, and what I've read on the Internet... ❞

what time she's put down and how long she is allowed to nap; what she is given to look at or play with at different times; when she is fed or cuddled or talked to. The idea is that you can quickly get her into a routine that disrupts your adult lifestyle as little as possible. The more out of control having the baby has made you feel, the more tempting these plans may sound, and they do work for some parents.

Following a strict routine

Many new mothers bombarded with differing explanations and advice about babies say, "I wish someone would just tell me what to do"—and some instruction books will do just that in hourly detail. Once a woman has committed herself to such a regimen, few further judgments or decisions are required of her. Following each day's routine is mindless. It's far from effortless, though. There are snags from the adult's point of view, as well as from the baby's. A rigid minute-by-minute program leaves little room for spontaneous fun with babies (you can't meet friends for lunch unless you can be sure of being home to put your baby down for her nap at the

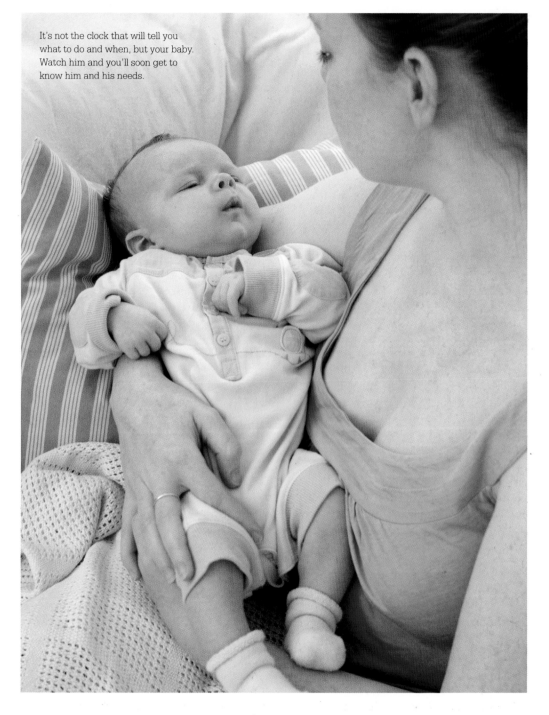

It's not the clock that will tell you what to do and when, but your baby. Watch him and you'll soon get to know him and his needs.

right time in her usual room and total darkness), so while it may make motherhood more manageable, it does nothing to make it more enjoyable. Furthermore, such a regimen assures mothers that they're right to do things they might otherwise have been uncertain about and had to figure out for themselves, insulating them from looking at things from the baby's viewpoint.

Watching the clock, not your baby

The price to your baby may be high. If the routine you want doesn't fit her particular developmental stage or personality, you'll be forcing her, and that's not good for babies or for their relationship with parents.

In a world where managers often outnumber practitioners—where a hospital may have more managerial than medical staff—it's not surprising if time management seems like an answer to life with a baby too. But your baby is a person, not a project. However natural it is to you to organize your baby care, organizing your actual baby is as different as it would be if hospital managers performed surgery as well as scheduling the operations. It's fine to manage your stock of diapers so you never run out, but it's not fine to try to manage your baby's pooping so she never needs a diaper change in the middle of the night.

A routine that your baby slips into, that knits her into the fabric of your being and knits being parents into the rest of your lives, will make life easier for you and may help the baby feel safe. But that routine isn't one you construct by the clock and impose on her whether she likes it or not, but one you arrive at together, watching her to see what she needs and finding ways of giving it to her that are comfortable for you too.

Listening to your baby

Babies cry so that a caring adult will soothe and calm them when they're upset or uncomfortable in some way, so it isn't crying itself that's damaging but crying that gets no response.

You only have to watch to see that it's very stressful for a baby to be left crying hard and

You may hear...

"There's nothing wrong with training a two-month old baby to sleep through the night. Mothers need their sleep, and a little crying doesn't hurt a baby."
The basic "training" technique is called "controlled crying," where the baby is put into his crib when parents decide, and left, whether he's crying or not. Someone checks on him at increasingly wide-spaced intervals (every 5, 10, then 15 minutes) but he's not picked up. Some babies only cry for a few minutes. Fine. They're happy to settle (they didn't need "training"), but some cry for an hour or more night after night. When they stop it isn't because they've learned not to cry but because they've despaired of anyone coming to their aid.

alone. What can't be seen—and has only recently been understood—is that stress is never good for babies, and a lot can actually be harmful. Since nobody can tell you how much crying is "too much" for your particular baby at this particular point in her day and time in her life, leaving her to cry for more than an occasional few minutes is a risk that's just not worth taking. There's nothing wrong with feeding and sleeping routines if your baby adopts them without distress. But if a baby doesn't take easily to rigid routines, "controlled crying" means too much stress too often.

At this stage in her life your baby cannot soothe herself, that's your job. There will be times when you put her in her crib, well fed and

From research

Early stress. When a baby experiences acute and continuing distress, a hormonal chain reaction begins. That ultimately stimulates the adrenal glands into releasing cortisol, a "stress hormone" that floods the baby's body and brain. That whole stress response system (known as the HPA axis) goes on pumping out cortisol until

someone turns it off by comforting the baby and making him feel better. High levels of cortisol that build up over time can be literally toxic to a young baby's rapidly developing brain. Repeated episodes can permanently affect his response system so that it becomes hypersensitive and he overreacts to minor stress with major fear and anxiety, not only as a baby but as a child and an adult too.

Why leave your baby to cry alone when going to pick him up produces pure joy.

drowsy and content to slip into sleep, and other times when she needs to be held safely in the comfort of your arms.

If you leave your baby to cry hard, alone, she will eventually stop. She can't go on crying forever after all. But at this age she won't stop because she's learned anything—her brain is not developed enough for that. And even when she's much older, the only lesson being left alone might teach her surely isn't one that you want her to learn: "Don't bother to cry because nobody will notice." If she cries herself to sleep she will drop off in despair and exhaustion.

An instruction-manual approach sometimes gives parents a sense of adult control and separateness and supports their use of authority over their baby ("you know best"), when what they most need is enough personal support, from each other, from family, friends, and professionals, to make them feel able to risk submerging themselves in a relationship with him or her. It is misleading to suggest to parents that they can conserve their adult autonomy by rationing and routinizing their attention to the baby, because however much they may resent the fact, their happiness and the baby's are inextricably entangled. A mother may resent her baby's crying; resent, even reject, the fact that she needs her—again. But ignoring ("controlling") the crying won't improve things for the mother, since refusing to respond to her crying baby does not only mean that the baby has to cry unanswered, but also that the mother has to listen to her crying. So being sensitive to a baby's needs, tuning in to her, treating her as she seems to ask to be treated, is not only better for the baby, but also better for the mother

Your baby can't soothe himself: That's your job.

and for their relationship. And that relationship matters more to the new baby's ongoing development than anything else in her world.

Babies' attachment to mothers

A very large, rapidly growing, and undisputed body of international research shows that a secure attachment to their mothers or whoever mothers them is crucial to all aspects of babies' lifelong development. An associated body of research demonstrates the importance of mothers being sensitive and responsive to their babies. The security of an infant's attachment to mother and the sensitivity of her care go together. Furthermore, findings emerging from the fast-moving field of research into infant brain development show that stress, including the stresses that lead to and result from insecure attachment, are likely to damage a baby's capacity to learn, and may, in extreme instances, damage it forever. When studies compare children of any age on any aspect of development—from language, to resilience, to sociable play—the sensitivity and responsiveness of their mothers in the first year explains more of the difference between the babies' achievements than anything else.

Nobody can be sensitive to another person all the time; nobody can always be responsive. You will sometimes fail to understand your baby's cues or be so sound asleep that you are slow to respond when she wakes in the night. But it is a fact, not merely an opinion, that the more a baby experiences parents as attentive, responsive, and loving, the more she will flourish today and the more resources she will have to cope with difficulties tomorrow; bear her in mind.

Bearing your baby in mind means that wherever you are and whatever you are doing

and thinking about, she is there, taking up a piece of your consciousness. And when you are directly paying attention to your baby, it means thinking with and for and through her; thinking of yourself in relation to her and about how the two of you can turn the next challenge into pleasure, rather than about a set of instructions, the time, or even your cooling supper or beckoning bed. This kind of attunedness is not at all the same as total indulgence. Indeed, as we will see, parents who are having problems with babies past the newborn stage wanting to be fed every hour or to be held constantly, often need to be clearer and more consistent without being less loving or more detached.

Being responsive to a baby soon grows into mutual responsiveness between child and parent. Infants are not out to "get at" parents. Watching and listening to babies and responding to them as swiftly and as positively as possible does not turn babies into bullies or parents into victims. On the contrary, it leads, naturally and without prior planning or a particular program, to negotiation between adults and infants and thence to the reciprocity on which all intimate relationships eventually depend. It is by negotiation (rather than by rules) that a parent arrives at the appropriate period of grace between this particular baby waking up and an adult arriving at the crib side. It is by negotiation that a mother can gradually stretch the time between feedings, or persuade her baby to accept her face and voice for reassurance when something startles her, instead of instant nursing. It is through months of these reiterated mini-negotiations that a baby learns that mother is not her, but someone separate. Someone who thinks about her needs and can be trusted, but who also has needs of her own. These lessons are the foundations of mutual regard. Laid in the first six months, they will support the parent/child relationship not only through infancy and as an alternative to rigidly programmed parental control, but through the toddler's confused and confusing developmental drive for autonomy and the child's increasing passion for peers, and into adolescence. And by then mutual regard is the only hope, because power-tactics no longer work at all.

From research

Separation and "disorganized attachment."
Babies' repeated experiences of being separated from their mothers or of their crying not being responded to are a leading cause of "disorganized attachment."

Settled babies' feeding

Whether your child is three weeks, three years old, or thirteen, you and he are on the same side over feeding, so worrying about it is a waste of energy and pleasure for both of you.

The pleasure part is important. If you watch your baby as he latches on at the beginning of a feed you can see his urgent hunger and the feeling of the milk going down inside him lessening it, and you can see the bliss of the actual sucking too. For the first minute or two he gulps, then his sucking settles into a steady rhythm, slowing down to little bursts of sucks followed by a breath, a rest pause and then another burst. Soon his face takes on an expression of drowsy satisfaction. The rhythm of his sucking slows, with longer rests in between. Eventually the rests are longer than the bursts of sucking, and he falls into what looks like drunken slumber, only the occasional suck showing that he isn't ready to end the feeding.

For some mothers with some babies, it is as easy and enjoyable as that sounds, and for others it will soon become so. You can be sure that breast-feeding is going well from your baby's point of view if he has begun to gain weight steadily; tends to be more rather than less contented as the days pass, and is increasingly alert when he is awake. And if feeding him is something you enjoy, even if you don't look forward to it in the middle of the night, it's fine from your point of view too. You could ignore the next few pages.

But it isn't always easy for everybody, and a sadly large number of women who had intended to breast-feed and got started with breast-feeding, abandon it during these very first weeks. If you might be one of them, read on.

Breast-feeding: common problems in the early weeks

Resisting the breast: If your baby suddenly refuses to latch on and suck, or keeps latching on and coming off again, fretful and apparently irritated, you'll probably be upset and miserable. When he rejects the breast it feels as if he is rejecting you.

It may set up a vicious circle too. The more upset your baby gets, the more you want to comfort him, but he is rejecting the most basic comfort you have to offer, so what can you do? Breast-feeding can be a wet and sticky business at the best of times, and this is not a good time. As he cries and roots, half latches on, fights away, has a quick suck, your milk is likely to let down so that you are dripping everywhere. And if it goes on for long, or happens several times in a row, your nipples may get sore, so that you begin to dread physical pain as well as emotional rejection.

This kind of behavior is not at all unusual. You may never know why your baby behaved like this at the breast—at one feeding or two week's worth— but one of the following may well be the explanation:
◆ Your baby may be getting "flooded" by the first flow of milk, unable to gulp fast enough to keep up with it, and feel like he is going to drown.
◆ He may be having trouble breathing through a stuffed up nose while sucking.
◆ If he was kept waiting, he may be past hunger.
◆ If your milk is not letting down readily, his sucking efforts may not be rewarded with milk.
◆ Thrush in the mouth is not unusual, and may make sucking painful. (Look carefully inside his mouth for white patches.)

If one of these explanations seems to fit, you may be able to prevent it in the future. Right now, though, you need to accept that something unknown has got this feeding off to a bad start, and begin again. If your partner, your mother or a reliable friend is present, the baby can be held out of sight and smell range of your breasts and soothed while you dry yourself off (baby wipes are for you as well as him!) and calm down. Then try a different place and whatever position the two of you have been finding easiest. If things

If your baby rejects the breast it doesn't mean he's rejecting you. When you've both had time to calm down, all will be well again.

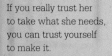

If you really trust her to take what she needs, you can trust yourself to make it.

went wrong while you were sitting at a café table in the park, you might want to seek some privacy. If your baby latches on best when you're lying down, you might try reclining on the grass.

It's quite likely that your baby still won't feed well, but, tired out by the whole experience, soon goes to sleep. Don't even try to wake him: Let the whole episode go by. By the time he wakes again he will be really hungry, and chances are he'll feed happily.

If something like this keeps happening, though, it's very likely to erode your confidence and destroy your pleasure in this new nursing business, so do be quick to ask for help from whomever you trust most for hands-on help with breast-feeding—whether it's a health professional, lactation consultant, relative, or friend. It's very likely that this kind of problem is caused, and can be cured, by your baby's position at the breast.

Milk intake

When you breast-feed your baby you cannot see or measure, let alone control, what's available to him or what he takes. That's why breast-feeding is often more anxious-making than bottle-feeding, especially for first-time parents who have never seen the demand-and-supply system in operation. Can your baby really be trusted to make and take what he needs? He almost certainly can, but you have to believe that your baby knows how often and for how long he wants to suck, and be willing to feed him whenever he asks—even if his last feeding was only an hour ago—and let him go on sucking for as long as he is swallowing.

Judging whether your baby is getting enough food

Not all babies thrive easily from the beginning. If yours does not, you'll obviously consult your child's pediatrician, but don't be too quick to assume that the problem is that your milk supply is low and your baby is short of food. That may not be the case even if it looks that way, because the traditional criteria for assessing newborn feeding behavior were built on observations of bottle-fed babies and may mislead mothers who are exclusively breast-feeding.

◆ Your baby may be demanding food very frequently, for example. Babies who do that are often assumed to be underfed but may in fact be making sure that they are not. And how frequent is very frequent? You can't arrive at a sensible answer to that question by comparing your breast-fed baby with your bottle-fed niece. Babies who are fed on cow's-milk formula sometimes go 3–4 hours between feedings when they're this age, but babies who are fed on human milk almost never do. For your baby, a two- or two-and-a-half-hour interval is entirely ordinary.

Two hours between feedings doesn't mean a period of two hours when your baby is asleep or away from the breast. Intervals between feedings run from the start of one to the start of the next—so if your baby starts nursing at 5:00am, takes both breasts, and finally finishes sucking at 5.45am, a two hour gap will mean that his next feeding comes up around 7:00am.

This means that feedings that take longer have shorter gaps between them, and breast-feeds often last longer than bottle-feeds.

◆ Producing very few soiled diapers with very scanty contents is often a sign that a bottle-fed baby is underfed, but does not necessarily mean the same if a baby is breast-fed. Some babies digest breast milk so completely that there is very little waste, so the fact that your baby soiled three or four diapers a day in his second week but now soils only three or four a week does not necessarily suggest that he is starving or constipated.

Babies have to grow, and that means that however they are fed, they have to put on weight (and length).

◆ Not putting on enough weight does suggest not getting enough milk, but how much weight gain and how much milk are "enough"? Again the "norms" for bottle-fed and breast-fed babies are different. Breast-fed babies may not gain as many ounces each week as is expected of bottle-fed babies. In the first 6–10 weeks though, breast-fed babies sometimes gain weight so rapidly and get so roly-poly plump that if they were bottle-fed there'd be talk of "overfeeding."

You want your baby's weight to show an upward trend—and that's the only indication you need that he's getting enough to eat—but a trend takes time to establish and stabilize, so you won't get help with sudden panics from his weight chart. For short-term reassurance that your baby is not starving, consider his diapers and make a careful count of how many he wets.

A baby who is exclusively breast-fed cannot go short of food without going short of drink: Milk is both. So the number of diapers he wets in each 24-hour period is a good instant measure of his feeding. If he wets at least six or, better still, eight per day, he is not short of food or drink. If you are going to rely on the wet-diaper-count though, bear in mind that it depends on frequent changes and careful inspection of super-absorbent disposable diapers. Their capacity is so great, and their stay-dry lining so effective, that one pee by a small baby is almost imperceptible. (If in doubt, weigh the used diaper in one hand against a new one in the other; if it's even a little bit wet it will be noticeably heavier.)

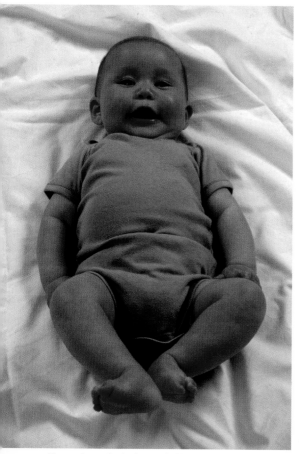

You can't overfeed a breast-fed baby unless you give her something extra. Plump? Yes, and *gorgeous*.

Parents talking about...

nursing

❝ I loved breast-feeding, and my son loved being breast-fed. He grew and he grew and before he was even three months old he was, well, plump. My husband said he was fat; my mom said he was "past chubby," and his doctor said I shouldn't feed him on demand as he was taking too much. Luckily I'd read enough to be pretty sure they were wrong (the doctor was elderly so she'd obviously trained a long time ago), and I just kept on feeding on demand and he kept on growing, and by the middle of the year he'd got bigger, not fatter. **❞**

Is your breast-fed baby taking too much milk?

Breast-feeding and overfeeding are a contradiction in terms. You absolutely cannot overfeed a breast-fed baby unless you give him something in addition to breast milk. Believe it. Don't let appearances deceive you. A hungry baby whose mother has a copious milk supply may gain weight faster, and look fatter, than the baby next door who is also breast-fed, or the one down the road who has bottles of formula. Don't compare them. However roly-poly he becomes, your baby is not, and will not become "too fat" (meaning fatter than he is programmed to be at this stage in his life) unless you start adding solid foods to his diet before he needs them, or giving him sugary drinks.

Is your breast-fed baby not getting enough milk?

Underfeeding in a breast-fed baby is unusual, despite mothers' worries about having enough milk. Still, it can happen, when you and your partner emerge from your babymoon and start to get other aspects of life going again, and so do the people who have been helping and caring for you. A spurt of physical activity, or even just the sudden stress of finding yourself alone with your baby and expected to cope all day, can make you very tired. Whether it happens when the baby is two weeks old or four weeks old, you may find yourself wondering how you will ever integrate everything you used to do with everything you have to do now or, in another mood, how you will possibly manage to fill your time without "real" (i.e. paid) work.

If you get tired, low-spirited and harassed, you're likely to make less milk, and meanwhile your baby is growing, so he needs even more milk this week than he did last. Put those two things together and you have a hungry baby (and an increasingly stressed breast-feeding mother). It's easy to cope with your baby's hunger from his point of view: just let him suck whenever he asks, even if he asks far more often than before. But that's not such an easy solution from your point of view, because the increasing frequency of his feeds is one of the reasons you are stressed out.

Underfeeding a breast-fed baby

You may not notice right away that your baby is short of milk. His discontent and crying, his frequent night wakings, and his every-two-hours demands for food in the daytime don't tell you very much because they are not new behaviors, but seem like a further chapter in his earlier unsettled behavior.

What's more, if you wake each morning with full breasts and a soaking bra, it may not occur to you that there isn't enough milk for your baby. The point is that there may not be enough *all the time* though. Babies often want most milk when their mothers make least—especially toward the end of a long and tiring day.

In fact if you look back over the past week, you may find that there's a pattern. Your baby is happy for reasonable periods between the times he nurses from, say, 5:00am to 4:00pm, but gets less and less contented in the late afternoon and evening—probably until you have had your first sleep of the night. This pattern isn't always due to a just-adequate milk supply dipping to inadequate at the end of the day, when older children need to be picked up from school, the house needs tidying up, and dinner needs to be cooked. It may not be because you have less milk at this time of day but because he wants more. Many breast-fed babies like to feed almost nonstop through the evening, even if their feeds are reasonably spaced both in the day and in the night.

What to do if your baby needs more milk

What to do depends on how determined you are to go on with exclusive breast-feeding. If you want to, you almost certainly can, but it will be time-consuming: The baby will have to be given the chance to increase the amount of milk you make just as he did at the very beginning when you were getting breast-feeding going. Your milk production is stimulated by his sucking. The more often he takes milk from your breasts, the more milk you will make, and the faster they will fill. When his frequent sucking has built up the supply to the point where it meets his needs, he will suck less often. Supply and demand; a simple system, but an effective one.

Breast-feeding while doing other things

The best way to ensure that there's plenty of milk for your baby now, and that your supply continues to be ample, is to make nursing him an enjoyable part of almost every aspect of your daily life.

◆ Teach yourself to breast-feed whenever and wherever: real multi-tasking!
◆ Have several comfortable nursing places.
◆ Make feedings restful and sociable.

(1) You can share breakfast with his father while your baby has his. (2) Even on maternity leave you can keep in touch with the world on the phone. (3) There's room for two: Cuddle your toddler while her baby brother sucks.

Helping your baby make more milk

Your baby won't stand a chance of building up your milk supply to match his growing demands unless you feed him whenever he wants and for as long as he wants each time. That may not be easy, especially if you and the rest of your household had thought the babymoon was over and begun to look forward to doing other things as well as nursing.

But nothing else, not even a half-hearted attempt, will certainly work, so pushing for the time and space you and the baby need is really worthwhile. You may find that space and time most easily if you declare a breast-feeding emergency and retire to bed with your baby for a couple of days. Nobody can expect you to do anything if you're in bed, can they? And they'd have to manage without you if you had the flu.

Declaring a breast-feeding emergency can give you and your baby time and space to increase your milk supply.

A couple of days spent resting yourself and not only feeding your baby whenever he asks, but also encouraging him to suck whenever he is willing, will certainly begin to build your milk supply. Of course you may not be able to abandon your household altogether, but even if you have to get up to get food for yourself (and the cat) or take your toddler and a load of toys and snacks into bed with you, it will still be worthwhile. As long as you are bed-based, there's no chance you will miss a cue from your baby that he'd like to nurse, and no likelihood that once he latches on you'll be tempted to hurry him. Does it have to be bed? Wouldn't a sofa do? Well it would, of course, but somehow being in bed is a more accepted escape from everyday life: You'll expect less of yourself, and less will be expected of you. There's nothing else useful you can do:

◆ Drinking more fluids won't help unless you were actually dehydrated.

◆ Special foods won't help (unless the luxury of delicious meals raises your morale). Women can—and sadly many have to—produce nutritious milk for their babies when their own nutrition leaves them on the borders of starvation. Of course good food is important for your health and energy, but it doesn't have to be the "real meals" you have no time to buy, cook, or eat. Bread and cheese, fruit and yogurt, interspersed with ordered-in Chinese food or pizza with salad will do just as well.

Signs that the "more milk campaign" is working

◆ Your baby may begin to leave longer gaps between feeds—either because he sleeps for longer, or because he sometimes wakes without immediately needing to nurse.

◆ He may not always want both breasts. At some feeds he gets so much from the first breast that he takes little or nothing from the second, or is simply too deeply asleep to latch onto it.

◆ He may become more likely to spit up milk with his burps.

◆ He may make more diapers wetter than he had been doing.

Even if you see all these hopeful signs—and eventually an excellent weight gain—don't expect more peaceful adult evenings and nights. Evening

Parents talking about...
building breast milk supplies

❝ That second month, there'd be three or four days when I had more milk than he needed, he'd begin to space his feeds out, and it was blissful. Then he'd do another bit of a growth spurt and for a couple of days he'd be back to almost nonstop feeding, but just when I was about to give up he'd settle again. My husband made the ultimate sacrifice to keep breast-feeding going: He drove us to stay with my mother for three whole weeks even though he could only be there on weekends. She pampered me, I nursed the baby, and it all came well. ❞

nursing marathons and frequent night feeds don't suggest that your baby is still not getting enough; on the contrary, they help to ensure that he does get enough. Some researchers have suggested that night feeding has an important hormonal effect on milk production.

Keeping up the increased supply of milk

The single essential way of making sure your milk supply remains ample for your growing baby is to go on offering the breast whenever he seems to be hungry, and (usually) letting him suck for as long as he likes. Try to keep your stress levels within reasonable limits (only you can know what's reasonable for you). Being relaxed and happy certainly helps lactation, which is why those peace-inducing hormones are released as you nurse.

Some things won't help

◆ Worrying. Worry, anxiety, and stress affect breast-feeding. If you try to breast-feed in circumstances where you cannot feel relaxed—perhaps in a restaurant where other diners are "eyeing" you disapprovingly—you're likely to find that although the breast is full and the baby sucks, tension prevents the "let down" reflex, so the milk does not flow in response to the stimulation of increasingly desperate sucking.

◆ Trying to keep the baby to a schedule that isn't natural to him today, even if it is one which he seemed to have settled on for himself a week or so ago. The baby's rapid growth means surges of appetite, and your breasts must have the stimulation of extra sucking if you want them to produce extra milk. At this stage in his life you cannot ration his sucking without rationing his food.

◆ Giving a bottle-feed as well. If you offer your baby a bottle and he accepts it, he will be less hungry than usual so he will not suck hard or long enough to tell your breasts to make the full amount of milk he usually needs. Don't even consider complementary bottles until or unless you have given up on producing more milk yourself.

◆ Giving a bottle-feed instead, or leaving a baby-sitter to give occasional bottles of formula. If your baby doesn't take the milk your breasts have made, they will make less. If you don't want to take the baby out with you, it is better to leave expressed breast milk and express again during your absence.

◆ Dietary supplements that claim to increase breast milk. Like herbal remedies and medicines that claim to increase your sexual performance, most of these are merely water, herbs, multivitamins, and magic. They may not hurt, but herbs can have side effects, and it's better not to take any "medicine" without your doctor's approval while breast-feeding). Unless your diet is very deficient in vitamins, they probably will not do you any good either.

◆ Birth control pills. Many combination pills decrease milk supply. You need to discuss an alternative method of contraception, or at least an alternative type of oral contraceptive, with your doctor. You might be advised to take a mini-pill now and return to a (marginally more effective) combination pill when you and your baby are completely adjusted to breast-feeding. By the time your baby is three to four months old, and his demands and your supply have been meshing smoothly for weeks, your supply of breast milk should be well able to override the slight and temporary reduction the changeover is likely to cause.

Bottles?

If you spend two or three weeks determinedly trying to increase your milk supply (and your baby's contentment) you will almost certainly succeed (with or without that bed rest!). But success has a price, and only you can decide whether it is too high. For some women, especially mothers of twins, breast-feeding can be an almost full-time activity for the first three months or so, until the growing baby's demands mesh with your breasts' supply and the whole system stabilizes. If you have a toddler or older child, you may feel that being fully available to her, as you used to be, is as much a priority as nursing the new baby. What's more, if there's nobody else around to take care of your household and visit with you, lying around while the baby sucks and dozes may be very lonely. If you're beginning to feel as if the walls are closing in, your marriage is in jeopardy, your job is gone forever, and your nipples are sore again, you may decide that you've given breast-feeding your best shot and that's enough.

It's principally your decision, of course, just as the original decision to breast-feed was necessarily yours. It's not only your decision though, unless you are on your own. Don't cut the baby's father out of it, unless he has put himself outside the situation by going away, actually or figuratively. If he hadn't realized how much of a struggle breast-feeding was for you and what it was costing, he may not have been doing all he could to help you. But faced with the likelihood of your giving up nursing in favor of bottle-feeding, he may realize he wants the baby to go on being breast-fed enough that he'll do anything he can to make that possible, and you may feel that more joint responsibility for the rest of parenting and some breakfasts in bed might make it worth another try.

Giving complementary bottles

You need to make a definite decision that's not just for now but for the next several months. You can ensure that your baby gets plenty of milk by "topping him up" with bottles of formula. But once you start regular complementary bottles, it's likely that the amount of milk he takes from the bottle will gradually increase and the quantity he takes from the breast will decrease, so that within a couple of months you might be feeding him entirely from the bottle. If you want to change over from breast- to bottle-feeding anyway, complementary bottles may be a good way to start. A gradual change from mostly breast with a bit of bottle, to mostly bottle with a bit of breast, and then all bottle, no breast, is much easier than a more abrupt swap. But if you're aiming to nurse your baby for most of a year or more and he needs complementary bottles, it's better if they contain expressed breast milk.

Feed the baby from the breast as usual, giving him both breasts, but when he has taken all he can, offer him a bottle of breast milk you expressed earlier in the day when you had more than he wanted. He may take nothing at some feeds, quite a lot at others.

If your baby refuses point blank to take any milk from the bottle, you may not know whether he is refusing it because he has already had enough from the breast or because, like many babies who have settled into breast-feeding, he dislikes the new method. The only way to be sure is to persist in offering the top-up for at least five days. If he is hungry, the baby will have come to terms with the bottle within that time. If he still has not accepted it, he probably isn't hungry. Check on his weight gain, though.

If your baby sometimes wants extra breast milk at times when you've got least, a bottle of expressed milk can solve the problem.

Non-exclusive breast-feeding: adding in bottles

Your baby can go on having most of the physical advantages of breast-feeding without you always having to be there to nurse him if you use bottles to feed him expressed milk. Provided you find expressing milk relatively easy, this part-breast-part-bottle-feeding system may work for you if you particularly want to keep on feeding exclusively breast milk (perhaps for some medical reason such as a family history of allergies), but you're eager to reduce your time commitment to nursing. Most of the emotional and social advantages of breast-feeding do depend on one-to-one nursing, of course, but having someone else feed the baby from a bottle some of the time may make it easier for you to go on being there and nursing him yourself most of the time.

If you're going to rely on bottles of expressed milk for part of your baby's feeding, spend time finding the type of breast pump that suits you. Expressing milk by hand is a useful technique in emergencies, but a nightmarishly slow way of collecting several ounces of milk at a time every day. There are manual and electric pumps available, ranging widely in cost and

If you've ever wondered why mothers who don't nurse carry big bags, even on short trips; here's the reason.

sophistication. Most hospitals and some manufacturers and drugstores rent pumps, so you can try before you buy. The most expensive may not be the kind you find most comfortable. If you can afford and manage a double electric pump, your expressing will take half the time.

Nipple confusion

Your baby may not cooperate with you in adding bottles to breast-feeding, even if the bottles contain breast milk. A lot of babies, especially those under three months, find it difficult to switch between the two, because getting milk from a breast and getting milk from a bottle feel completely different and require different sucking techniques. Breast-feeding means taking in a large mouthful of warm, soft, nipple-plus-areola; the nipple on a bottle is a smaller, cooler, stiffer bulb of rubber, latex, or silicone. That contrast alone is enough to cause problems: If the baby tries to suck at the breast the way he sucks a bottle, he'll make your nipples sore and get no milk. Likewise, if he tries to latch onto latex the way he latches onto you, he'll take the bottle's nipple so far into his mouth that he'll make himself gag.

People may tell you that bottle-feeding is "easier" for babies so once they have discovered it, they won't work at breast-feeding. However, babies who are accustomed to nursing are often difficult to persuade into taking bottles, so it may simply be that they like to feed the way they're accustomed to feeding. Whatever the reason, introducing a bottle to a breast-fed baby can spoil his latch and lead to poor nursing and breast problems. Since your breast-milk supply depends on your baby's sucking (which the supply of milk in a bottle does not) don't risk it. It's best not to introduce your baby to a bottle at all—even for expressed breast milk—until your milk supply and his technique are both well established. Although some mother-baby pairs can cope with occasional bottles at three weeks, you'd do better to wait until six weeks if you possibly can and twice that long if breast-feeding is a real priority for you. (see p. 170)

Even when your baby is six weeks old or more, don't assume that introducing a bottle will be easy. It may take considerable tact and patience, so make sure you will be available for at least a week from the time you first offer a bottle to the time you leave him with no alternative. Your baby may accept bottles best if it is you who offers them. After all, he is used to you feeding him. But he may accept bottles better from his father or a caregiver—anyone other than you—because when you feed him he can smell the milk he is used to. You may need to experiment with types and stages of nipple, too.

Bottle-feeding: problems and solutions

When you feed your baby formula instead of breast milk, you have more control over what he eats and how much, and he has less. For many mothers the best thing about bottle-feeding is always having plenty of formula available to their babies whether they themselves are available or not, and being able to see exactly how much is taken at every feed. Bottle-feeding rather than breast-feeding your baby means that you are far less likely to worry about him being underfed—but more likely to overfeed him.

Overfeeding

When bottle-fed babies get too fat, it is not because they were allowed to drink as much properly-made formula as they wanted, whenever they wanted it, but because they were given extra foods or sweet drinks as well as their bottles, or because those bottles were made up extra-strong. Unless your doctor specifically recommends it, your baby should definitely not have anything except formula before he is four months old, (preferably six) and that formula should always be made up exactly according to the manufacturer's instructions.

Milk is a baby's drink as well as his food, and like the rest of us, a baby can be thirsty without being hungry. Breast milk adjusts itself accordingly, but formula does not. Bottle-fed babies sometimes welcome drinks of cooled boiled water, especially when the weather is hot or they are feverish.

If your baby does have extra drinks, keep them to plain water and hope that it becomes a pleasurable habit that largely replaces fruit drinks now and sugary sodas later. Although those vitamin C–enriched baby fruit juices "contain no added sugar," sugar is already there, in the form of fructose, or natural fruit sugar. Like any other form of sugar, fructose will eventually be bad for your baby's teeth and will give him extra calories along with vitamins he probably doesn't even need. Modern baby formulas usually contain adequate vitamin C, and there will be still more of it in any multivitamin drops your doctor recommends. So if you choose to give him fruit juice, it will be more for pleasure rather than for health; stick to one drink a day, very highly diluted.

Underfeeding a bottle-fed baby

In the rich world where formula is affordable, underfeeding is rare in bottle-fed babies, but it can happen. If your baby cries a lot, gains weight slowly, and seems generally discontented, he may be hungry.
Check the following points:
◆ You may be assessing your baby's needs too rigidly. If you prepare the number of ounces your baby "ought" to need in 24 hours, divide it equally between the number of bottles he usually takes, and then wait for him to drain each one, you are not allowing for the fact that, like anyone else, he will be hungrier at some times than at others. If a bottle is emptied, how can you be sure that the baby would not have liked more? Emptied bottles are a reproach, not a cause for congratulation. Put at least 2 ounces (60 ml) more than you think your baby will drink into each bottle.
◆ You may be scheduling feeds instead of relying on your baby to ask for food when he needs it. It will usually take him around three hours to digest a bottle-feed, so he won't often demand to be fed much more often. But that doesn't mean that if he does ask, you should refuse. His appetite will vary from feeding to feeding, so he won't always finish his bottle. If he can't make up for a small lunch by having an afternoon "snack" but is made to wait until the next "correct" mealtime, he won't be able to make up the lost nutrition because his tummy can't hold enough extra milk. For example, if he only drinks 3 ounces (85 ml) of milk at lunchtime instead of the usual 6 ounces (170 ml), a couple of hours later he will be hungry. If you make him wait until afternoon feeding time, he will not be able to drink 6 ounces (170 ml) plus the 3 ounces (85 ml) he missed earlier. His stomach simply will not hold

9 ounces (255 ml) of milk. Repeated day after day, this kind of situation can lead to a great deal of fretfulness as well as to low weight gain.

◆ You might need a nipple with a larger hole. While your baby is really hungry he will keep sucking as hard as he needs to, even if the milk comes slowly. Once he's had 2–3 ounces (60–85 ml), though, the acute hunger pains stop and his motivation dwindles. If he gives up and goes to sleep, he will wake and demand more food a couple of hours later; if this becomes a pattern, he may become a baby who demands frequent feeds, doesn't drink much of them, and is not gaining much weight. Milk should drip rapidly from the nipple when the bottle is inverted, and your baby should get at least half his bottle in the first five minutes of steady sucking.

◆ You may be dealing with an exceptionally sleepy baby. This will right itself in a few weeks as he grows up enough to be more alert, but in the meantime you may have to help him realize when he needs food. If he doesn't wake himself, wake him for a bottle at reasonable intervals and use the things that will interest him most—your face and voice—to keep him awake while he sucks. If you can't help him stay awake though don't keep trying to pour milk into his sleeping mouth. There's no point in trying to make him take more at each feed, just offer him the bottle often and he will become more alert with time.

He's taken all you gave him but it wasn't all he needed. Empty bottles are a reproach.

Settled babies' sleeping

Settled babies still sleep exactly the amount they, personally, need. Unless he is ill, in pain, or extremely uncomfortable, your baby will do his sleeping wherever he finds himself and under almost any circumstances.

Making him comfortable will help him sleep as much as he wants to, but you cannot *put* him to sleep. On the other hand, if you can't make him very comfortable because you're in a crowded bus you need not worry about him being kept awake. If he stays awake, it is because he does not need to sleep.

Disturbances to sleep

Don't impose an unnatural hush on your household every time your baby goes to sleep. Ordinary sounds and bustling activities around him will not disturb him at this early age, but if everyone walks on tiptoe and talks in whispers because he is asleep, there may come a time when he cannot sleep unless they do. He will sleep through whatever sound level is normal for your family, and it's better that he does not come to expect unnatural quietness.

Outside stimuli can wake the baby of course, but will usually only do so because they change very suddenly. Your baby may go to sleep quite happily with the television on, but wake when it is switched off. His toddler brother playing around the room will not keep him awake, but may wake him by coming in unexpectedly.

At this stage though, it is internal stimuli that are most likely to wake him: hunger, pain, passing a bowel movement, or burping. Sometimes the jerks and twitches of his body as it relaxes toward deep sleep will disturb him, too.

Helping yourselves to get more sleep

Human beings are diurnal creatures. We all sleep by night and are active by day. All except new babies, who do not seem to have a clear, in-built mechanism instructing them accordingly, but

> # Twin tip
>
> **A lot of parents like their twins to share a crib,** believing that they settle better together. But some find that just about now the babies may begin to disturb each other. If you want them to go on co-sleeping, a larger crib may temporarily solve the problem. But if you plan for them to sleep in separate cribs eventually, it might be sensible to separate them now so they don't always expect to sleep together.

have to learn. Babies start off sleeping and waking randomly through a 24-hour period. It takes time and sensible handling (see p. 188) to persuade them to do most of their sleeping at night and most of their being awake in the daytime. The majority begin to adopt this pattern fairly rapidly, if not as rapidly as their exhausted parents would choose!

Almost all new parents (and some others) suffer from lack of sleep and from constantly disturbed sleep. It is not just that new babies wake to be fed. All babies wake (some more often than others), and most of them insist on parents knowing about it when they do. There are babies who sleep all night, every night, from six weeks of age (so I'm told), but while you can cross your fingers for such a baby, don't hold your breath. It may be not months but years before the two of you share a whole, unbroken night.

Apart from the imposed-routine approach already discussed, there are two very different approaches to this problem-area, and one may suit you better than the other. The first approach accepts that this small new person is not just part of your daytime life but your night life, too. Having your baby in bed with you will not stop him from waking up or save you from night feedings in the first weeks. But if he is sharing your bed with you, feeding your baby won't disturb you as much as it will if you have to get up and go to him. Your baby is likely to go back to sleep more quickly too, because he is where he best likes to be—close to you. In the first few weeks, having your baby with you probably optimizes the establishment of breast-feeding and minimizes the amount the baby cries.

Babies who sleep in "family beds" all night long from early on do tend to wake more often than other babies as they get older, but as they get older still, they may wake but not need to cry because they already have you there.

But "family beds" have downsides, the principal one being that once you start having your baby in bed with you, or at least once he has had three months or so of this arrangement, you are very unlikely to be able to persuade him that a separate crib in a separate room is preferable. However much you enjoy co-sleeping with your six-week-old, you may find that you feel differently later on. A baby or toddler in your bed does cut down your privacy, and much though you love him, being with him 24 hours a day, by night as well as day, can make you feel as if the non-parent in you has been totally submerged. It's fine to change your mind;

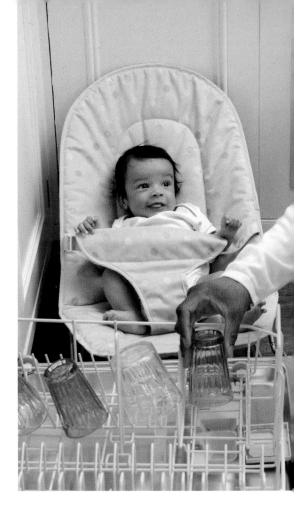

changing your baby's mind is another matter.

The second approach is just as welcoming to the baby into your daytime life but aims to minimize his place in your night life and your

From research

Helping your baby to "sleep through."
Research suggests that careful management of your baby's nighttime sleeping from six weeks on can help her discover how to settle to sleep on her own, both at the beginning of the night and when she awakens in the small hours. Evidence shows that these three steps much reduce the likelihood that she will still be crying for you whenever she wakes at three months:
◆ Make as much difference as you can between your baby's daytime environment and the night:

Cut down the light levels in the room and avoid active social play.
◆ Settle your baby for the night in her crib when she is sleepy and relaxed; don't go on feeding or rocking her until she is sound asleep.
◆ When your baby wakes and cries for a feeding, go to her immediately but gradually introduce some delay between the waking and the feeding, perhaps by changing her diaper or singing her a song before you offer food.

Note that this approach has no effect whatsoever before six weeks, and that at no time does it involve leaving your baby to cry.

Don't wait until he goes to sleep: Ordinary chores that are boring for you may be as good as a puppet show for your baby.

because sometimes letting your baby sleep with you and sometimes trying to insist that he stay alone guarantees misery for all of you.

Daytime sleep

When first-time parents bring their baby home they often find it impossible to relax, think about anything other than the baby, or get on with anything that doesn't concern him while he is awake. Only when the baby goes to sleep can ordinary adult life start again. So of course if he does not go to sleep, or if he keeps waking up, parents feel that there has been no ordinary adult life: Nothing has been accomplished all day.

That feeling is very natural while you are coping with a brand-new and unpredictable baby, but it's important to get yourself over it as quickly as you can, because it is only for a very few weeks that being asleep is a baby's usual state, and being awake the exception. Your baby is a human being joining a human household. Very soon, like the rest of you, being awake will be his usual daytime state, and sleep—in the form of separate naps—the exception. You have to teach yourself to accept and enjoy the baby as an (almost) ever-wakeful member of the family and instead of saving everything you need to do until he falls asleep, find ways to do a lot of it while keeping him pleasant company.

Once you take it for granted that your baby is a person, to whom you can chat while peeling potatoes or recount the gist of that maddening phone call, baby care and at least the domestic aspects of your life will join up.

bed. That can be hard work at the beginning, because it means doing everything you can to help him sleep happily alone: going to him whenever he cries for you, but never taking him back with you as he gets older. It leaves you much freer when he sleeps well but gives you no peace when he doesn't. An imminent tooth, a cold, or a nightmare will have you going back and forth between your bed and his crib, and later still when he can get out of bed and come to yours, you may find yourself taking him back to his room, again and again.

Nobody can make this choice for you. You may not be able to make it and stick to it either: Even once you have decided on the second approach, a bad week may find you taking your baby into bed with you at 3:00am after all because nothing seems to matter except being allowed to get your head down. It's worth being aware that there is a choice to make, though,

Twin tip

Make sure you have a stroller downstairs that's big enough for two and two playmats and two bouncy chairs. You can't tuck two babies under your arm while you go to grab something from another room or carry two in a sling while you water the garden, so if they are to watch what you do, you need to be able to move them from one safe place to another.

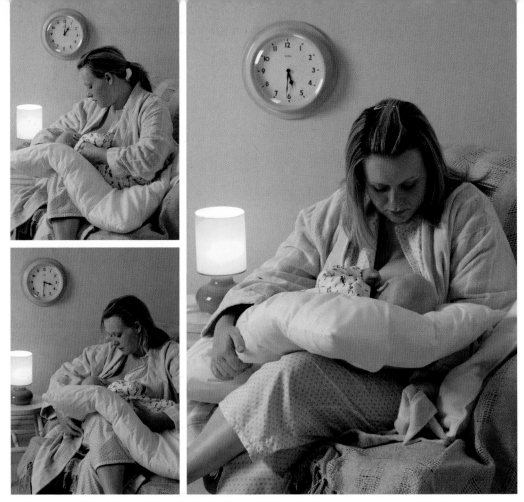

Just for once, do look at the clock: If you had woken him at 11:00pm just before you went to bed instead of waiting for him *to wake* you *at 1:00am, he might have only woken you twice.*

Night feeding goes on…

An astonishingly large number of the parents you meet have babies who regularly "sleep right through the night" before they are six weeks old—or so they tell you. Don't believe everything you hear. Most babies don't, and yours probably won't. Sleeping "through the night" sometimes turns out to mean midnight to 4:00am!

If you are breast-feeding, your baby will probably nurse so often that the number of feedings seem irrelevant and you lose count. Bottle-fed babies often go rather longer between their harder-to-digest feeds, and because you have to buy and mix and pour and warm the bottles, you probably will keep track of the number. Most babies need at least six bottles in a 24-hour period until they are around six weeks old, and many will need five until they

are somewhere around four months. As long as four hours is the longest your baby ever goes between feeds, you are bound to have to wake up at least once during your normal sleeping hours.

Night-waking (your baby's and therefore yours) is often even more of a strain than parents expect and other people realize. The lost hours of sleep are not the principal problem, because they can often be made up with early nights or afternoon naps. The dragging exhaustion comes from the constant interruption of your sleep: the disruption of your sleeping patterns. Being woken twice or three times every night for weeks on end, even if your baby feeds efficiently and settles swiftly, can make you feel as if you are sleep deprived, even if your hours of sleep add up to a manageable number.

Planning his feeds around your sleep

If you're to get all the sleep you can while keeping your baby calm and content, you'll need to adjust your approach to his night-time wakings to his age and stage of development. For the next few weeks, keeping him waiting for feeds will always mean more crying for him and less sleep for you. But later on—perhaps from around three months—going to him the instant he stirs may actually mean that he wakes right up and has a feed, when if you'd held back for a minute or two he might have re-settled himself.

If you can stop thinking about these early night feeds as anything to do with discipline (if the baby goes longer without a feed he's being a "good baby"; if he wakes an extra time he's not) you may be able to juggle night feedings so that they suit you all. The trick is to feed him before he is ravenous rather than trying to make him wait when he is. Don't listen to anyone who says that is "spoiling"—it's simply good sense and self-interest. If you can accept that, you will often be able to anticipate a demand for food and prevent it from coming up in the small hours by waking the baby up and feeding him early instead of waiting for him to wake you. It works something like this: If you usually fall into bed at midnight, dreading the fact that your baby will wake you for food both around 2:00am and around 5:00am, you can wake and feed him just before you go to sleep—and if you do, he's unlikely to wake again before 3:00am and then will probably sleep at least until 6:00am.

When your baby reaches a point where he needs either a late-night or a crack-of-dawn feed but not both, you can try the same feed-juggling technique to persuade him to accept your choice. If you want to get rid of the late-night feed so you can get to sleep earlier yourselves, don't wait until midnight; wake him a few minutes earlier each night until eventually that late feed merges with the evening one into a single feed around 10:00pm. You'll soon be (almost) counting on (almost) six unbroken hours of sleep.

If you prefer to go on with a late bedtime and get rid of the small-hours feed you can gradually push his 6:00pm-ish feed toward 7:00pm, and then leave him to sleep until around 11:00pm or midnight. That way you can probably persuade your baby to give you that precious six-hour sleep before he next needs feeding, waking at a comparatively civilized 6:00am.

You can't "teach" your baby to sleep through the night

Juggling feeds doesn't always work. A lot of babies are still having six (and seven and eight) feeds at six weeks, though you probably won't hear about them from your exhausted friends. And even when they reach three months old some babies wake in the small hours and at the crack of dawn even if they were fed at midnight.

If yours is one of those babies, you'll probably find your patience and good sense are under threat, but try to hang onto them and ignore any pressures other people may put on you to resist your baby's demands. This is not a moral issue, it's a pragmatic one. Your baby wakes and cries because he's hungry. You're going to feed him sooner or later, and you'll save both of you a lot of misery if you feed him sooner. Feeding will stop his crying immediately, and it is the only thing that will do so. If you try to delay that feed—make him wait—you'll also delay your own return to sleep.

"Teaching" babies to sleep through the night by leaving them to cry is a common recommendation, but it's premature and makes no sense during these first months. If you leave your hungry baby to cry, he will get more and more hungry and more and more tired. By the

---

Parents talking about...

night feeds

❝If you think you've got it tough, try twins. The sleep deprivation was worse than anything you can imagine. It almost tipped over into mental illness. It gets easier, though. From about four months our babies got predictable. It wasn't that they slept all night (when will that be?) but that they always slept two chunks of three hours. Not enough, but oh, so much better than nothing.❞

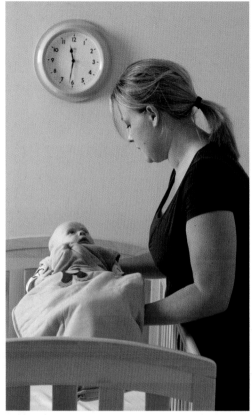

...It worked! Putting him peacefully down at 11.30pm meant he stayed asleep until 3:00am.

Parents talking about...
organizing better nights

❝Jake and I were beginning to feel like sleepwalkers. Our daughter, Jewel, wasn't a bad sleeper, in fact she slept quite a lot. But she didn't sleep any longer between feeds in the night than in the day. Most days she'd have a feeding around 5:30pm and another around 9:30pm, but then she'd wake between 1:00 and 2:00am and again at around 5:00am.... I knew it was no good trying to delay a feed when the baby was hungry—it would just mean more crying for Jewel and even less sleep for us—but might offering Jewel the first night feed before she was hungry (and before we'd gone to sleep) mean that we all got more of what we needed? I fed her as usual at around 9:30pm but instead of waiting for her to wake at 1:00 or 2:00am, I woke her around 11.30, just before we went to bed. After a couple of confused nights when Jewel woke at 1:00am even though she had just been fed and wasn't hungry, she took to sleeping through to around 4:00am. Not a civilized time to be awakened, but far better than both 1:00am and 5:00am.❞

time you decide to feed him, he may be so tired and upset that he can't take a full feeding before he falls asleep, so he will wake again sooner than he would have done if you'd fed him before. If you don't decide to feed him but leave him to cry for half an hour or more, he probably will go back to sleep not because he's learned anything, but because he's exhausted. There's a lot of pain for both of you in that scenario, and no gain even for you. Revived by a half-hour nap, and now ferociously hungry, your baby will start to cry again, and you'll be awake once more.

When a baby is hungry, nothing but food will do

If your baby is bottle-fed, water instead of milk may put him back to sleep for a few minutes if he was only a little bit hungry. But sucking water only temporarily fools him into thinking he's

been fed. By the time you are back in your bed and getting sleepy, he'll realize that his tummy is still empty and cry again.

Giving your baby an extra-large feed in the evening will not help unless you were actually underfeeding him before. Baby food manufacturers, well aware of parents' need for more sleep, sometimes write advertising copy that suggests a more food = more sleep equation. But a baby's hunger and digestion do not work like an internal combustion engine. An extra-large feed won't keep him going for longer before he needs another. If he has as much milk as he wants at his evening feed, he won't want any more. If you get extra calories into him by subterfuge—putting cereal into his bottle, for example—he will still digest the whole feed at a normal rate. The extra calories will affect his figure but not his sleep.

Growing

After a few days of losing weight and a few more regaining it, most babies gain something like 6–8 ounces (175–225 g) per week, until they are around three months old.

Of course not every baby's weight behaves like that—or behaves like that all the time—but that is the average rate of gain, not only for babies who were born average-sized (in the middle of the weight chart) but also for babies who started out big (at the top of the chart) or small (at the bottom).

Babies also grow in length of course, and the circumference of their heads increases too, but those changes are so gradual that to track them, measurements have to be accurate to a few millimeters—and on a wriggling baby, that isn't easy. Health professionals will take these measurements at your baby's check ups, and that is often enough. The relationship between these various aspects of growth is important, though. A baby who gets heavier more quickly than most babies but gets longer much more slowly will be getting fat rather than growing large. A baby who is long for her weight may just be tall and slim, but if her weight drops down from near the top to near the bottom of her chart, she might be underfed.

Individual growth charts are only useful if they are completed for long enough for there to be several individual points to be joined up so that you can see how the resulting curve that you draw compares to the percentile curves already printed on the chart, and if your baby is being compared with an appropriate population. Ask your pediatrician.

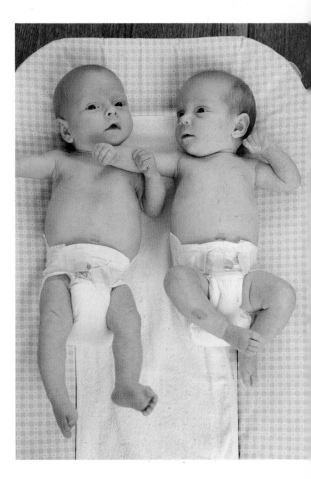

Twin tip

Pre-term babies have missed out on some of the growth and development that should have happened in the womb and will take some time to catch up. How much time depends how pre-term the baby was, and you will probably be advised to think of him as the age he would be if he had been born at term. Bear in mind, though, that 37 weeks is regarded as full term for twins, so if your babies were born at 37, or even 36 weeks, you can take their actual birthday as being their development birthday. Even if twins are born at term, though, they are likely to be smaller than single babies because they have shared the resources available in your womb. If those resources were not shared equally between the two of them, their sizes, weights and progress may be very different.

The charts presented here are World Health Organization growth charts, containing weight-for-age percentiles for the first year of life. These WHO standards for the optimum growth of all children are derived from international measurements of healthy, breast-fed babies whose mothers were not poor and did not smoke. Since 2006 they have been adopted in 106 countries including the UK. In the United States, the CDC growth charts used by pediatricians since 1977 (and primarily based on formula-fed children) were revised in 2000, to more accurately reflect the proportion of U.S. babies that are wholly or partially breast-fed.

Why change growth charts?

The growth patterns of formula-fed babies are different, and their cumulative weights over time somewhat higher, than the expected pattern of gain for breast-fed babies. Many breast-fed babies start out with rapid weight gains so that some who were born at around the 50th percentile may have gained their way onto the 75th by eight weeks. Weight gain may then slow down so that the baby's measurements return to where they began. On a weight chart where percentiles are based on formula-feeding patterns and these are regarded as the norm, such a slow-down may seem to suggest that a baby is not getting enough to eat. Some breast-feeding mothers have even considered supplementing their breast milk with formula to make their babies gain faster, like the formula-fed babies. But looked at against the expected weight gains of thousands of breast-fed babies, that pattern is clearly normal—and now thought also to be desirable.

CDC and WHO growth charts

Separate charts are used for boys and girls, since their birth weights tend to be slightly different.

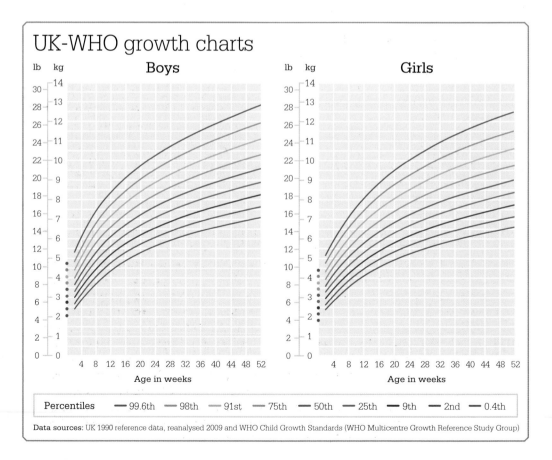

UK-WHO growth charts

Boys — lb, kg — Age in weeks: 4 8 12 16 20 24 28 32 36 40 44 48 52

Girls — lb, kg — Age in weeks: 4 8 12 16 20 24 28 32 36 40 44 48 52

Percentiles —— 99.6th —— 98th —— 91st —— 75th —— 50th —— 25th —— 9th —— 2nd —— 0.4th

Data sources: UK 1990 reference data, reanalysed 2009 and WHO Child Growth Standards (WHO Multicentre Growth Reference Study Group)

Percentile curves are the same shape for all populations, but the actual measurements vary depending on the population from which the measurements were taken. CDC growth charts are based on the birth weights of millions of infants born nationwide, length-related data from the birth certificates of nearly one million infants born in two states, and the CDC Pediatric Nutrition Surveillance System. For UK-WHO growth charts, the population was 8,600 healthy, breast-fed babies between two weeks and four years of age studied by the World Health Organization in six countries, including the United States, and a sample of British babies born between 32 and 42 weeks.

On each chart the dark green line in the center is the 50th percentile. This is always the average, and is drawn so that out of any randomly chosen 100 of the population being studied, 50 (50%) will weigh more and 50 (50%) will weigh less. Likewise the orange lines, one from the top, are 98th percentiles, drawn so that only 2% of babies will be heavier (and 98% will be lighter), while the purple lines, one from the bottom, are the 2nd percentiles, drawn so that only 2% of babies will be lighter (and 98% will be heavier). The 75th and the 25th percentiles (pale green and light blue lines respectively) are drawn so that they divide up the space between average and very large or very small: 25 babies (25%) will be heavier (and 75% lighter) than the 75th percentiles, and 25 babies (25%) will be lighter (and 75% heavier) than the 25th percentiles.

The same statistical definitions apply to all percentile curves, and as many can be added as are thought useful. Here a 0.4th and 99.6th have been included so that the weight gain of the very smallest and largest babies can be predicted.

Varying growth patterns: breast- and formula-fed babies

Babies who are exclusively breast-fed sometimes gain weight very rapidly in the first few weeks. After three months, however, as the comparison chart above shows, they tend to gain weight more slowly than the rest. If their weight gain

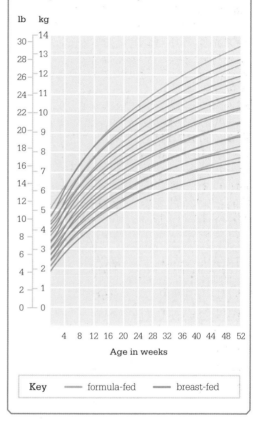

Comparison chart

Differences between expected weight gains of exclusively breast-fed and mainly formula-fed boys.

Age in weeks

Key — formula-fed — breast-fed

is being recorded on a chart based on norms for breast-fed babies—such as UK-WHO growth charts—everyone can see that this slowing is normal, but if their weight gain is being recorded on a chart based on formula-fed babies, or on those who were fed breast milk exclusively only for relatively short periods, such as the CDC charts, slower weight gain may look like inadequate weight gain—especially as the difference (shown here in the blue and the yellow growth curves) increases to as much as 2.2 pounds (1 kg) by the end of a year. It is not that breast-fed babies are lighter than they should be, though, but that formula-fed babies are heavier.

Settled babies' crying

Although all babies cry, some cry more than others, especially in their first few weeks outside the womb, as you may already have discovered. Almost all babies who were born at term reach their personal crying-peak at around six weeks and cry at least a little less by three months.

If your baby cries a lot it may be because she starts crying often, or because once she starts she's difficult to comfort so she goes on a long time—or it may be both. More than three hours in a 24-hour period for several days in a row over several weeks is classified as "excessive crying."

In this first half-year at least, real crying (as opposed to grumbling on the way to sleep) should never be deliberately ignored because it always means that your baby is uncomfortable or unhappy. People who are looking for a reason to ignore crying babies sometimes say that they cry "to exercise their lungs." That's nonsense of course, because lungs don't stop working for a moment from birth to death. Your baby cries because she needs you to take action on her behalf. She will stop as soon as you have restored her comfort and equilibrium. Doing that is central to your job as her parent; she cannot do it for herself.

From research

Programmed to cry. Human babies have evolved to signal distress by crying. A baby will cry whenever his internal state is one of discomfort. He will cry in reaction to major discomfort such as pain, or minor discomfort such as too-bright sunlight. The crying signal is not just to alert parents to the baby being upset, much less to tell them what is the matter, but to ensure that they do something about it. Young babies are helpless to regulate their own internal states: They rely on parents or parent substitutes to act as external regulators; to restore their equilibrium and make them feel better.

Although crying always means that action is needed, in these first weeks it doesn't always mean that something is wrong. A lot of crying is thought to be "developmental": not caused by anything specific that has happened to the baby but by the fact that she hasn't yet adapted to life outside the womb; isn't yet able to sort out one sound, sight, or sensation from another, or is momentarily overwhelmed by some aspect of the complicated developments that are taking place in her brain and nervous system.

The many occasions when your baby cries because she needs something specific may be easier to deal with; when you can understand what it is that she needs, you will probably be able to give it to her and have the satisfaction of seeing her restored to calm. Feeding her when she's hungry and watching crying turn into contentment is as pleasurable for you as for her. It isn't always that

Sometimes you can hold your baby in perfect equilibrium.

When she's overcome by internal stresses, the tactile comfort of face to face and chest to chest may be the best you have to offer.

Bottle-feeds need preparation, so however hard you try to anticipate your baby's needs, you can't always meet them instantly and so he may sometimes cry from hunger.

easy, though. Try as you may, you may not be able to work out what your baby needs. You offer everything you can think of, but the crying goes on and on and nobody can feel satisfied.

Although you probably wish that your baby never cried at all, she'd actually be far more difficult to care for if she didn't. How do you know when your baby's uncomfortable or unhappy? Because she cries. She would only stay silent when she needed you if she was desperately ill, severely chilled, or smothering. How do you know that your baby doesn't need anything right now so you can relax and think about other things? Because she's not crying.

When crying goes on and on

The sound of your baby's crying is meant to grab your attention and galvanize you into action, but it is not meant to go on and on whatever you do: It's meant to stop when it's answered, like a ringing phone. Coping with a baby who keeps on crying and cannot be comforted is definitely one of the hardest aspects of parenting, and the longer the crying continues the more likely you are to feel panic-stricken by your helplessness, and less and less loving and sympathetic to a baby who, by rejecting all your efforts to help her, even seems to reject *you*. When crying goes on and on, many parents come to feel frustrated and useless, even angry; to feel that their baby is doing it deliberately to torment them, that she *will not* stop.

From research

"Numbed into silence." A small and tragic minority of babies do not cry when they are distressed. Some have been abused and are afraid to attract adult attention. Others have been left to "cry it out" for so long and so often that they have given up hope of getting attention. Either set of experiences is thought to trigger a "freeze" response to stress. Such a response is sometimes said to have evolved from prehistory, when infants who had been lost or abandoned by adults were less likely to attract the attention of predators if they kept silent.

Causes of crying and ways of comforting

Although your baby may spend twice as much time crying as your friend's baby, and half as much time as your niece, many of the circumstances in which they begin to cry will probably be similar.

Effective ways of comforting crying babies are part of their relationship with their parents, so you and your sister may adopt different strategies. However when the "cause" of a crying episode is clear, there may be an obvious "cure." Even when the "cause" is a mystery, there are some techniques that are worth trying:

◆ **Hunger:** The commonest cause of crying and the easiest to deal with. If your baby is hungry, milk and only milk will stop the crying. Your baby may suck a bottle of sweetened water or a pacifier, but the comfort of sucking, even combined with a sweet taste, will have only a momentary effect. She needs food going into her stomach, or she will start to cry again after a minute or two.

◆ **Pain:** This certainly causes crying from the first minutes of life, but it is often difficult to be sure whether a crying baby is distressed by pain or by something else. If your baby stops crying when she is picked up, and immediately passes gas from one end or the other, she may have had an uncomfortably distended belly that is now relieved, or the gas may have had nothing to do with the crying, being passed merely by chance when she was picked up.

Your baby will probably react more to some kinds of pain than to others. A bottle or a bath that is even a few degrees too warm will make her howl, but minor knocks and bangs, especially to her hands or feet, may pass unnoticed in these early months because the myelin sheathing of some nerves is not complete.

◆ **Shocks and frights:** Any sudden movement that makes your baby feel like she's falling will evoke her startle reflex and make her cry; she may even turn pale and tremble from shock.

◆ **Mistiming:** Your baby's mood and state dictate the amount of any kind of stimulation she can enjoy. Games she enjoys when she is awake, content, and well-fed may be too much for her when she is sleepy, irritable, or hungry. When she is feeling sociable she loves to be played with, but when she is not, trying to "cheer her up" will have the opposite effect.

◆ **Overstimulation:** Too much of any kind of stimulation may overwhelm her: too much

When your baby's feeling vulnerable, even being picked up from her familiar chair can be enough to startle her.

tickling, bouncing, or hugging; loud sudden noises, unexpectedly bright lights, sharp or bitter tastes, or rough toddler kisses. Your baby will obviously cry from hunger if a feeding isn't forthcoming when she needs it, but mistiming the rate at which she can get the milk can also make her cry. If food comes too slowly because a bottle's nipple has too small a hole or you take her off the breast to burp, the distress of hunger overrides the pleasure of feeding. Sometimes a baby who was crying because she was hungry stays hungry because she is crying too much to suck. Many babies are easily irritated if they are handled when they are hungry, so a bath or diaper change when your baby needs a feeding is also likely to cause crying.

◆ **Making the transition from wakefulness to sleep:** Small babies often have difficulty in getting from being sleepy to being soundly asleep. Changing her surroundings when she's just settling down makes it more difficult, so if you're going out in the car, put her in her car seat before she begins to drop off so that she can go to sleep to smooth motion, or delay the expedition until she is asleep. Many new babies jerk and twitch when they are in that drowsy

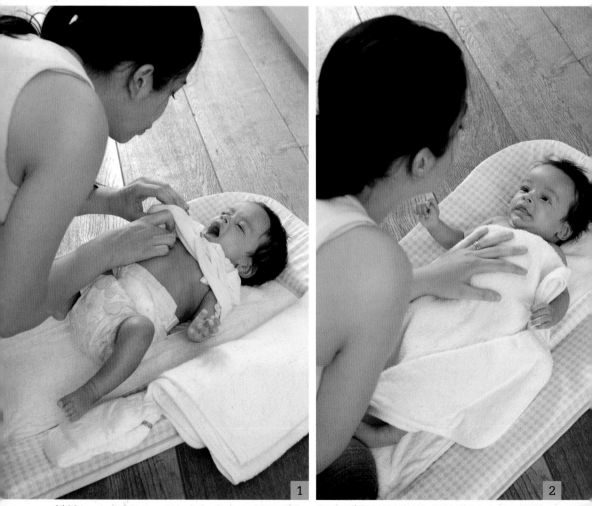

(1) Many new babies cry piteously for the loss of their clothes; they hate their skin being exposed even in the warmest air. (2) Luckily it's only a bare chest and tummy that cue distress: cover him with something warm and textured and the crying will (probably) stop.

state of near-sleep. A few startle themselves awake over and over again, crying, drowsing, jerking, and crying again. If this is why your baby is crying, being swaddled will almost always resolve it. *(See p. 102).*

Crying for contact comfort

Babies come out of wombs where they are held tightly in a warm, soft environment. For a few weeks at least, many are upset by too much physical freedom.

◆ **Being undressed:** If your baby cries when you take her clothes off, don't assume that it's entirely because you are inexperienced and clumsy. A lot of babies hate being undressed and become more and more upset as each layer is removed, often howling when that final layer comes off. Your baby doesn't react like this because she's cold—she'll cry however warm the room. She is crying because having her bare skin exposed to space and air makes her feel uncomfortably unprotected.

Your baby will stop crying as soon as she is dressed again, but in the meantime you can probably keep her calm—or even calm her—by laying a towel, a shawl, or any warm textured material across her chest and tummy.

◆ **Lying on hard surfaces:** You can often prevent crying for contact comfort by making sure that all the surfaces the baby lies on are warm and soft. Plastic laminates and sheets make life easier for you but they are horrible for her. So cover all plastic mattresses and mats with a textured fabric such as a towel. Even if you never use cloth diapers for their intended purpose, it is worth having a few just for this.

◆ **Being put down:** If your baby cries until you pick her up, stays calm while you hold her, but cries again when you put her down, don't assume that she is manipulating you into picking her up and that you shouldn't "give in" because it will "get her into a bad habit." Your baby isn't crying to be picked up: She is crying because she has been put down and deprived of contact comfort. Small babies are instinctively happiest when somebody holds them. In many parts of the world, grandmothers and older sisters take turns with mothers to free them for heavy

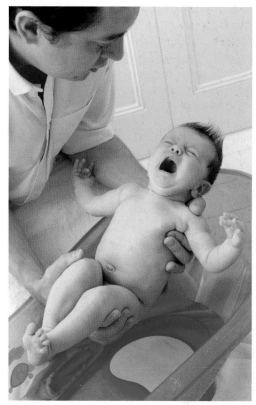

A baby has to be naked to go in a bath; but is the routine worth it if it upsets her this much?

physical work, but most chores are carried out with the baby slung on the mother's back.

Unless your crying baby is hungry, picking her up and cuddling her will almost always stop the crying. If it does not, then holding her against your shoulder, so that her stomach and chest are pressed against your breast, probably will. Holding your baby quite firmly against you, face to face, is an all-purpose comfort that works more often than it fails. If the contact comfort of being held doesn't quite suppress the crying, try walking with the baby in this position. Adding rhythmic movement to holding usually leads to peace.

When neither of you can hold and walk your baby, swaddling her will often provide the contact comfort she needs, the blanket giving her something similar to the feeling of warmth and security she gets when she is held closely in your arms against your body. *(See p. 102.)*

If all else fails…

If you've considered all these causes of crying and tried all these "cures" and your baby still cries, for no reason you can fathom, you may want to stop trying to understand and solve the problem, and instead try one of the blanket comforting techniques that may soothe your baby no matter what has made her cry. Note the words "try" and "may." It is very important to your baby that you respond to her crying and do your best to restore her equilibrium and make her comfortable again, but it's important for you to realize that there may be nothing you can do that will hasten the end of this episode.

Rhythm

When babies are tense, even overwrought, they can often be helped to relax by constant rhythmical stimuli. The rhythm seems to work like a warm quilt thrown over the baby's distress, blocking it

Carrying your baby in your arms is fine for him, but a carrier or sling makes it easier for you.

> ## Twin tip
>
> **These ways of rocking a crying baby** aren't always possible with two. If both your babies are crying together, bouncy chairs, infant swings, or baby gliders may do the trick. You can put one baby in a seat and rock it with your foot while you cuddle the other, or put each of them in a seat and rock with a hand for each. If none of that works as well as being held while rocking, see if you can buy or borrow a rocking chair large enough for an adult to sit in with a baby in each arm.

out. Rhythm won't help if there's a simple reason for the crying—such as hunger—that you haven't spotted. But it probably will help if your baby is crying because she's feeling generally irritable, or is tired but too tense to go to sleep.

◆ **Rhythmical sounds:** Don't bother buying purpose-made baby-soothing CDs: Gentle rhythmical music on the radio or from your collection works just as well. Make sure it continues until the baby is really asleep; a change in stimulation when she is drowsy may wake her right up again. Burring sounds—such as a fan heater, or tumble dryer—often work excellently, as does the sound of a car engine. But since most babies sleep peacefully in cars while they are running but wake as soon as the engine is turned off, a desperate drive around the block in the small hours may not really solve your crying problem!

◆ **Rhythmical movements:** Almost all babies are calmed and soothed toward sleep by being rocked. If it doesn't work for your baby you are probably rocking too slowly. Your baby's first experiences of being rocked were inside you, so try walking briskly with her in your arms or in a sling: lots of rocking and contact comfort. There are many commercial carriers available, but for soothing crying babies a simple sling made out of a small sheet or blanket is probably as good as a store-bought model. A stiff canvas carrier puts a barrier between her body and yours. A sling holds her warmly against you.

The best blanketing
technique of them all…

Babies who are helped to get a comforting hand to their mouths sometimes discover that they can get them there themselves.

Sucking

Sucking will only stop a hungry baby's crying if it brings her food, but if she isn't hungry "nonnutritive sucking" may soothe her better than anything else. Try offering her your (clean) finger, with the pad facing the roof of her mouth so her tongue prevents your fingernail from hurting her. If she sucks eagerly on a finger she might like a pacifier.

◆ **Thumbs and fingers:** You may have seen an ultrasound picture of your baby sucking her thumb or fingers in the womb, and she may have sucked them for comfort from day one. That's rare, though. It's several weeks before most babies can get their hands into their mouths without help. If your baby cries a lot and is difficult to comfort, and you'd prefer not to give her a pacifier, you could try helping the baby get a hand to her mouth to see if she calms herself by sucking it. She may not find her own small digits nearly as satisfactory as your fingers, though.

◆ **Pacifiers:** The use of pacifiers has become increasingly widespread in the last 20 years. Just as many parents buy bottles before babies are born—assuming that breast-feeding won't work out—many buy pacifiers as a matter of course, assuming their baby will need one.

Advantages and disadvantages of pacifiers

Advantages:

◆ Once she takes to it, a pacifier will soothe her to sleep, and often soothe her after a scare or when she is irritable.

◆ If she goes to sleep with a pacifier in her mouth and it stays put, disturbances will make her start sucking again instead of waking her right up.

◆ If she uses a pacifier she probably won't suck her thumb.

Disadvantages:

◆ Once she is used to the pacifier she may not be able to do without it. She may want it for years, and you'll find it difficult to ban it, because when she's upset and crying it's more effective than anything else.

◆ If the pacifier falls out of her mouth when she enters into deep sleep, any disturbance may mean that she wakes and cries for it. Since she will not be able to find it for herself, she will always need your help in going back to sleep.

◆ Using a pacifier in the daytime will stop her from exploring playthings with her mouth, and may limit her sound-making.

◆ Unless you are very vigilant about sterilizing them, pacifiers are unhygienic.

◆ You may be tempted to plug your baby's mouth at every protest, instead of trying to find out what she is protesting about.

◆ Sucking her own thumb or fingers is more hygienic and aesthetically pleasing, and it gives a baby independent control of her sucking-comfort. You can't take them away from her, and you won't have to keep finding them for her.

Most babies don't need pacifiers though, and are better off without them.

The problem with pacifiers is that using them is habit-forming—perhaps even more for you than for your baby. If your baby is inclined to misery, a pacifier during her first six months, until she begins to put toys and finger foods in her mouth and to chat to herself and "talk back" a lot to adults, might make an important difference to her contentment—and yours.

Unfortunately, though, after six months (or even six weeks) she will have gotten so used to the pacifier that it will probably be extraordinarily difficult to limit its use to bedtimes, let alone take it away from her altogether. Sucking her pacifier helps her keep upsets low-key: Take the pacifier away and the upset will peak, and nothing will help her deal with it but that pacifier.... If your baby takes to a pacifier and regularly uses one when she's two months old, she is likely to be using one a year or two later—and not only in her crib, either. Even if you don't mind what it looks like, that will be unhygienic, bad for her speech development and her teeth, and liable to make it difficult for her to resettle herself when she wakes in the night.

Twin tip

Pacifiers. Because there are two of them, twin babies may have to wait for attention more often than singletons. If they cry and fuss a lot and sucking seems to help, twins are excellent candidates for pacifiers—unless you dislike them.

Parents talking about...
difficulties with pacifiers

❝ When I had my first baby I simply didn't believe that if I gave her a pacifier I wouldn't be able to control how much she used it and for how long. "When you don't want her to have it any more, throw it away. What's the problem?" I said to myself. However she was still carrying pacifiers (yes, several) around with her night and day when she was three and I got pregnant again. You know what? This baby isn't going to have a pacifier at all. ❞

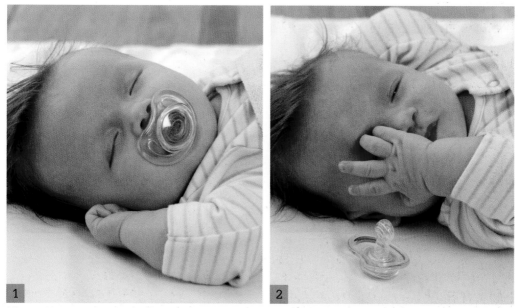

(1) His pacifier helps soothe him into peaceful sleep, and that's great. (2) But when he's deeply asleep it falls out, and the next time his sleep lightens, he'll miss it and have to cry to you to give it back.

Colic?

Coping with a three- to six-week-old baby who cries excessively and is difficult to comfort is so stressful that many parents long for an explanation (a "diagnosis") and latch onto the idea of colic with relief—even if they realize that it is not a very scientific term.

Your baby fits the description "colicky" if she regularly cries in a more distressing way at certain times of day, such as the late afternoon and evening. During those episodes she does not just cry, she shrieks. She appears to have acute abdominal pain, drawing her knees up, lifting her head, and going red in the face. Nothing you do comforts her for more than a minute or two, and it may be two or three hours before she settles.

Colic or not?

Don't jump to the conclusion that your baby is suffering from colic just because she cries in the evening for the third day in a row. She may be suffering from some other kind of distress, and if you're fixated on the possibility of colic there's a risk that you'll miss it.

◆ Crying and grumbling after a late afternoon or early evening feed does not suggest colic if she eventually goes to sleep with no screaming.

◆ Ordinary crying, even if she cries really hard and draws her legs up to her belly, does not suggest colic.

◆ If any help you offer brings the crying spell to an end within 30 minutes, it was not colic. If a feeding ends it, she was hungry; if a burp settles her, she had gas; if cuddling and rocking soothes her, she was lonely or tense.

◆ A crying/screaming jag is not colic if it ends in less than 30 minutes and the baby then sleeps or stays happy for at least 15 minutes before she cries again. (A bad day, yes; colic, no.)

◆ Occasional brief bouts of screaming that may occur at any time of day do not suggest colic.

◆ Whatever patterns of behavior your baby displays that are typical of colic, if she also vomits or has diarrhea, she has a different condition—an illness—but not colic.

From research

Colic. The name sounds like the name of an illness needing diagnosis and treatment. However there isn't an illness called "colic" (though adults can have various painful conditions that have "colic" in their descriptive name, such as renal colic). The kind of "colic" your baby might have (also sometimes called "evening colic" or "three-month colic" or, more accurately, "paroxysmal crying") is not an illness but a very distressing pattern of small-baby behavior. Some researchers reject the notion of "colic" as an entity, seeing it only as the extreme end of the continuum of ordinary newborn crying. Some see it as largely a temperamental matter, with babies who are especially sensitive to their environment reacting with colic to stress, to change, and perhaps to pollution by cigarette smoke. On the other hand, some health professionals believe that colicky babies do have especially acute stomach pain, and that it is usually caused by excess or trapped wind. They may recommend giving the baby drops of a medicine called simethicone (e.g. Mylicon) to break down bubbles of gas and make it easier to pass. Pediatricians stress that colicky babies remain healthy and thriving, eating and growing normally and with no clinical signs of digestive difficulty. There is no generally accepted cause, let alone cure, for colic, and no ill effects on babies—only on their parents' feelings.

Rhythmic music and movement and a double hug: Sometimes all you can do isn't enough.

From research

"Colic," lactose intolerance, and gastroesophageal reflux disease (GERD).
Research that is relevant to colic is ongoing, though no complete explanation has been arrived at. Some babies are thought to have difficulty digesting lactose, the natural sugar that is in all milks, including breast milk. Adding lactase to bottle-feeds or eliminating dairy from nursing mothers' diets helps some babies with apparent colic. However, lactose intolerance causes diarrhea, so lactose intolerance is unlikely to be the cause of your baby's trouble unless he has diarrhea, and if he has diarrhea he does not have colic.

GERD is the commonest medically diagnosable cause of excessive crying in this age group. In many new babies, the valve at the top of the stomach is immature, and in some babies it allows milk to be regurgitated. The milk is now mixed with acidic digestive juices, which burn the baby's esophagus and cause acute discomfort. Thickening the baby's milk with a product recommended by the pediatrician—by adding it to bottles or giving it to the baby before breast-feeds, can help.

Although the pain and screaming of GERD are sometimes thought to be due to colic, the two conditions are easily distinguished: GERD causes vomiting that is clearly different from ordinary spitting up, and the pain is always worse after feeds, not just in the evening and if the baby is laid flat.

Lactose intolerance, GERD, and intolerance to cow's milk as a whole should all be diagnosed and treated by your baby's doctor. Elimination diets (yours if you are breast-feeding; your baby's if you are not) can lead to inadequate nutrition. The American Academy of Pediatrics considers soy protein-based formulas appropriate for babies whose nutritional needs aren't met from breast milk or cow's milk–based formulas. Don't speculate with friends. Investigate with your doctor.

Surviving colic

While a baby is colicky, she may be unreachable by any of the comforting techniques you use to good effect at other times. It is your helplessness that makes "colic" so horribly difficult to cope with.

Once your baby has been checked by her doctor and you've been assured that she's flourishing, try to accept the fact that colic doesn't have a known cause. If you keep looking for one you will confuse every other aspect of your baby care. Why? Because you will find advice that the cause of "colic" is overfeeding and that it is underfeeding; that the problem is in formula feeds that are too strong or too weak; that your baby is having her milk too hot or too cold, too slow or too fast…. If you are receptive to all that, you are certain to change your baby's feeding routines and your own feeding techniques. Those suggestions couldn't all be right, but one of them might be. It doesn't stop there, either. Other favorite suggestions are allergies, hernias, appendicitis, gall bladder trouble, and gas. And of course "nervous exhaustion in the mother" (which from your point of view may seem more like a result than a cause).

If any one of these contradictory explanations for colic was correct, why should the trouble occur after one and only one feeding in a 24-hour period? However you feed your baby, you do not do it in a different way at 5:00 or 6:00pm, nor would any physical problem in your baby manifest only at that time of day. Of course your own stress and tension may play a part in this, as it does in anything to do with your baby, but if that was what was making your baby colicky, why would it still happen when her father or her grandmother bottle-feeds her?

Although friends and relatives may be eager to offer widely differing advice, try to confine yourself to suggestions from your doctor. She might suggest trying simethicone drops before feeds, changing to a different formula if you are bottle-feeding, or experimenting with your own diet—by eliminating dairy produce, for example—if you are breast-feeding. But if none of that makes any difference, try to accept that if there was a real cure for colic, everybody would know of it.

You need to be there for your baby, but you need someone to be there for you, too.

longer than three months.

Even once they know that there's nothing they can do to cure or even comfort their "colicky" babies during attacks, most parents feel that they have to go on trying: That they cannot leave the babies to scream alone. It's a good thing parents do feel like that, because research shows they're right. Trying to comfort a baby doesn't stop her colic attacks, but it does moderate them. Babies whose parents keep doing all they can scream less (and may grumble more) than babies who are left on their own.

If you try everything to comfort your baby, some techniques will clearly interrupt (though not end) her misery. If you put the most effective-seeming techniques into a regular sequence, such as walk-and-rock; offer a suck; rub her tummy; walk-and-rock, you may find that all those interruptions added together actually reduce the sum total of shrieks. And even if nothing you do seems to make a practical difference, the fact that you are doing *something* makes an enormous emotional difference. If she is screaming in your arms, you may feel that nothing could make her worse, but put her down in her crib and leave her for a minute and you'll hear a note of desolate despair enter her screaming.

Letting her know that you're there for her is vital, but being there is enormously stressful and hard work, too, so the more you can share these hours, the better. Some couples get through it better if they do it together; others take turns—maybe 30 minutes on and 30 minutes off watching television in another room. Taking turns makes it possible to provide attention for an older child, too.

If you're on your own, do try to find some company or respite rather than facing evening after evening without any. You might be able to arrange a schedule of family and good friends to spend the colic-hours taking turns with you. When there's nobody else around and you can't think what else to do, putting the baby in her stroller the moment she starts to scream and going out for a long walk might help. And some parents swear by loud music to drown the baby out, and dancing to it with the baby in a sling so that she gets rocked and you get exercise.

Two can cope better than one

You'll probably get through the next couple of months most easily if you can resign yourselves to them being difficult and try to support each other. Try not to blame yourselves, each other, or your baby, and hang onto the fact that however painful it may look, colic is not doing your baby any lasting harm and is not going to go on much

Settling into their own bodies

In half a year your baby will be sitting up (or almost) and in a year he'll be standing (or nearly), so it's not surprising that within a month of being born he's already beginning to take charge of his body.

Muscle control moves downward from his head to his wobbly neck, and over a couple more weeks it moves down to include his shoulders. He's growing all the time, too, which means that his head gets a little less heavy relative to the rest of his body. By around six weeks of age he'll mostly be able to hold his own head up as long as you keep still while you hold him, or move very gently. He'll still need your supporting hand when you pick him up and put him down though, or when you tip him off-balance by maneuvering him into his car seat.

As long as your baby's usual position is curled up, his range of vision is limited; he won't be able to see things that are directly above him. If you show him something at about 8 inches (20 cm) from his nose, he will focus his eyes and indicate his interest with his body. If he was lying still, he will start to wriggle; if he was kicking, he will "freeze to attention." If the toy is moved slowly, still within the limited range of his easy focus, he will follow it with his eyes. If it is moved too fast or taken too far away for him to see it clearly, he will lose interest; indeed the minute he loses sight of the toy, he has forgotten that it ever existed.

Why head control matters

As your baby's head control improves, all his typical newborn positions and postures alter. These are small and gradual changes, but they make a big difference to what he can do by the time he's around three months old.

◆ When he's on his back he begins to uncurl from that newborn fetal position and lie flat with the back of his head on the mattress.

◆ Lying flat he has a clear view above him—he'll begin to enjoy mobiles and faces hung there—and he can turn his head to enlarge his view.

◆ Lying flat on his back frees both his arms and both his legs and is the first step toward kicking and rolling over.

◆ When he is placed on his tummy, he begins to stretch his legs out instead of keeping them

It is not only what she can do that is changing, but also how happy she looks doing it.

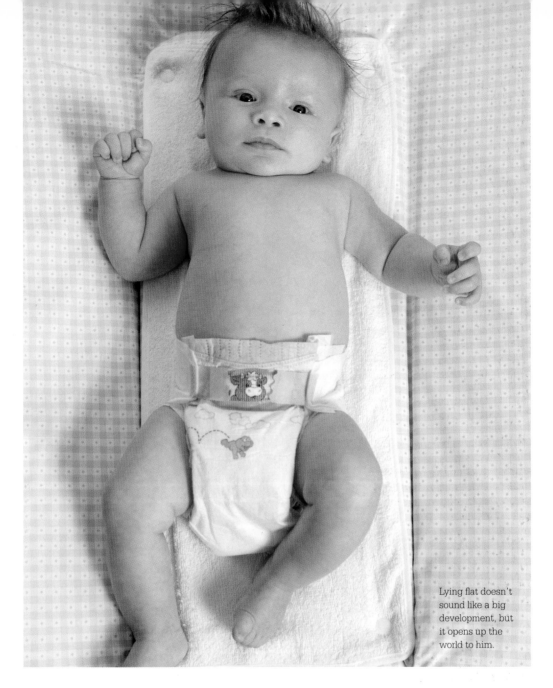

Lying flat doesn't sound like a big development, but it opens up the world to him.

bent under him, and to turn his head to either side instead of always to one preferred side. He can even lift his head enough to see what he's lying on.

◆ When you hold him against your shoulder, he doesn't immediately curl in and rest his head under your chin; instead he begins to keep himself upright for a few seconds so that he can look around.

From research

Babies' easiest focusing distance. 8 inches (20 cm) has evolved as babies' easiest focusing distance. It cannot be a coincidence that this is just about the distance that separates a mother's eyes from her baby's eyes when he is nursing.

Early playing: looking first, doing later

Until your baby opens his hands (at about eight weeks) and begins to play with them, he is not ready to play with toys—although he'll love to look at them.

Until your baby is ready for manipulative play, he can use any number of things to look at, and it's probably good for him to practice focusing his eyes on different things at different angles. His easiest focusing distance is only about 8–10 inches (20–25 cm), so if you're going to hang mobiles or dangly toys for him, they need to be close. His head is usually turned to one preferred side when he's lying on his back, though, so he may see things better if they are tucked between the mattress and the side of his crib or stroller on that side. Your baby may surprise you by the concentration with which he'll study a black-and-white cloth "first book," a vinyl pattern card, or perhaps large photographs of faces. Still, your real, animated adult faces—smiling, talking, singing, and questioning him—will certainly be the most interesting objects in his world, so he'll probably enjoy as much face to face "conversation" as there is adult time available.

Looking from the toy to his hand and back again, the baby is figuring out the distance and getting ready to try a grab.

Hands: first and best playthings

An indirect but important consequence of learning to support his own head and lie flat when he's on his back is that your baby will now be able to "find" his hands. He isn't ready to use them to hold onto things or to reach out, and he won't be until they stop being loosely fisted all the time, but somewhere around six weeks he'll find his hands by touch. When his two hands happen to come into contact, he'll grasp one with the other, pulling the fist open and playing with the fingers. He doesn't have any idea that those hands are part of him, and he doesn't lift them up to look, or even recognize them if a waving arm brings one hand into his eye line. He treats his hands as if they were toys.

Miraculous rattles

A couple of weeks later his hands will be open some of the time. He still uses one to play with the other as if it was an object and he still doesn't bring them up to look at them, but if you put a really lightweight rattle into one of them, he'll grasp that and finger it just the way he fingers the hand itself. Now, when he's waving his hands around, he'll wave the one with the rattle in it; the rattle will make a sound; he'll follow the sound with his eyes; and hey presto! see his hand for the first time, and the rattle it's holding.

For the next few weeks rattles or rattly toys will be really valuable to your baby. Don't go for big grand expensive ones: they just need to be easy for a small hand to hold onto, too light to hurt your baby when he drops them on his face, and reliably rattly when waved around. That sound attracts his attention so that he looks toward it, sees what his hands are doing and begins to understand that the waving hands and the sound are somehow connected. By the time he is three months old or thereabouts your baby won't need the sound of a toy to guide him to his hands—although he may still enjoy it. He will have found them by eye as well as by touch and he'll play with them many times a day, often for minutes at a time, spreading his arms apart so the hands drop out of sight, bringing them back together again, pulling the fingers, and concentratedly watching them.

Although your baby still focuses most easily on objects that are close to him, he becomes quicker to achieve focus and better at following a moving object with his eyes. Soon he will turn his head to keep something in sight.

Beginning to connect seeing with doing

When the time comes that your baby always watches his hands when he is playing with them, you will know that he has made a connection between what he's seeing and what he's doing. Soon he will not only look at an object that interests him and try to keep it within view, he will also try to do something about it, usually taking a vague swipe at it with whichever hand is nearest. Watch carefully and you'll sometimes see him looking consideringly from his hand to the object and back. He's practicing controlling his hands and estimating, by eye, the distance between them and the toy he wants.

Your baby can use lots of opportunities for reaching out to things, especially if you arrange for him to experience plenty of success and a growing sense of his power and control over his own body and the outside world. He won't yet be very efficient at getting hold of things, because he will usually overshoot. You can help him toward success by holding a toy for him, waiting until he has definitely reached toward, it and then putting it in his hand.

Baby gyms and play frames come into their own at this stage. If you lie your baby on a mat and hang things above him, he will look: wave a hand vaguely toward something, and sometimes, semi-accidentally, connect. Hang things close enough to him that he can easily touch them if he stretches out (about 10 inches/25 cm is usually about right) and choose things that are light enough not to hurt him if they should come loose, such as soft pom-poms and lightweight rattles. When your baby's hand does touch one of these objects it will swing; it won't take him long to make the connection between touch and result, and to do it on purpose, glorying in the huge discovery that "I do this, and that happens." Don't leave the same old objects hanging there until he's bored of them. Hang different things that will behave in different ways when he swings them. That ball feels soft; the rattle makes a noise....

Becoming sociable

Human babies are born completely dependent on adult care but helpless to insist on it. If you got so bored of taking care of your baby that you just walked away and left him, what could he do about it?

Nothing except cry, and until or unless you have bonded with him, the crying might drive you away rather than keep you close. That bonding business is what does most to ensure care and survival for your baby; it has ensured the survival of all babies and therefore the human race. Babies themselves do a great deal to make mothers bond with them—from having round, chubby-cheeked "baby faces" to gripping onto fingers. It's that bond that almost guarantees that you will do all you can to protect and care for your baby; prevents you from abandoning him; compels you to cope with another and another and one more bad night; keeps you trying to help him through even the longest crying jag.

A lot of the early caring when your baby was newborn may have felt more like duty and responsibility than love, but your baby's development absolutely depends on secure loving attachment between you, so he is biologically programmed to play his part in building it. Day by day and week by week it will become increasingly clear that apart from food, the most important things in his young life are the people who take care of him: you.

Looking for faces

Your baby finds people's faces and voices fascinating, and by now he will be beginning to seek them out. When a face comes near enough for him to see it clearly, he studies it with extraordinary concentration. If there's no face and no object close enough for him to focus easily on it, he'll gaze toward anything that is lit or moving—the curtains across a bright window perhaps. But if there are several things he can comfortably look at, he will choose to pay attention to much more subtle stimuli than brightness or movement. And if there's a face, or even a simple eyes-nose-mouth sketch of a face on a balloon, he'll look at that. From a group of objects, he won't choose the most brightly colored but the most visually complex. A sheet of paper with a complicated black-and-white pattern on it (drawn in lines at least .1 inch or 2 mm wide), rather than a bright red rattle; a bread basket rather than a simple cube. He is programmed to give his attention to complex patterns and shapes because he must learn a complex visual world.

People are the most important part of that world, though, so while drawing face-patterns on paper and watching him study them ("hairline" to "mouth" and back to the "eyes") is fun, patiently offering him your face to study is much more important.

Listening to voices

Meanwhile, your baby listens to your voice as intently as he looks at your face, and it won't be long before he links up his looking and his listening. Right now, if he was still when he heard your voice he may start to kick excitedly, and if he was kicking he may freeze into immobility as he listens. Soon, though, he will turn his eyes and his head to see the person who is talking. If you pick him up, he stops crying. If you cuddle and walk him, he usually remains content. It's clear that he likes you, enjoys you, needs you, and his newly sociable-seeming behavior may be a welcome boost to your confidence in yourselves as parents.

Smiling

Smiling is your baby's trump card to keep you caring. The very first smiles you see may not be aimed at you; in fact they may not be aimed at anybody but at the ceiling light your baby is

Smiling: your baby's trump card in
the game of "keep them caring for me."

Smiles that your baby aims straight at you are key to your developing relationship: This is what it's all about....

gazing toward. That doesn't mean the smile is "just gas" though. It means that like most babies, your baby's first smiles aren't directed at something he sees but at something he hears— probably your voice, chatting as you change his diaper. When he has studied your face sufficiently; learned about it, there will come a day when his careful scanning ends as usual by looking into your eyes, only this time it will culminate in a vital social gesture: his first smile.

The first smiles your baby does aim directly at you are key to your developing relationship because few adults, and even fewer parents, are immune to the charm of those slowly-developing toothless grins. However bad a night he's just given you and no matter how many times he's spit up on your shirt, he's the most beautiful and the most lovable baby in the world.

When your baby smiles straight at you, into your eyes, it looks like love—but of course he cannot truly love anyone yet because he does not know one person from another or even himself

from anyone else. Early smiles are not about "I love you, Mommy," but about "Adults have to take care of me and my still largely-primitive brain is programmed to make sure they want to." The more your baby smiles at you, and makes noises and waves at people, the more you and other people—even passers-by and people in the checkout line, will stop and smile and talk to him. And the more attention people pay him, the more he will respond, so that his social responses make a self-sustaining, benevolent circle. He smiles so you smile; you smile so he smiles.

Although these first smiles only look as if they are meant for you personally, it's fine to behave as if they are, and indeed they very soon will be—because your baby will move on over a very few weeks from being interested in people in general, to recognizing and attaching himself to particular people. By his quarter birthday or thereabouts, you'll be able to see that although your baby is still friendly to almost everyone, he likes his parents best. In fact by that stage he is ready to begin consolidating the passionate and personal emotional attachment to you that will be the foundation of his mental health and happiness.

Hearing and talking

Babies react to sounds—and therefore clearly can hear—even before they are born, but it's during the second month after birth that most begin to react to an increasingly wide variety. Sharp bangs and crashes have always made your baby jump and still will, and if music soothed him in the womb and as a newborn, it will probably soothe him now, but he also begins to react to a wide range of sounds that are neither alarming nor delightful. These newly noticed sounds are "neutral" in the sense that how your baby reacts to any one of them depends on his mood and state when it begins. If you start the dishwasher while your baby is feeling cranky and fretful, the noise will probably act as the last straw and make him cry. But if you turn that same appliance on when he is feeling happy and playful, it will probably just add fuel to his smiling and kicking. It is as if these neutral, medium-range sounds tend to make babies feel more strongly whatever they were feeling before the sound began. People's voices are the exception though. As long as they are friendly, not angry or scared, voices, and only voices seem to interest and please all babies, always.

First social sounds

Babies make a few non-crying sounds of their own from soon after birth, but they have nothing to do with communication. They are not even deliberate. Your baby may sound contented after nursing and he probably is, but those little gurgles aren't expressions of contentment but the result of a very full tummy and a nearly-asleep, half-open mouth.

Babies make their first truly social, communicative sounds two or three weeks after they have differentiated listening from looking and usually while they are being held by a playing, talking adult. Once your baby responds to that kind of situation by smiling back at you and wriggling, it won't be long before he'll add some sounds of his own, so that as he gazes at

> ## From research
>
> **Impaired hearing.** At this early age it's easy to miss the fact that your baby is not hearing as he should, because even babies who are profoundly deaf "coo" just like babies with normal hearing do. The early sounds that come out of your baby's mouth do not depend on sounds going into his ears.
>
> If a baby does have impaired hearing, early recognition and help is really important, so all parents should be alert to the possibility. Don't assume that your baby's hearing is normal because he startles if someone slams a door or drops a saucepan; all but the most profoundly deaf will hear very loud and sharp sounds. However, a baby with a slight hearing impairment may not hear gentle conversational voices, so if your baby doesn't turn his head to look for your face when you speak to him, take notice. Babies do not always look for the face they can hear talking—sometimes they are busy with something else—but if your baby never does it, watch to see if he turns to other sounds, such as the TV or the dishwasher. If he does not seem to, talk to his pediatrician.

you, smiling and kicking, he suddenly begins to produce small, soft, liquid trills of sound. After a couple of weeks of that—perhaps as his three-month birthday approaches—he will differentiate smiling from talking. Now, if you smile, he smiles back. If you do both at once, so does he. It's astonishingly sophisticated discrimination to have learned in a few weeks.

The more babies are talked to, the more vocal they are. Babies who are cared for by people who don't talk much at all, or whose parents or care providers often talk to other adults or to older children at the same time as them, "talk" much less. The language used by the adult makes no difference at this stage; only the quantity and the communicative intent.

Of course, babies do not only talk when they are talked to; they also talk when they are on their own in their cribs or strollers. "Talking to

Taking turns in talking about love.

themselves," combined with playing with their hands, is most three-month-old babies' best solitary entertainment. But the more social conversations your baby experiences when he is with other people, the more of this "practice talking" he will do when he is alone, too.

This is yet another demonstration of the fact that babies who are given plenty of attention by adults tend to be more contented and less demanding than babies whose parents ration the attention they give for fear of spoiling.

Getting conversational

Your baby's early social sounds are not what we usually mean by "talk," because he isn't trying to tell you anything specific. But a baby who's looking at you and making sounds is "talking" in the sense that he is deliberately using his voice to interact with you. What is more—and more surprising—is that even at a few weeks of age he follows the basic rules of conversation. When you say something to him, he makes a sound back to you and even pauses to leave space for your answer. Say something more and he'll wait, as if giving you your turn, until you leave a pause. Only then will he take his turn by making some more sounds. It may sound improbable but it's true. Hearing is believing, so try it.

Putting looking, listening, and smiling together

New babies look and they listen, but it's not until about four to six weeks of age that they link the

From research

Social sound-making. If people had ever doubted that this kind of sound-making is social, research has proved it. Experiments show that babies will not react in this conversational way to any sound other than a friendly human voice. Scientists have tried "answering" each sound a baby makes with pleasant sounds such as a bell tinkling. None of the sounds made any of the babies "answer," nor did they increase the amount babies talked to themselves.

From research

The importance of talking. It's widely known that the more babies are talked to the more they talk, but while that is true, there's a less widely known truth: The more babies are talked to, and talk, the more certain areas of their brains develop.

two so that they always try to look at what they're listening to. Like starting to smile, this happens overnight, or from one minute to the next. One day your baby lies on his changing mat gazing absently toward the ceiling as he always does, while listening intently to what you are telling him, or the song you are singing. The next day he listens while gazing at the ceiling just as before, but he smiles. After a week or so of this there comes a day when he listens just as intently, but instead of gazing at the ceiling, he begins to search with his eyes for the source of your voice, looking for what he is hearing. Go on talking—or singing or whatever you were doing before—while he searches. When he succeeds in linking his listening and his looking, he discovers your talking, smiling face and smiles to the sound and the sight. In another couple of weeks he will smile back if you smile at him, even if you don't say anything.

Why early sociability matters

A baby's smiles don't only look loving, they make adults feel loved and loving too. In fact, being smiled at is so rewarding to many parents that it makes up for a lot of the hard work. Parents say things like "Now he's really getting to be a person." And the more a baby responds to them in other ways—stopping crying when they pick him up, calming down when they carry him around, kicking when they tickle his tummy—the more time they will spend cuddling and playing with him. Sadly, a less responsive baby—perhaps one who was born prematurely or had newborn problems—is likely to get less affectionate attention, although he needs it even more.

A member of the family

Loving and being loved

Your baby's quarter-year birthday may be a watershed for you all. By the time a baby is three months old, most of the stresses of being a new parent have usually subsided along with the often-chaotic behavior of a newborn.

You have gotten used to being this baby's parents and she has got used to living outside the womb. And whatever difficulties you may have had even once she was "settled"—with breast-feeding, perhaps, or with colic—they will be on their way out, or at least past their peak, while the pleasures of smiley, cuddly, cooing play begin to replace them.

The first nine months of your baby's existence—your pregnancy—transformed two cells into a baby and you into a mother. Now the next nine months will complete another transformation. By the end of that time, your child won't be a tiny baby any more, but almost a toddler, sitting up and nearly walking, babbling to you and almost talking, eating real food, drinking from a cup, and playing with anything she can get hold of. Babies' development on all fronts is so rapid that it's fascinating to watch, but you are not a spectator, you're a participant. Your influence over how your baby develops and what kind of person she is becoming is just as powerful in these coming months as it was during the months she grew inside you.

Learning who's who

At the beginning of this period, your baby, who has always enjoyed interacting with people in general and still does, will be beginning to know one person from another and to recognize and attach herself to particular ones. Around this time it will become heart-warmingly clear that she knows you both and likes you best.

Mother love

A baby usually selects her mother for her first love, if she is available at all. But the privilege doesn't automatically go to, or stay with, a baby's biological mother; it has to be earned by mothering her, and that doesn't just mean taking physical care of her. However expertly a baby is fed and cleaned and dressed and kept safe, her needs will not be met unless someone takes personal, emotional care of her: smiling and talking gently and affectionately to her; holding and stroking and cuddling her. Of course the chances are that you'll care for your baby both ways, physically and emotionally, but if you only had time to do one or the other, you would more certainly keep your prime place in the baby's

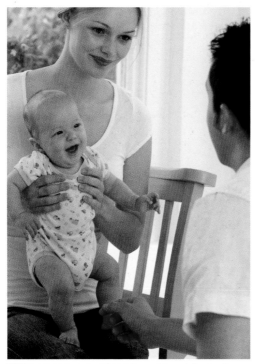

By three months parents get the smiliest smiles, and although Mommy's there 24/7, "Daddy's home" can be the thrill of the day.

From research

Attachment to parents. Attachments to fathers and mothers are different. Secure attachment to mothers is promoted by the sensitivity of their care in the first year, whereas secure attachment to fathers is promoted by the quality of their play, supporting and gently challenging babies' and toddlers' explorations.

world if you concentrated on loving talk and play than if you lavished the little time you had on giving her superb physical care. Of course physical and emotional care are linked, especially in feeding, her greatest pleasure in life, but someone to feed her, even someone who feeds her whenever she is hungry, isn't enough. Your baby needs someone who has her somewhere in mind all the time, whatever else she is doing. Your baby will fall in love with you, and it won't only be because you come to her with helpful concern when she cries, but also because you notice and respond—with pleasure and in kind—when she smiles and makes sounds. Even at this early age, your baby needs loving companionship from someone who plays with her, laughs with her, and carries her around to see the world. Someone she will have fun with because that person finds her fun.

Secure attachments

Secure attachment to both of you is of lifelong importance to your baby. At least one special person to attach herself to is an absolute necessity for every human baby—and more than one is better, safer. There's growing evidence that to a baby, having a father who is closely involved with her, as well as a mother, is a big advantage that lasts into adulthood.

There are babies who, while they are not obviously deprived, as babies reared in orphanages are deprived, never know what it is to be central to anyone's life. Such babies may be "well cared for" in every way except that they get very little emotional response. Some of them may be looked after by one caretaker after another so that even

the ones a baby could have become attached to aren't around long enough. Some of them do become attached to someone, but then lose her. Losing a beloved caregiver suddenly, especially later on when there is strong mutual attachment, always puts a baby's development at risk. It is difficult to overemphasize the importance of these first love relationships. It is through them that babies learn about themselves, other people and the world. It is through her attachment to you that your baby will experience emotions and learn to cope with them. The more secure her first "primary attachment," the more confident and competent she will be in exploring the world today, and the more resilience she'll have in coping with whatever life throws at her in the future. It is through this baby-love that grown-up kinds of love become possible for her. If one far-distant day she gives a child of her own the close, intimate loving care he needs, the long-forgotten roots of their relationship will be in your relationship with her right now.

Two parents are better than one

Although a baby's primary attachment is usually to her mother, that doesn't mean that the father is neglected or unimportant. If you and he are both willing and able to care jointly for your baby from the beginning, she is likely to be equally close to each of you, and because all her emotional eggs are not in one (maternal) basket, she'll be safer, too. Don't expect her to respond in the same way to each of you, though. You are different people and you'll have separate relationships with her. She may giggle more readily or go to bed more easily for one of you than the other. She may even play favorites. Although babies are usually most relaxed with their mothers at the very beginning, by four or five months some suddenly direct special favor toward their fathers. Rather unfairly, a father who has not been much involved in day-to-day (or night-to-night) baby care is especially likely to strike the baby as fresh and interesting, especially if he comes home at the end of the working day with untouched stores of energy for play, just when the mother's are running low.

Shared parenting

Figuring out how to share your baby's care isn't always easy, practically or personally. It may be especially difficult for fathers, however much they want to participate fully.

Family-friendly working hours are often even more difficult for fathers to arrange than for mothers. Furthermore, although most women would welcome more help than they get with the domestic aspects of caring for a baby, many value the fact that carrying, birthing, and breast-feeding a baby is an exclusive female role and don't want to give away any of their autonomy as mothers.

Whatever the issues between you, and however you resolve them, now and in the future, remember that you are both the parents of this baby and that you are mother and father, not mother and (male) assistant mother. You are different people of different genders in different roles. However you each fulfil your role, both of you are enormously important to your child.

Your baby's three-month birthday may be a watershed, but what's on the other side of it? For some women the next six months or so of

Twin tip

The birth of twins usually ensures that, willy nilly, the father is equally involved in baby care. A lot of the time two babies require two adults, so it's not a question of father "helping" mother but of both of you being equally competent to do everything (except actually nurse).

From research

Father-baby relationships. A close relationship with a father matters more than his practical baby care. Research studies from the last 20 years show that children who had lots of contact with their fathers did better in almost every way than those who did not. When thousands of babies were followed into adulthood, for example, those with closely involved father figures had higher levels of education and more close friends of both sexes and were less likely to smoke or to have had trouble with the police. Similarly, women who had had good relationships with their fathers at the age of 16 grew up to have better relationships with their husbands and a greater sense of mental and physical well-being.

their babies' lives are the epitome of mothering. Nobody has ever loved or needed them as much, and there is enormous satisfaction in feeling unique and irreplaceable. Mothering a baby as her first year passes isn't only an emotional experience, either, or even an emotional experience backed with practical physical care. Your baby needs intellectual care, too: talk and play, toys and treats, help in understanding whatever she has just noticed, and opportunities to practice each new skill. It's an enormous commitment, of course, yet because the baby is at a relatively easy stage—neither unpatterned and incomprehensible as she was when she was a newborn, nor awake all day and into everything as she will be six months from now—many mothers passionately enjoy it.

But some women don't enjoy this period of mothering at all. If your baby's dependence, her constant need of you, gives you cabin fever, you are not alone. By the time she is five or six months old, you may long for some time—even a little bit of time—when your baby doesn't need you for anything: not for practical care like a diaper change or a snack and not for emotional care either. Spending all day (and often some of the night too) paying attention to her feelings and anticipating her needs can leave you feeling drained.

Fathers matter, now and
forever—not just as part of
a parent-package, but as
their unique selves.

Mothers matter, now and forever, and the more joy you give your baby the more you'll get.

The more you can give, the more you'll get

The more you understand your crucial importance to your baby now, and the enormous importance of these months to the rest of her life, the more obviously worthwhile all this physical and emotional effort will seem. All the developments that must take place in your baby during this first year are waiting inside her, but they cannot be manifest without your help. The more you play and talk and cuddle and sing with her, keeping her happy and interested and busy, the more completely she will fulfil her potential for brain growth, development, and learning. You'll gain and so will the whole family, because your baby will be as cheerful and easy as she's capable of being at this stage in her life, and that means that most of the time she'll be a pleasure to be around.

But if you try to hold yourself aloof, resenting and rationing the attention she gets from you, your baby will often be discontented and bored and the whole family will suffer, you most of all, because she will seldom be much pleasure to anyone. The truth, however unwelcome it may be, is that your happiness and your baby's are intermingled. When you make her laugh and purr with pleasure, you'll feel happy too, and because you're happy it will be easier to continue being sociable with her. But when you are fed up with going back and forth to the nursery trying to settle her to sleep and choose instead to leave her to cry, listening to her crying will make you miserable too. So trying to tune in, understand, and meet your baby's needs is not only vital to her, but also better for you and for the family she's now part of.

Thinking about outside work

In these next months of her life, your baby is gradually building her special relationship with you. Once that attachment is formed, you won't threaten it if you give some of your time to paid work. If you are not going to take care of your baby full time yourself, though, she will still need to have a sense of being your primary concern, and the person who will be there for her when you are not—whether that's her father, her grandmother, or a paid caregiver—will need to be genuinely warm toward her and enthusiastic about caring for her. Indifference, perhaps from a bored teenage au pair, can be damaging. As long as anyone else who looks after her does provide high-quality, consistent, and loving care, though, (see p. 276) having you share her care will do your baby no harm and will not touch the ever-deepening attachment relationship between you.

Although some people talk of "full-time mothers" as if being with a baby 24/7 was "natural" or "traditional," all mothers, everywhere in the world and at every time, have had help from other people, especially grandmothers and older children, in caring for their babies. What is different in modern Western societies is that more non-maternal childcare is paid for rather than familial. Good care will keep your baby's development moving forward even when you are not there, and it's right that it should; missing some "firsts," like the first time your baby sits up

From research

Attachment Theory. Understanding of the immediate and long-term importance to babies and young children of their earliest relationships has been structured by Attachment Theory for more than half a century. The theory, which continues to be developed, is based on careful observation of children's and their parents' various styles of interaction during a "Strange Situation," in which babies and toddlers are observed in an unfamiliar playroom, and two brief separations from their parents and a visit from a stranger.
◆ **Secure attachment** (known as category B) The baby is happy to be reunited and quick to settle into interested play.
◆ **Insecure-Avoidant** (A) The infant turns or moves away from the returning parent; the mood is flat and play is half-hearted.
◆ **Insecure-resistant/ambivalent** (C) The baby both seeks contact with the parent and angrily rejects it and remains upset.
◆ **Disorganized** (D) There are no consistent strategies for maintaining the relationship with the mother, who is not seen as predictable but frightening.

Many studies have found that infants who had secure attachments to their mother tend to be more cooperative, socially competent, and self-confident children than infants who had insecure attachments. These insecure relationships in babyhood do not predict specific difficulties in later childhood but are a risk factor, increasing children's vulnerability to stressful events and experiences. Category D, added some years after the first three, is regarded as a disorder in its own right.

unassisted, is inevitable and, in the long run, unimportant. Good care means loving care, and although some mothers find it difficult to accept, your baby needs to love a caregiver. She won't love her better than you. Once babies know their mothers and fathers from everybody else, they love them best and go on feeling that way.

More feeding

By the time they reach three months, many babies are well-settled into a routine of feeding, from breast, bottle, or both, and may even be beginning to sleep for longer stretches at night.

Don't expect this "progress" toward more widely spaced feeds to carry smoothly on, though. Your baby's need for food keeps increasing, because she keeps growing.

If you are enjoying hanging out with your baby, now is the time when breast-feeding really comes into its own from your point of view as well as hers. Even if you had problems getting started in the first couple of months, feeding your baby is likely to be easy and pleasurable by now. And compared with formula-feeding, it's economical both of time and money. Nothing to buy, or remember to buy. Nothing to mix or warm or wash. And nothing to take with you when you go out, or wish you'd taken with you if you get delayed while out. Until she begins to be mobile, your baby is easier than she will ever be again to take with you wherever you want to go.

If you don't always want to take your baby around with you though, or you're already heading back to work, you may want to introduce your baby to bottles. Breast-fed babies are often reluctant to feed from bottles, so it's sensible to get them used to it gradually and before their acceptance is crucial. A hungry baby who rejects a bottle at 10:00pm when you are out to dinner may get very upset, but if she refuses a bottle at 10:00am when you're at work she (and whoever is looking after her) will be far worse off.

Adding bottles to breast-feeding

Fill occasional bottles with expressed breast milk rather than formula for as long as you possibly can. Most of the enormous benefits of breast-feeding are in the milk, not the container. Unless you find expressing breast milk unusually difficult, there shouldn't be a problem stashing enough milk for occasional bottle-feeds in the refrigerator (3–8 days at less than 39°F/5°C) or freezer (6–12 months at less than -0.4°F/-18°C), but providing milk for regular daytime bottles because you are back at work is different. If you find expressing easy—which is probably a matter of finding the pump that's right for you—and if you can have privacy, time, and fridge space at work, it's perfectly possible to go on feeding your baby exclusively with breast milk. You just express and store the milk she'll have while you're at work on Tuesday during Monday, and Wednesday's on Tuesday, and so on. Those are quite big "ifs" though, and expressing can take a lot of time from your working day, too. If you have problems with fitting pumping into your work routine and there is no particular reason, such as a family history of allergic illnesses, to avoid giving your baby formula, giving breast milk when you are with her and formula when you are not may prove to be a much easier option.

Formula-feeding for a couple of feeds five days a week means the end of exclusive breast-feeding, but probably doesn't need to mean the end of all nursing. By the time your baby is 4–6 months old, you may well find that

Parents talking about...

babies refusing bottles

❝ No means no." I'd tried Jake with a bottle before, so I knew he wouldn't like it, but I thought he'd accept it when he got hungry enough. He didn't though. He got hysterical, and my mom was so upset for him and angry with me for leaving her in that position of being helpless to comfort him that she nearly gave up on babysitting for us! ❞

A breast-fed baby under six months is blissfully portable; wherever you want to go, she'll be happy to go along with you.

your supply of milk is independent of nursing or expressing throughout the day, but keeps up in response to the stimulation of your baby feeding in the early morning and through the evening and night. By that stage your baby will probably nurse at night and take bottles of formula by day without getting confused between the two kinds of nipple or rejecting either.

Growing

After gaining something like 1 ounce (28 g) a day or 6–8 ounces (175–225 g) a week in the first three months, babies' rate of growth usually slows down a little. In the second three months your baby will probably gain around 4 pounds (1.8 kg) overall and around 2.2 inches (6 cm) in length. Of course not every baby's weight behaves like that—or behaves like that all the time. If you check the chart on p. 136, you'll see that babies who are exclusively breast-fed, many of whom gained faster than average in the early weeks, now tend to slow down more than formula-fed babies. If you are using a CDC growth chart based on formula-feeding, your breast-fed baby's weight gain may look slow in comparison. The faster gains of bottle-fed babies are not the ideal, though. Don't decide that your baby is gaining "too little"; it's more likely that formula-fed babies are gaining "too much."

Regularity of gain is still far more important than quantity. A baby whose weight gain, week by week, has put her just below the 50th percentile, so that her accumulating points show a weight curve that neatly follows that one, is unlikely suddenly to gain so little that she drops right down to the 9th percentile. Indeed, if she did she might be short of food. However, if that baby started out just below the 50th percentile but has always gained more slowly than most babies, so that her upward weight curve has always been flatter than the average on the chart, she is probably a baby who is meant to gain more slowly than most. If you are in any doubt about your baby's growth, take her to the pediatrician, where her weight gain can be considered along with her length and the circumference of her head.

You may hear...

that babies need solid foods because milk alone does not give them enough iron.
That's true, but it's not relevant until the iron stores they were born with are exhausted—usually around the middle of their first year. If a baby were being fed on liquid cow's milk, or on evaporated or condensed milk, he might need extra iron sooner. But while there is not a great deal of iron in any kind of milk, the iron in milks that are appropriate for feeding babies—breast milk and baby formula milks—is so easily absorbed that a little may go far enough.

From research

Delaying mixed feeding. It is best to delay non-milk foods until 26 weeks because:
◆ Before that your baby's digestive system and kidneys probably will not be sufficiently developed to handle other foods.
◆ Non-milk foods before six months offer your baby no health benefits and may prevent her from absorbing maximum nutrients from breast milk.
◆ Earlier introduction of non-milk foods may increase your baby's risk of developing allergies, infections, digestive problems, and obesity in later life.

Why—and when—your baby may need non-milk foods

Since the balance of nutrients in breast milk or formula is exactly right for babies, they could, in theory, go on living and growing on milk alone. In reality, though, a milk-only diet wouldn't work because milk is so diluted. As the baby grows she needs more food-fuel—more calories. For several months she can easily increase what she gets by increasing the amount she drinks at each feed. Around now she may even begin to reduce the number of feeds she needs from six to five, and may seem to be moving toward four every 24 hours. That "progress" can't last though; she keeps getting bigger and if, like many babies, she has a growth spurt around four months, the amount of food she needs will go up again within a few weeks. Instead of continuing to reduce the number of her feeds, she increases their size until she is taking almost as much as she can hold (probably around 7–8 ounces/200–225 ml) almost every time. Once a baby is completely filling her belly with milk at every feeding, she is getting all the nourishment she can from the number of feeds she is having, so if and when she needs even more calories she can only get them by more frequent feeding or by having something different. Since you don't want her to start waking for extra night feeds or reduce the intervals between daytime feeds, it's time to move toward something different. No non-milk food is as perfectly balanced as breast milk—though it can provide her with iron, the one nutrient that is scarce in milk—but because "solid foods" contain less water, the calories are concentrated into a much less bulky package, so a very little can boost her food intake without overloading her already full stomach. Of course you will need to choose first non-milk foods carefully, and there are several groups of foods that should definitely be avoided during this first year (*see p. 177*).

Introducing food that isn't milk

Introducing non-milk food is not "weaning." Your baby's early solid foods are not instead of any of her milk but in addition to all of it. You are not switching her from a milk diet to "real food" but adding tastes of "real food" to her milk diet, and those early tastes are even more for education than for nourishment. Solid food is potentially more concentrated than milk, but the teaspoons of purée she'll start with won't do as much for her hunger as a few extra sucks of milk.

Many people will tell you that four months is the right time to start giving your baby spoon-foods. That's probably what your older sister did with your nephew and what your friends with babies still do. And there are shelves and shelves of baby food in supermarkets labeled "suitable from four months," so why not? Because since 2003, some official advice, based on international research, has been not to give babies anything

Your baby is interested in everything you do, but she wouldn't really like your cup of tea—and she certainly shouldn't have it.

except breast milk or baby formula before they reach the age of six months.

The American Academy of Pediatrics has conflicting advice on this topic. The AAP recommends delaying the introduction of solid foods to four to six months of life, but the AAP's Section on Breastfeeding recommends exclusive breast-feeding for the first six months of life. There are a great many parents who start even earlier than four months. Studies suggest that as many as one baby in 10 has his first tastes of non-milk food at six to eight weeks.

Why is the new advice being ignored?

Mostly because people believe that additional food (especially "something solid in her tummy") will help babies sleep longer at night. It's nonsense. Two teaspoons of vegetable purée or a mouthful of banana won't give her enough extra calories to make any difference: An extra ounce or two of milk will.

◆ **Those "suitable from four months" labels are misleading (and ought to be banned).** Four months has been the accepted start-time for so long that there are lots of grandmothers out there telling their children, "It didn't do you any harm." (Maybe it didn't, but the evidence is that it's a risk.) Also, the fact that the AAP says that parents can begin to introduce solid foods to their babies as early as four months (despite its simultaneous six-month exclusive breast-feeding recommendation) probably gives many parents the confidence to move in that direction.

If your baby is eager to pick things up and put them in his mouth, he may soon be ready to try it with something edible.

◆ **Peer pressure.** Even if you don't actually feel pushed toward giving solid foods early, you may feel uncomfortable when you're the only one in your moms' group who doesn't bring along a little pot of purée.

◆ **It's been said that the research and its recommendations only apply to the developing world.** In fact, of the 20 studies, 11 were conducted in developed countries and nine in developing countries.

◆ **People misjudge the signs of readiness for solid food.** And therefore believe that their own baby is the exception who is ready early.

Real and fabled signs of readiness to try non-milk food:

Fabled
◆ Doubled birth weight.
◆ Increased hunger.
◆ Renewed night waking.
◆ Watching you eat.

Real
◆ Being able to sit or at least to support head and shoulders sitting in a high chair.
◆ Being able to reach out and grab.
◆ Putting things she's grabbed in her mouth.
◆ Loss of the tongue-thrust reflex.

If your three-month-old baby watches every mouthful you eat and seems to be begging to share, harden your heart and refuse her. After all, you wouldn't give her a taste of your wine or beer, would you? In a couple of months though, giving her a first friendly taste of something suitably bland—smooth vegetable soup that you haven't sprinkled with salt and pepper, for instance—off your finger can tell you a lot about whether she really is ready for non-milk food. If the moment the food on your finger touches her tongue, the tongue and the food both come thrusting out, the tongue-thrust reflex that protects very young babies from choking, by clearing foreign bodies, including food, out of their mouths, is still active, and she is not ready to eat; only to suck milk. On the other hand if she grabs your finger, sucks it like a lollipop and looks disappointed when it stops tasting of food and reverts to tasting of finger, she might soon enjoy half a teaspoonful of something of her own.

First non-milk tastes are astonishing,
but is this one delicious or disgusting?

If twin babies can both manage finger foods and spoon-foods, you can feed one while the other feeds herself, and then swap…

Introducing non-milk foods early

There are a few (very few) exceptions to the "not before six months" advice. They include some (but not all) premature babies (including many twins) who may benefit from solid foods from as early as five months from their actual (not their corrected) birthdate, and some babies with feeding problems such as reflux *(see p. 99)* or other medical conditions that make sucking difficult. If you think that your baby should start non-milk foods before six months, consult her pediatrician before you begin.

If you are positively advised to start mixed feeding early, your baby's first foods will only be solid in name; mixing them to a creamy texture with her accustomed milk is the way to make them seem acceptably familiar. Don't take your attempts to "make it familiar" so far that you mix the new addition into your baby's bottle, though. That's force-feeding: making it impossible for her to get her usual quantity of milk without the added cereal as well. If you are ever tempted to add anything, food or medicine, to your baby's bottles, remind yourself that those bottles stand in for breasts and you couldn't add anything to breast-feeds.... Give these first tastes of other foods to your baby from a tiny spoon or, if she finds that difficult, let her suck it off your finger.

> ## Twin tip
>
> **Your babies may be ready to start tastes of solid food at very different ages.** Try to follow each baby's lead, remembering that the twin who stays with milk alone for another month or more is only missing the experience, not important nutrition.
>
> When both babies have solid food, many parents sit them side by side and feed the two of them with one bowl and spoon. If you've managed to wait until they're old enough to pick things up and put them in their mouths, it might be better to let one baby play with finger foods while you help the other with spoon-foods, and then swap.

Foods to avoid

Even if you decide not to follow the recommendation to delay introducing any solid foods until your baby is around six months, there are certain foodstuffs that she really should not have before that age, as well as some that she shouldn't have at all this year.

Foods to avoid altogether until your baby is at least six months old. These foods are especially likely to cause digestive upsets, intolerance or allergies:

◆ Any food containing gluten (bread, cereals made of wheat, pasta).
◆ Eggs (or foods containing them).
◆ Fish and shellfish.
◆ Strawberries, oranges (and other citrus fruits), and their juice.
◆ Any milk (to drink or in cooking) that has not been modified for babies.
◆ Anything made with cow's or goat's milk (yogurt, cheese).

Foods to avoid for the whole of the first year:

◆ Added salt and salty foods (stock cubes; potato chips, bacon, salami), since salt puts a burden on infant kidneys. It's better for her future diet and health if she does not come to expect savory foods to taste salty.
◆ Honey: Very occasionally honey contains a type of bacteria that can produce toxins—poisons—in a baby's intestines, leading to a very serious illness called "infant botulism."
◆ Nuts (whole ones are a choking hazard until age five; products containing peanuts are best avoided to age three if there is asthma, eczema, or hay fever in the family).
◆ Shellfish (because of the risk of food poisoning); shark, swordfish, or tilefish (because of potentially dangerous levels of mercury).
◆ Cow's milk as a drink; (it's fine to use it in cooking once your baby is six months old).
◆ "Slimming foods." Babies need some fat, so avoid low-fat dairy foods; they shouldn't have artificial sweeteners, and too much fiber can reduce their absorption of minerals.

Getting started with non-milk foods

Your payback for waiting to introduce solid foods until your baby is coming up to six months old is that the whole mixed feeding business is very much easier. Instead of propping her on your lap or in her bouncy seat and using a tiny spoon to put purées in her mouth, scraping them off her chin and back into her mouth as she ejects them, you can sit her in a high chair, put small pieces of soft-cooked vegetable (carrot, potato, cauliflower) and/or pieces of ripe fruit (banana, melon, pear, avocado), in front of her and let her pick bits up and play and put them in her mouth. Once she's discovered that as well as being fun to squish in her hands, these taste good when she gums them, you can add strips of toast, slivers of chicken, small chunks of flaked fish, even pasta. Yes, it will be very, very messy. You'll need a splat mat on the floor, and unless it's warm enough to take the baby's clothes off, a long-sleeved apron to cover them.

...of course that won't stop them from wanting whatever the other one is having.

Baby- or parent-led eating?

Some people start mixed feeding by offering only finger foods, letting babies do it all themselves. That's usually called "baby led" mixed feeding and contrasts with spoon-feeding purées where you are more active and the baby is more passive. Your baby is more likely to be enthusiastic about food if she has finger foods from the beginning and nobody tries to persuade her to eat anything, or more of anything, than she actively goes for, but you will probably introduce spoons as well. Some foods that are good for her and that most babies like—yogurt, baby cereals, soup, spaghetti sauce—are very slow to eat by the "dip a fist in and suck it" method.

If you're going to spoon-feed your baby and she's over six months old, make sure you have two spoons so that she can take part. At the beginning it's one spoon for you to use, the other for her to wave and bite. When you first start, don't put whole spoonfuls in her mouth (she'll probably gag and may be put off). Put the spoon

From research

Chewing without teeth. Your baby doesn't need to have teeth before she can chew. In fact the eight teeth that are all she'll probably cut during the whole of this first year aren't chewing teeth but incisors, or front, biting-off teeth (see p. 208).

to her lips and let her suck it off. If she likes the taste and can manage swallowing the food, she'll probably lean forward and open her mouth for you to put the spoon in. Soon she'll grab the spoon, but even when she can get the spoon to her mouth she won't be able to fill it and get it there the right way up. Now's the time for a swap system. You load your spoon, take it almost to her mouth and put it in her hand so she can put it to her own mouth while you take and load her empty one.

The swap system keeps your baby busy and interested as well as fed.

Helping your baby to eat —now and in future

Make sure your baby enjoys her meals and snacks. Enjoyment is really important. Early tastes of solid foods are intended more for education than for nutrition, and the most important lesson of all is "food is fun…and delicious!"

◆ Go slowly. Don't ever (now or next year) try to force food into her mouth when she is rejecting it or keep pursuing her with the spoon when she's trying to avoid it by turning her head away. You may put her off the whole business for days.

From research

Distraction doesn't help babies eat.
Exciting games with flying spoonfuls of food have the opposite of the intended effect, because when a baby is excited, her highly aroused state shuts down her appetite.

◆ Don't rely on her appetite to tell you how much she needs. Ever since she was born you have been able to rely on your baby's hunger to tell you when and how much milk she needed, but in the early stages of eating other foods you can't. Being hungry doesn't make her want food, it makes her want milk. It doesn't make her want to eat off a spoon but to suck—the only way of assuaging hunger she has ever known. She will discover the comfort of food from spoons, but it will take time.

◆ Don't assume that crying means she doesn't like it. Until your baby has learned about solid food curing hunger, it may mean the opposite. She may be crying because she does like it and is hungry and unlike the smooth flow of milk when she's sucking, the pauses between spoonfuls interrupt her eating.

◆ Be alert to signals that mean "enough." Dribbling the food out, gagging, or crying may all be signals to stop, but they may also be the result of bad feeding technique or a baby who is not very good at eating yet. Turning her head

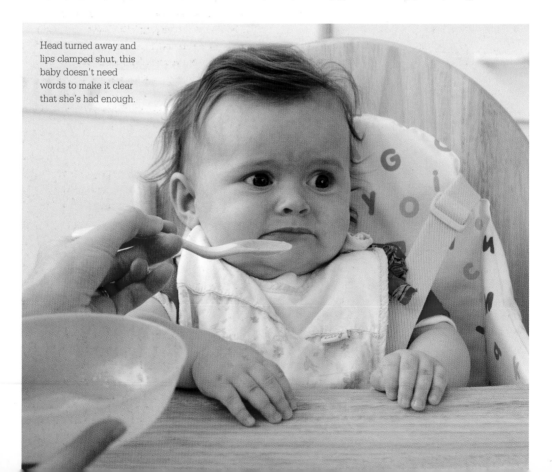

Head turned away and lips clamped shut, this baby doesn't need words to make it clear that she's had enough.

away from the proffered spoon or closing her lips against it definitely means she does not want it.

◆ Let her see the foods the rest of the family eats and their enthusiasm. As she gets older, sharing the pleasures of family eating will be the very best way to introduce her to new foods.

◆ Positively encourage her to handle and play with food and to put it (however inefficiently) in her own mouth. The more she feels in control of her eating, the more tastes and textures she'll willingly try.

◆ Be tactful in your timing and ready to be flexible. Don't expect her to eat in this new way when she's desperate with hunger: She needs to suck milk first. Don't wait to offer solid food until she's had the whole of her milk feed, though, or she may be too full and sleepy to bother. At meals when she's especially hungry—such as breakfast—a sandwich system often works best: first some milk from breast or bottle, then some solid food, and then the rest of her breast- or bottle-feed.

Staying safe

Babies often choke on a piece of food but almost always cough and dislodge it.
Serious episodes in which a baby seems unable to shift the obstruction or actually stops breathing are very rare indeed. Be aware of the risks and take sensible precautions by all means, but don't let fear of choking spoil early mixed feeding or make you nervous about which finger foods you give your baby.

◆ Serious choking is most likely if a firm roundish object gets wedged in the baby's windpipe. (Small toys—especially marbles, beads, and buttons, are more dangerous than food.) Don't give your baby whole grapes, olives, cherry tomatoes, raisins, popcorn, whole corn kernels, cherries, candies, or, of course, nuts (which are also allergy risks).

◆ Lumps of food that need to be chewed before they can be swallowed are also risky for babies who can't be relied upon to chew. Finely grate raw vegetables (such as carrot or cucumber) and finely chop meats such as chicken.

◆ Always sit your baby up in a high chair or booster seat at a table to eat, and always make sure you or another adult sit with her. If she begins to choke on something, you need to fish it quickly out of her mouth with your fingertips.

◆ It's better not to give your baby anything to eat in the car if you're driving. If you're keeping a careful enough eye on her you won't be watching the road!

◆ Don't let babies or toddlers crawl or walk around with food. You won't be able to watch closely, and if a child falls, the food in her mouth is very likely to "go the wrong way."

Helping a choking baby

These techniques are much better learned from a first-aid course than from a book.
Seriously consider attending such a course, and make sure that any care providers you employ are trained in Baby First Aid. This is only an outline, and it's unlikely that you could follow and act on it in a real emergency: It takes practice.

If the baby is unable to cough, cry, or breathe:

◆ Lie her face down along your forearm, using your lap for support, with her head slightly lower than her body. Hold her chest in your hand and her jaw with your fingers.

◆ Use the heel of the other hand to give five quick, forceful blows between her shoulder blades.

◆ If you can see the object blocking the airway, try removing it with your fingertips. This applies only if you can see it.

◆ If the object hasn't been dislodged you will need to give chest thrusts. Turn her face up, supporting the head and place two fingers on the middle of the breastbone just below the nipples. Give up to five quick thrusts down, compressing the chest ⅓ to ½ the depth of the chest.

◆ Continue this series of five back blows and five chest thrusts until the object is dislodged. If the baby loses consciousness, shout for help and give infant CPR. Call 911 after one minute of CPR. Continue giving CPR until help arrives.

Using jars of baby food

Just as reality dictates that you'll use both baby-led and spoon-feeding to introduce non-milk foods, so some of those foods will probably be home-cooked while others are commercially prepared.

When you cook from scratch for the rest of the household, a baby over six months can (usually) have the same food. It isn't difficult to extract a portion for her before you add salt, and to chop it up for her to eat in her fingers or purée it with a hand blender for her to eat with a spoon. But suppose you are not cooking from scratch? Your baby is probably better off with a jar of baby food (and maybe some finger-food vegetables) than with a serving of a take-out or supermarket-prepared meal complete with salt and who-knows-what additives.

Apart from their cost, the main problem with commercially prepared baby foods is that as well as not lending themselves to self-feeding, they are usually much sweeter and smoother than "real food," and each variety always tastes the same. None of that matters with occasional use, but the baby who eats jars at every meal all week may be reluctant to tuck in to family food on weekends.

Choosing ready-made baby foods

Read the labels when choosing commercially prepared baby foods: The name on the jar won't always describe the food that's in it, and the nutritional quality—and therefore the value for money—may not be at all what you expect. A leading manufacturer's "apples and pears," for example, contains eight ingredients—including apple juice, yogurt, modified corn flour, rice flour, vegetable oil, and vitamin C—but no fruit. More a thickened fruit juice than a fruit dessert.

A lot of apparently simple baby foods contain amazingly long lists of additives. Another "baby dessert" from a different manufacturer had this list of contents: rice, oat, wheat, soy and corn flours, malt, sugar, skimmed milk powder, apples, maltodextrin, vegetable fat, apple, pear, apricot, and plum juices, caseinate,.calcium carbonate, malt and vanilla extracts, dextrose, citric acid, yeast, vitamin C, cinnamon, niacin, zinc sulphate and iron. Can you even guess what dish the recipe

Parents talking about...

the timing of meals

❝James is always awake by 5:00am, and if I can get to him fast enough he'll have a breast-feed and then sleep again so we can get ready for work in peace. He has breakfast at daycare at 9:00–10:00am and lunch rather late, so, with the help of a drink and a snack he lasts until dinner with us at around 7:00pm. ❞

❝I'm still on maternity leave, so there's no special rush in the morning. Clara has breakfast with the rest of the family at around 8:00am. I give her lunch at about 12:30pm—that's her best meal for eating solids—and then an early dinner served specially—at about 5:00pm. She usually wakes around 11:00pm for a breast-feed, but if she hasn't woken by the time we want to go to sleep, we wake her. ❞

is for? It's a good idea to know which additives are which and why they are in there:

◆ **Thickeners:** Whenever a liquid—such as water or juice—is the first ingredient listed, there will be "thickeners" included: cheap substances put in to make highly processed runny "food" spoonable. Commonly used thickeners are modified corn flour, rice starch, wheat starch, gelatin, carob gum, and xantham gum.

◆ **Improvers:** Manufacturers are not allowed to put as many additives in baby food as in adult food, but they add "improvers" such as emulsifiers, maltodextrin, hydrogenated vegetable fat, citric acid, caseinate, calcium carbonate, and demineralized whey. The inclusion of several of these certainly means that the food is very highly processed.

◆ **Flavorings:** In "desserts," watch out for sugar in different forms (and by different names) such as: sucrose, glucose, dextrose, lactose, fructose, and maltose. In main course combinations, look out also for meat extract, hydrolyzed vegetable protein, yeast, or vegetable extracts. Again, lots of added flavorings mean a processed product with rather little natural food.

New foods, new mealtimes

By seven months or thereabouts, most babies are ready to eat some solid food at all three main meals and to begin to adapt to family breakfast, lunch, and dinner times. Most babies still need "snacks" from the breast or bottle in between, and your baby certainly won't be able to go without feeding from dinner to breakfast. She'll need either a late night breast-feed or bottle, or an early morning one; hopefully not both any longer, and whichever you prefer. If your household wakes early and you like to go early to bed, you will probably prefer the early morning. If you hate being woken early in the morning and always go to bed late anyway, it will probably suit you better to feed her just before you settle down for the night.

The beginning of weaning

Once your baby shows, by gesture, that she often wants to start a meal with her solid food rather than breast or bottle, or that having sucked and then eaten, she does not want any more milk, you will know that she is beginning to shift her allegiance from milk to "real" food. Now you can offer bigger helpings of solid foods (perhaps two tablespoonfuls rather than two teaspoonfuls) and be prepared to abandon the "sandwich" system. Make changes very gradually. This is the beginning of weaning, but it's baby-led weaning. Your baby is doing it herself because she wants to; nothing is being forced on her. If you let your baby set the pace, you will probably find that what she wants meal by meal, and how rapidly her eating pattern changes week by week, are both variable. There may be days or even weeks when weaning seems to stall and she wants almost nothing but milk—and plenty of it. And there may be particular meals in each day which she eats much more readily if you give her some of her milk first—reverting to that sandwich system. If you can manage to go along with what she seems to want without worrying or hurrying, the milk/food combination she takes will be what she needs. And if niggling anxiety begins, remind yourself that as long as she is having four breast-feeds or bottles in a 24-hour period, milk will go on providing almost all the nourishment she needs.

Those solid foods are still extras.

Your baby will eventually establish an eating-sucking pattern for herself. Every baby is different, of course, but many wake up so hungry and thirsty and amazed at being awake that they need to suck before eating. If this first feed of the day is breakfast, that will mean that your baby has as much breast or formula milk as she wants and then has her real food afterward. However, this feed may not be breakfast but a milk-only feed being given now, in the early morning, rather than last thing in the evening.

In the middle of the day many babies are less interested in sucking and more in eating. If you start your baby's lunch with her solid food and then offer the breast or bottle afterward, you may find that she takes very little and eventually none at all; that's the time to drop that milk feed in favor of drinks of water from a cup. For many

Milk first, food first, or a sandwich system? Follow your baby's lead.

babies, dinner follows the excitement of play and bathtime, and starting with sucking helps them to quiet down and get ready for the solid part of the meal. After that, a long, hopefully increasingly sleepy suck will help her get ready to settle to sleep. She may or may not have a milk-only feeding later on.

Milk is still central to your baby's nutrition, and sucking is bliss, but when it comes to her solid foods try to think of her as eating rather than being fed: of yourself as helping her do it herself rather than doing it to her. That means tolerating lots of dabbling in food and finger painting on the high-chair tray, but it also means that she feels in control and enjoys herself at meals, and that's crucial to avoiding food fads and food refusal later on. What's more, being allowed to make as much mess as she needs to now means that she'll be feeding herself with relatively little mess by the end of the year. Practice makes perfect.

Drinking without sucking

Don't go overboard about drinks at this stage. Your baby is still getting all (or certainly almost all) the liquid she needs from her milk and from puréed and semi-solid foods. She doesn't need to get much extra fluid from a cup, she just needs to discover how to drink without sucking. Don't try to persuade her to drink more than she wants by giving her a long, soft-spouted cup that makes it more like sucking than drinking.

Since your baby is still getting almost all the liquid she needs from breast or bottle and those sloppy foods, there's no need to try to make her drink more than she wants. Above all, don't try to make her want more by filling that cup with juice.

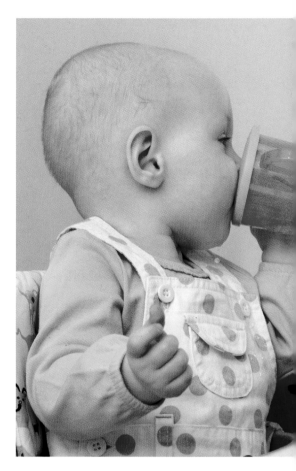

Moving weaning along

Once your baby regularly has her food before her milk and starts to eat more and suck less, she is beginning to change from a mostly-milk to a mixed diet, and if you want to, you can encourage her. For instance, you might add a second "course" to her lunch and give up offering

From research

Fruit juice. More than one small drink of fruit juice daily, even if it is high quality and well diluted, is a threat to your baby's future teeth and figure and also bad for her current nutrition. Babies and toddlers who drink juice all day, whenever they drink anything other than milk, fill their tummies with almost-empty calories, so they are less hungry for the nutrient-rich foods of their meals. The best drink for a baby, either to go with meals or when she is thirsty between meals, is plain ordinary tap water. You can bring up your baby to take drinking water for granted if that's what you give her from the beginning. That's probably the most important single thing you can do to prevent later dental cavities and obesity.

Drinking without sucking is an important new skill, but does her water taste nicer?…

weaning from the breast tends to be gradual and painless, with the baby suckling less and the quantity of milk you make dwindling to match. However, it's more likely that your baby will go on nursing for as long as you will let her.

If, like many mothers, you plan to stop breast-feeding when your baby is somewhere between six and twelve months old, and you are around most of the time, she can continue to take all her milk from you until she's ready to take all of it from a cup. Try to delay the beginning of weaning from the breast until her single-minded passion for nursing has slackened a bit at least at daytime feeds (probably by around nine months), and then make the change gradually. If, for example, she eats well at lunch and only sucks briefly afterward, you could drop that breast-feed; give her a drink of water from her cup instead, and move her straight from her high chair to her stroller for a distracting outing so she doesn't think about nursing. A few weeks later you might do the same at dinner time (maybe helped by the distraction of her father's arrival home), leaving her bedtime and early morning feeds until last. Hopefully you will never have to refuse the breast to your baby when she's asking for it. It's a pity if you do—there's no way she could understand your denial, and it might seem to her that you were refusing closeness as well as milk.

Ending all breast-feeds

If you need to wean your baby from the breast before she is seven or eight months old, especially if you are going back to full-time work, it may be difficult to decide if she can manage with solid food and cups of milk or whether she needs bottles. At around 28 weeks, many babies eat enough solid food and drink enough from a cup to get through the day without feeling hungry or thirsty, so if you're happy to go on with early morning and evening nursing for a few more weeks, you may be able to avoid bottles. Your baby is still very young for life with no sucking though, so if you want to stop nursing altogether at that sort of age, she should probably be offered bottles. It's an offer that may well be refused, though.

a breast- or bottle-feed at that meal in favor of water from a cup. Weaning is not only about the quantity of milk your baby takes, though; it's also about how she takes it. Weaning will not be completed until your baby has stopped nursing or using bottles. When that is going to be is largely up to you. If you left it up to your baby, she might go on for years.

Weaning from the breast

Babies are weaned from the breast at widely different ages—three months tô three years—and although mothers will tend to believe that their timing is the right timing, the truth is that the only right time is the one that feels right to you and your baby. The two of you may not agree. Your baby may get bored with breast-feeding and prefer a cup long before you had planned to stop nursing. Your feelings may be hurt, but baby-led

Weaning from bottles

As your baby gets older, she is likely to get more and more attached to her bottle, for comfort sucking as well as for milk. Since that source of comfort isn't part of you, and can easily be refilled with milk, it can be very difficult to refuse her another and another bottle. As she gets older and more able to think of and ask for a bottle at any time of day or night, she may drink so much formula that she doesn't get healthily hungry for meals. So don't assume that bottles will be comfort objects (rather like pacifiers) and useful non-spill cups right through toddlerhood. You will need to exert some control over when, how, and for how long your baby uses bottles. That doesn't mean that she should give them up the moment she eats from a spoon and drinks from a cup, though. If she's had bottles "on request" for more than half a year and then they're suddenly withdrawn, you're all in for an unhappy time. Besides, comfort sucking is as good for bottle-fed babies as it is for breast-fed ones. Be aware of some of the pitfalls, but go ahead gently.

Treating bottles as if they were breasts

You don't have to wean your baby very early in order to avoid long-continued dependence on a bottle. All you have to do is treat the bottle as if it were a breast, and wean her from bottle-feeding exactly as you would wean her from nursing:

◆ Don't let your baby take a bottle to bed with her, however desperate you are for a quick and peaceful bedtime. She might choke; her new and future teeth will certainly suffer, and once she's discovered this lovely way of getting to sleep she's likely to demand a refill not just every night, but every time she wakes.

◆ Don't let her carry a bottle around in her hand or dangling from her mouth: she has to suck her bottle on your lap as if it were a breast. If she does carry her bottle around, it will restrict her play and her "talking," and milk that's been at room temperature for a couple of hours is the perfect breeding ground for germs.

◆ Don't let your baby drink anything but milk from a bottle from around four months, well before you want to wean her from her bottle.

Treat the bottle as if it were a breast… (1) and (2) She'd like to suck her milk while she toddles around. But she couldn't do that if it came from a breast. (3) So make sure she cuddles up as if she was nursing.

By six months all drinks (water, or juice) that are extra to her meals should come from a cup. Like breasts, bottles only hold milk.

◆ Give up bottle-feeds in the order in which she gets more interested in solid foods. That probably means abandoning her lunchtime bottle at around seven months.

◆ Once she sleeps through the night, give up either the late night or the early morning bottle so that she is having three meals a day plus snacks. Milk can be an excellent snack, but milk from a cup rather than a bottle. Otherwise she can snack on hard finger foods with a drink of water from a cup.

Giving up bottles altogether

Once your baby is having only two bottles each day—probably the first after the solid part of her breakfast and the second after dinner—it's time for the parent-upmanship that can keep bottles in their proper, and pleasurable, place. If you treat your baby's bottles exactly as if they were breasts, she will wean herself from them at the time that's right for her.

Give those two bottles for as long as your baby wants them, but only if she drinks them on somebody's lap with that person holding the bottle for her. As her first birthday approaches, your baby's increasing drive to be independent will make her more and more determined to hold the bottle for herself and her increasing passion for mobility will make her long to crawl around the room with it. She couldn't put those two things together if it was a breast that was in question, so don't let her discover—even once—that she actually could take the bottle with her around the room.

There may be times when she is very obviously torn between her desire to suck and her desire to get moving, and, anxious not to provoke a battle of wills, you are tempted to let her do both at once. Don't. If tonight you let your baby combine the two activities she enjoys most, she'll know it's possible and is bound to demand to do the same again next time.

You can help her with that choice—whether to suck or crawl—by letting her change her mind and crawl back for another suck as often as she likes (after all, a breast-fed baby can do that too). Do be sure, though, that each time she comes back for more milk she gets right up onto your lap and lets you hold or at least help her to hold the bottle (as she would have to do if she was nursing).

Don't abandon the idea of the bottle as a pretend breast whatever the circumstances. It can be very difficult to resist offering a bottle of water or juice when you especially want your baby to have extra fluid (perhaps because she's feverish) and you think she will take more from the bottle than she will happily take from a cup. The trouble is of course, that if she gets the bottle this once, she's likely to fuss for one next time.

More sleeping

Although your baby will still be inclined to go to sleep while he is feeding and to be unwakeable once he is full, the relationship between feeding and sleeping has probably slackened a little by three months.

It isn't always hunger that wakes him now. Sometimes he wakes up just because he has had enough sleep for the moment. And instead of having one particular "wakeful period" in the day—as he probably did when he was (even) younger—your baby is likely now to have two or even three daily wakeful times. A good feed makes him inclined to sleep, but as he gets older his naps get progressively shorter and more and more dissociated from his feeds.

Getting the sleep he needs

For the next year at least you can be sure that your baby will get as much sleep as he needs, even though you almost certainly will not. Whatever his sleeping (or non-sleeping) patterns, they aren't difficult for your baby, only for you. Provided they are well and not in pain, babies in this age group sleep when they need to sleep and stay asleep until they are ready to wake up; only parents or care providers care how much that is. Your baby can't yet keep himself awake on purpose (although he can get overtired and therefore unable to settle), and of course he can't wake himself up on purpose, now or in the future, any more than you can.

From research

Safe naps. Recent research into sudden infant deaths shows that three-quarters of the (tiny number) of babies who died in the daytime had been left to sleep in a room on their own and that many of them had been placed on their side. It's important to use the SIDS safety guidelines (*see p. 190*) for daytime naps as well as for night-time sleep.

Helping your baby differentiate night from day

Babies are not born diurnal. Sleeping mostly by night is a biological adaptation that only starts in the first days of life and usually takes three or four months to complete. If your baby does not yet sleep any more soundly or for any longer periods at night than in the day, you may need to help him make a difference between night behavior and day behavior.

◆ Consider whether there are outside sounds that may be disturbing him in the night. Accustomed background noises won't wake him, but sudden unexpected ones may. Don't leave a phone close beside him.

◆ If he shares your bedroom, make sure that *you* are not disturbing *him*. If you respond instantly to his every small sound, you may be turning every period of light sleep into an awakening.

◆ If you've moved a bigger more energetic baby to a bigger crib, he may feel dwarfed and exposed by the extra space he's suddenly surrounded by and he may start kicking the covers off, however carefully you've tucked the edges under the mattress. Try putting him to bed in a light cotton sleep sack, the kind that is shaped like a nightgown with the bottom closed. A sleep sack will give your baby a safe, cozy feeling and keep him from getting chilly, even if his room gets cold in the small hours. It won't make him too hot as long as you count the bag itself as a layer and dress him accordingly. Starting to use a sleep sack now may also mean that your baby does not even try to climb out of his crib later on.

◆ As he gets older your baby needs to spend more and more time awake, so if he sleeps a lot

A big crib with high bars can be scary.
Putting your baby in his usual little bed in the big
crib can be a good way to introduce the change.

"Co-sleepers" or "bedside beds" can be a safe and companionable compromise between family beds and separate cribs.

From research

SIDS: Sudden Infant Death Syndrome.
By definition the causes of sudden infant deaths are unknown. But while they cannot therefore be prevented, you can take steps to reduce the already tiny risk.

◆ Have the baby in your bedroom for at least six months and supervise him during daytime naps.

◆ Don't share a bed with your baby if you have been drinking, take drugs, or if you are a smoker.

◆ Put your baby in his crib on his back to sleep. Lying on his back does not make him more liable to choke. Lying on his side is less safe. Once he can roll himself over from back to front, he will be past the peak risk age. He should still be put down on his back but can safely be left to choose his own sleeping position during the night.

◆ Either use a sleep sack instead of blankets or put him in the crib with his feet at the crib end, covered by a blanket no higher than his chest, with the edges tucked under the mattress.

◆ Don't let your baby get too hot—don't overheat rooms (if it's too warm for you it is too warm for him)—or use a comforter.

◆ Don't put him to bed in outdoor clothes (perhaps because he dropped off in the car and you don't want to wake him).

◆ Don't put your baby to sleep anywhere where his head might get trapped and obstruct his breathing—such as on a sofa or armchair or in a crib whose mattress does not fit closely, or with a pillow.

◆ Seek medical advice quickly if your baby seems in any way unwell. If he has a temperature, remove some or all his coverings.

of the day, he is bound to choose the evening or night for wakefulness. It's unlikely that your baby will sleep through the night (even with a feed in the middle) until he sleeps for twice as long at night as he does during the day—say 14 hours in a 24-hour period, 10 at night and 4 by day. If you are taking care of him yourselves, you may need to adjust the pattern of his daytime naps and be sure that you offer him as much stimulating play as he enjoys. If you share his daytime care with somebody else, such as a nanny or a group daycare, you may want to make sure that your baby is being encouraged to be alert and playing even when he doesn't demand attention. Babies in daycare who are passively undemanding sometimes get less stimulation than they could use, because staff do not realize they are bored.

◆ Your baby may not share your view of when night ends and day begins. Many babies wake appallingly early, and unless they still have an early morning feed, nothing will put them back to sleep. Their night is over. Right now the best you can hope for is a glorious cuddle in your bed that gives you time to wake up slowly (and to remember what being a parent is really about). By the time your baby is seven or eight months old, if somebody visits, puts on a light, and gives him some books and toys, he may be happy to stay in his crib for as much as 20 minutes, playing and talking to himself.

Starting to sleep in a big crib

Bassinets and newborn cribs stop being safe places for your baby to sleep as soon as he approaches their weight limit or begins to make energetic efforts to roll over. Some babies take a few days to get used to being surrounded by the space and the bars of a standard-size drop-side crib. It may help if you start by putting him to sleep in his usual little bed but with that little bed inside the big crib.

A crib is a place of safety that it's difficult to manage without, even if your baby is not going to sleep in it routinely every night because you all share a family bed. Once your baby can roll over, and eventually crawl, he can only be safe in his parents' bed if one of you is in it with him. If you don't have a crib—or a co-sleeper with a

Twin tip

If twins have been sharing a bed that wasn't designed for two their increased kicking around may mean that they begin to disturb each other; this is about the time when you may want to separate them into their own cribs or a twin-designed bedside-bed. All babies should be in the same room as their parents until they are at least six months old, but after that you may want to move them out into a room—or even two rooms if you have them—of their own.

From research

Twins and SIDS. There's no extra risk of SIDS when twins share a crib. Both need to be placed feet to crib end, which means they will need to be side by side rather than head to toe.

fourth side you can put up—how will you ever be able to put him to bed early for a grown-up evening, or be able to leave while you take a morning shower before getting him up?

Safe co-sleeping

The ideal way to organize family sleeping is to use bedside beds, sometimes called co-sleepers. They offer a compromise between having your baby in your bed and having him completely separated from you. Bedside beds tend to be more expensive than ordinary drop-sided cribs (presumably because they are still scarce; there's no obvious other reason) and may not be worthwhile if you plan to move your baby into his own room soon after he is six months old. If you like having him close by, though, they are an excellent investment as long as you can make enough space alongside your bed. Be sure to buy a version that has a fourth, adjustable side that keeps your baby safe when you're not in bed but drops down and under when you want the beds linked.

Planning for future naps and nights

Bedtimes that are reliably peaceful both for you and your baby are so important that you will probably be extremely reluctant to do anything to upset them. Even your baby's awakenings in the night seem more tolerable if you can count on him to settle to sleep, or back to sleep, quickly and easily.

Your baby still tends to go to sleep when he's full of food so he'll often nurse, or suck his bottle, until he's so asleep that the nipple falls from his mouth. Once asleep he may not surface again even if you hold him up to burp, so you're likely to put him into his crib already soundly off. It's a luxurious transition from being awake to being

As long as he is comfortably full of food and already sleepy, your baby may be content to go into his crib…

asleep for your baby, and from baby-focus to grown-up matters for you.

That's no longer a win-win way to put your baby to bed though; in fact it is important to re-think it before he is much older. Your baby needs to be able to put himself to sleep—or back to sleep—rather than relying on someone else to do it for him, and if you regularly put him into his crib fast asleep, he has no opportunity to practice. In fact, if you nurse or pat or rock your baby until he is asleep and then put him in his crib, he is not *going* to sleep, you are *sending* him to sleep. And however nice that may be for both of you right now, it is not worth the sleeping difficulties it is certain to lead to in the future.

If you always let your baby suck until he is completely unaware, and you then put him down without him realizing it, when he wakes during the night—as everyone does—he'll find himself alone in his crib instead of in your arms. He doesn't know how he got there. He doesn't know what happened or where you are or what to do next. He has no experience of snuggling himself down, closing his eyes, and going to sleep, so of course he cries. He cries for you to come and pick him up and put him back to sleep the way you put him to sleep in the first place. If you come quickly and pick him up, he may be able to drop off while you hold him in your arms, but even that may not be enough. He may need you to start from further back in his going-to-sleep routine, giving him another breast-feed or another bottle so that he can drop off again while he is sucking.

Getting your baby to sleep, or back to sleep, by nursing him or giving him a bottle is misleadingly easy. A few minutes sucking and you can probably put him down without any sense of struggle. But the next time he wakes, the whole pattern repeats. And if you let it go on and on the pattern may still be repeating every time he wakes next year. Many toddlers have two or three breast- or bottle-feeds every night because although they don't wake especially often, there is no other way to resettle them.

You need to make sure that your baby knows how to go to sleep on his own even if you don't always leave him to do it. The trick is to let him get sleepy in your arms, so that he doesn't mind

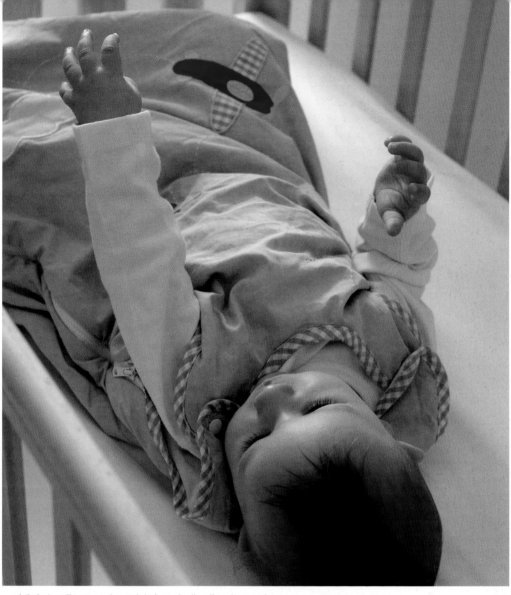

...while he's still just-awake and drift gradually off to sleep on his own.

being put down—but to make sure that he is just awake enough to realize that he is in his crib and on his own, and perhaps even to feel positively comfortable.

If, like many parents, you dread disrupting a going-to-sleep routine that has served you well, you could start by making a point of putting him down awake for daytime naps when it does not matter so much if you have to go back to him. But while that may be a good way of getting him used to going to sleep on his own, once he can do it for an afternoon nap you need to get him used to doing it at night as well. Otherwise

you'll find yourself going on giving him the breast or a bottle whenever he wakes in the night, even when he no longer needs feeding between supper and breakfast. You might even be tempted to give him a bottle in his crib, and once he's learned that that's a possibility he's likely to fuss every time until he gets one.

By the time your baby is able to roll over to make himself comfortable and is weaned from all but one or two feeds a day, you want him to be able to drop off again when he surfaces in the night, unless some discomfort or dream means that he really requires your help.

Coping with sleeping problems

However carefully you have followed those suggestions for helping your baby settle and re-settle himself to sleep without needing you to feed or rock him, not all babies will always (or ever) oblige.

Under the immediate stress of conflict between a crying baby and imminent visitors (or a favorite TV show) it's easy to lose sight of what matters in the long term and do whatever will work right now. However, what works today is likely to mean months of trouble in the future, so try to think through the whole matter during a calm daytime moment, together with anyone else who ever cares for your baby.

You want your baby to settle calmly into bed and drift contentedly off to sleep on his own, every (or almost every) night. And if that's what you want, leaving him to cry cannot be the right answer (even if you can tear yourself away), because he is certainly not calm or contented but abandoned and panicky. He'll probably be even quicker to fuss when you try to leave him tomorrow. But if leaving him crying isn't the answer, neither is getting him up again. You need to help your baby feel safe on his own and able to settle himself into sleep, not "rescue" him as if you agreed that he shouldn't be alone.

There are long-term answers that really do work. Unfortunately they won't solve your situation right now, and they do involve quite a lot of consistent effort. You want your baby to know that you are always there for him, that you will always respond to him when he cries; but you want him to learn that when it is night, it is time for sleep, and you will not pick him up and feed or play with him. You give him the emotional reassurance he needs but you do it your way (you are the grown-up after all), not by giving in to what he immediately wants.

If you settle your baby down, sleepy but conscious, and he doesn't drift off but starts to cry, go straight back to him. If he is not yet six months old he will not and cannot keep himself awake on purpose, so it's probably enough to pat and soothe him until sleep overtakes him. If that seems like a lot of trouble compared with just nursing him until he is asleep, think of the future.

If your baby is coming up to six months and, far from settling on his own more easily, is even more reluctant, you might need to be more proactive now, because in three or four more months he may be so passionately attached to you—yes, "clingy" is one word for it—that he finds it really hard to let you leave him.

Techniques to try:

"Hanging in there": Follow your baby's usual routine, ending with putting him into his crib with a kiss and a cuddle. Stay next to him. If he cries, stroke his hand but don't pick him up. Smile and look loving but don't chat. Stay with him until he falls asleep.

◆ Repeat the same thing for two or three nights until he seems more relaxed about it, then move yourself a little bit away so he can still see you but you can't actually touch him.

◆ After that, you might try sitting in a chair on the other side of the room reading a book.

◆ Finally, try being around and in and out, maybe sorting clothes and generally tidying.

◆ Don't hurry these stages. If your baby becomes anxious that you're going to vanish, it may set the whole process back.

"Popping in and out": It sounds something like "sleep training," but this technique is importantly different. You are not trying to teach your baby that it's no use crying because you won't come, no matter how long he goes on. You're trying to teach

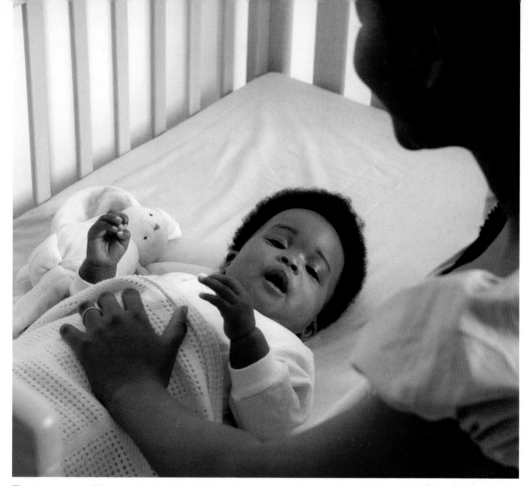

The time you spend "hanging in there" tonight is an investment in peace for all the nights to come.

him that you will always come when he cries, at night as you do in the day, but that when it is the night you are not going to pick him up or play.

◆ Settle your baby down, kiss him good-night, and leave the room. If he cries, go back in—but only for long enough to speak to him reassuringly. Don't pick him up or touch him. Leave again. If he cries again, or is still crying, go back again, and again, and again.

◆ Even with you popping in and out your baby may cry and keep on crying, but that's because you are refusing to do what he wants—get him up—not because you've gone away and left him. It may help to remind yourself that it's not crying that is so stressful for babies but crying that goes unanswered.

◆ Popping in and out may take up most of your evenings for as much as a week, but longer is unusual, and two or three days is often all it takes. If you really can't bear your baby to be so upset, you could always convert "popping in and

out" into "hanging in there," which may take a lot longer but shouldn't involve any crying.

However well your baby sleeps when he is three or four months old, or however successfully you help him find out that he can go happily to sleep on his own, don't assume that you've solved all sleep problems forever. Later in the year your baby's attachment to you may become so strong that he can scarcely let you out of his sight to go to the bathroom for two minutes let alone to go downstairs for the evening. And even when he goes to sleep and doesn't need to be fed again until the morning, the fact that he is able to surface and resettle himself doesn't mean that he will always want to. Sometimes he will want you to know he's awake. Finally, these new sleeping routines aren't very deeply embedded in him: Anything that disturbs him—from a vacation trip to a week of teething-misery or a heavy cold—is likely to upset them so that you have to start all over again.

More about crying

By the time your baby is three months old, crying will be starting to play a smaller and smaller part in her (and therefore your) life.

Instead of sometimes seeming like a behavior in its own right—almost one of her activities and something she might go on and on doing no matter what you try—her crying will become a reaction to things that will stop when you change them. Instead of crying a lot today because she's having a crying day, your baby will only cry more today than most days if more than usually upsetting events or feelings overwhelm her.

As your baby grows up, and especially as she passes her half birthday, she's much less likely to cry about ordinary happenings—even things that used to frighten her, such as sudden loud noises. Sometimes now, sights and sounds and movements that are unexpected will actually make her laugh. When she is worried by something your baby will often seek reassurance by looking uneasily at the adult who is with her, and perhaps making whimpery sounds. She'll only embark on full-fledged crying if nobody tells her it's OK or, worst of all, if she can see that the adult she is looking to for reassurance is also alarmed. She is beginning to be very sensitive to adults' facial expressions. (See p. 199)

But although your baby probably cries less overall, and certainly less readily and less often than she used to, there are new causes of crying coming up in the next six months. They are all linked to particular aspects of her development, and if you can recognize and learn to help her with them from now on, your sensitive handling will certainly make life easier for all of you right through toddlerhood.

Being away from you and alone

The trigger for a majority of babies' crying episodes from around four months is being left by the adults they are attached to. And if it is often being left by a parent or caregiver that starts off the crying, it is being left to cry unanswered that is most likely to keep it going. Being left crying, ignored by an adult—perhaps because parents are taking a "cry it out" approach to sleeping difficulties—probably leads to longer nonstop crying sessions than anything else.

Sensitivity to separation isn't something your baby is soon going to grow out of: It will probably continue to increase well past her first birthday and keep going in her second year. It is not only at night that babies object to adults leaving, either. Many babies object just as strongly to being left when they are up and playing in the daytime as when they are in their cribs at night. Some babies are sometimes so sensitive to being left that even the single minute it takes a parent to get something from the next room causes crying. Continual fusses about what feels to an adult like nothing are wearing. It's tempting to slip out of the room meaning to be back before your baby notices. Don't risk it. Babies seem to have antennae that track parents' every move. Chances are, your baby will notice that you've gone out of the room—and if she does, she won't only howl this time, she'll keep an even closer eye on you the next.

If having you leave is likely to upset your baby, being left alone is usually far worse than being left with another familiar adult. So while the big separations, such as having a parent leave to go to work or being left by a parent at daycare, are likely to cause some crying, a good and loving caregiver can usually ensure that it is very brief.

Babies' fears

Right now your baby may still be a little fearful of a great many things, including loud noises, strange sights, and sudden unexpected movements. However, over the next two or three months she'll cope much more robustly with those aspects of daily life and begin to enjoy new adventures such as being taken into a noisy environment like a train station, riding on an airplane, or being introduced to a horse. Along with her growing confidence in coping with life in general, though, may go increasing sensitivity to one or two specifics. Completely unworried by most loud noises, she may suddenly be terrified whenever the dishwasher starts. Loving rough and tumble play, she may intensely dislike having a sweater pulled on over her head or being maneuvered into her car seat. Thrilled by baths or any kind of "water play," she may panic when the water is emptied out and she sees it running down the drain.

This kind of fear adds difficulty to daily life and sometimes seems irritatingly irrational: Why should the dishwasher bother the baby when none of the other appliances do? But you don't have to understand (or share) fears in order to respect them. What matters is not whether they are sensible, but that they are real. Don't ever be tempted to "prove" to your baby that "there's nothing to be afraid of." You cannot ever make a baby or child—or most adults for that matter—fearless by frightening her, and if you carry her right up to that dishwasher, that's what you'll do.

The more often your baby has to face something she's afraid of, the more intense her fear will become. The more you can help her to avoid or keep a distance from things that frighten her, the faster those fears will die down—though at this stage in her life she may acquire another fear to replace each one she loses. Perhaps the dishwasher could be run only at night for a while. The plug doesn't have to be pulled from the bath's drain while she is in the room, and you could take to getting into the back of the car with her in your arms and putting her into the seat from there. Be careful not to give your baby the impression that you share her fears, though. The less she is aware of the trouble you are taking, the better. When she has to come face to face with something scary you've been helping her to avoid, it must be clear to her that you haven't been avoiding it because it is dangerous or because you are frightened of it, but because she is.

Typical fears and other causes of crying

◆ **Fear of the unexpected:** During the second half of the first year, as your baby comes to know one familiar person from another and all of them from strangers, she begins to build up expectations about different individuals and how they behave, and to make the routines, rhythms, and rituals of daily life into patterns in her mind. These expectations are new and powerful, and she is very aware of them. When something happens that seems to contradict what she thought she knew and understood, her confidence drains away, and anxiety and fear seep in. Imagine a baby who has learned that when she's having dinner and she hears a particular set of sounds (key in door; door closing; footsteps), her father is coming in and will pick her up and hug her. Now imagine that on this occasion it is not her father who comes in but someone she has never seen before. The chances are that the moment she saw him the baby would start to cry, but not because he is a stranger (she often smiles happily at visitors who are new to her) but because he arrived at the time and in the space where she was picturing her father. She may react similarly to any contradiction of established expectations. If she usually has her bottle warm, for instance, she will probably cry with outrage if you offer it fridge-cold. She doesn't dislike cold milk; in fact that may be the way she likes it when she drinks it from a cup. But cold milk to suck from her bottle is completely unexpected and therefore out of order.

Experiences which are totally new to your baby can't contradict any specific expectations, of course, but may still be more than she can cope with. Her very first ride on a bus, her very first taste of ice cream, or her very first meeting with a cat in a friend's house may all make her cry. They'll be fun parts of her life later on, but not until she is used to them.

Your baby has experienced very little in her short life thus far, so a lot of objects and happenings are new to her. Helping her to come to terms with them and supporting her from alarm to interest, is important, because

Put your baby in a baby bouncer and watch surprise and alarm quickly give way to delight as he discovers the joys of independent jumping and twirling.

experiences that are novel now that will broaden her horizons and enrich her life as she gets older. Warning and reassuring her will be easier when she is old enough to understand your actual words, but even at six months you can do it with your intonation, facial expression, and body language. If she has that first bus ride sitting on your lap, with your face directing her attention out of the window, your interested voice telling her what you can see, and your familiar trusted arms holding her steady, she may enjoy it from the first minute to the last.

◆ **Helplessness:** As far as we can tell, babies feel what they feel as strongly, and want what they want as passionately, as we do, but there is much less that they can do about it, being small, physically incompetent, and unable to use language. Often when your baby cries, it will be because she is in a situation where she very much wants to take action but cannot do so herself. Her crying tells you that she needs you to take action on her behalf.

When you go out of the room, she wants to go with you, but she can't crawl yet so she can't follow you, and she can't talk yet so she can't ask you to take her along, so what can she do except cry? In the park, a colleague of yours whom the baby does not know stops to chat. She asks if she can hold her and the baby feels your arms starting to pass her over. She cannot prevent you. She cannot say, "no!" All she can do is howl.

The more sensitive you and anyone else who cares for your baby are to subtle signs of frustration or distress, like changes in facial expressions, the less often she will feel so helpless that all she can do is cry. If you notice her face dropping as you start to leave the room, for example, and you pause, she *can* ask you to take her with you, holding up her arms to be picked up. Preventing your baby from feeling painfully helpless won't always be all up to you, though. As she gets more and more competent—both physically and socially—so she'll be more able to act for herself. Learning to crawl, for example, is not only an enormous pleasure but also a big boost to her independence. Suddenly, if she wants to follow you she can; if she wants that toy she may be able to get it. She is liberated from her most extreme dependence, and so are you.

◆ **Getting frustrated:** By the time your baby approaches her first birthday, more of her crying may be caused, or partly caused, by frustration than anything else. Even when it is clear that her crying means she is sad—perhaps about being left alone in her crib at bedtime—there is an element of frustration in it. You have left her in her crib and she cannot get out. The more your baby becomes able to go where she wants and find herself interesting things to do along the way, the more often you will have to prevent her, and the more infuriatingly frustrating she will find it.

Imagine that you get her up from a nap and put her to sit on the floor in the living room. Something catches her eye and she crawls off to investigate. What she has spotted is a nearly but not quite empty mug left on the floor beside the sofa. You get there just before her, put the mug out of harm's way and before she can build up a real protest you carry the baby into the kitchen, where she struggles to get down again. You put her down beside the collection of toys she was playing with earlier, but she can see something much more interesting: the cat eating from his bowl. As soon as you release her, she crawls after

The stress of being a baby: (1) One minute he's happily holding and mouthing a toy, (2) the next minute half of it has gone and he's got nothing to suck. (3) Two seconds later the whole thing has vanished, and he doesn't have any idea where it is.

him. The cat can take care of himself, so that's not a worry, but his escape makes the baby unhappy. Grumbling, she turns her attention to the food and gets a hand in it before you can get there. This time she is acutely frustrated at being stopped and when you pick her up and wash her hands in the sink, she is furious. You put her down again and she heads straight back to the cat's food bowl. You pick it up and put it on the counter and she howls.

Small dramas like that recur relentlessly with a baby this age. Crawlers are explorers, and however carefully their homes are arranged and vetted they have to be constantly checked, both for their own safety and the safety of other people's possessions. Such times are wearing on adult (and baby) patience though. Once your baby has found something she really wants to do—like reach into that cat food—she gets focused on it, and of course she cannot begin to understand why you won't let her do as she pleases. Your best help is her distractability. There's no need to have long drawn out battles about the undesirable games your baby gets fixated on. Be brave: Pick her up and take her right out of the room. Yes she probably will screech with fury, but in a few seconds the whole issue will be forgotten—for the moment.

A certain amount of angry, frustrated crying is inevitable, because you have to stop your baby from doing things that are dangerous or destructive. Furthermore she will—and must—frustrate herself by attempting tasks that are maddeningly difficult for her. But too much frustration, whether by restricting adults or her own immaturity, will not help her development. One of the demands of good parenting is finding and continually readjusting the balance between too much frustration and too little.

If your baby is struggling to push over the safety gate at the bottom of the stairs, you know that she cannot succeed, so her efforts can only end in frustrated tears. Distract her. But if her next self-imposed task is getting your shoe off your foot as you sit on the sofa, don't just take it off for her. She can get a long way toward success on her own, and subtle assistance such as wiggling your toes may allow her a triumph.

Frustration tolerance varies in babies just as it does in older children and adults, but it's by no means fixed at this age, so even if yours is a baby who succumbs to the slightest setback, don't assume that she always will. She may become a calm, even a placid child.

But while your baby's reactions to fear and frustration now tell you little about how she will be as a child or an adult, they do reflect and affect her current experiences of daily life. Babies who cry easily and often and are difficult to comfort and distract must be assumed to be less contented than babies who are slower to plunge into misery and easier to help out. Furthermore, a baby who never seems happy for more than a minute at a time or content for more than five, is difficult for parents or caregivers to care for cheerfully, so there's a risk that you'll all make sad circles between you. So it's worth trying to figure out what it is that most often upsets your baby in case there is something about her environment or her care that you can change for the better. Most of her crying is about being separated from you, being afraid, needing you to take action for her that she's helpless to take for herself, or being angry and frustrated. Once you have taught yourself to decipher her signals so that you know which is which, there may be a great deal that you can do to ease things for her.

◆ **Babies who are wakeful can get bored:** Sometimes babies cry a lot because they don't sleep as much as their parents expect, so they are often put down for naps they don't need, or left bored in their beds because they "ought" to be sleeping. There really is no exact "ought" for babies' sleeping hours or routines. An average of about 16 hours sleep in a 24-hour period spans a normal range from around 12 hours to 19. If you expect your baby to sleep 16 hours when all she needs is 12, or you very much want her to nap for

From research

Boredom is stressful. Researchers suggest that brains react to understimulation as a stress and will take action to change it.

Extra time awake means extra time for play; make sure there's lots for him to do.

two hours twice a day so that you can "get things done," the mismatch is likely to mean a lot of crying. That mismatch may mean physical frustration as well as boredom. Babies who are awake need to be active, and very wakeful babies are often especially eager to use their bodies. If your baby must spend time alone in her crib or stroller when she's awake, at least make sure that wrappings and coverings aren't restricting her physical freedom. If the house is not warm enough to leave her uncovered, a sleep sack will keep her warm but still able to move around.

Being free to move around will only help your baby to be happy for a few minutes at a time, though. Interesting things to look at will also help

if you hang them close enough that she can see them clearly, swipe at them, and eventually touch them on purpose. Interesting means ever-changing. Don't stick to the same old mobile day after day: Hang up different things and change them frequently.

Even with physical freedom and things to look at, your baby will cry if she's left long alone and awake. She'll cry because she is lonely and bored without people. If she is always with somebody companionable when she is awake, she'll probably cry a great deal less.

Caring for a wakeful baby, especially a breast-fed one, is easy if you make the most of her portability. In these few months until she acquires mobility and requires food and drink other than breast milk, she is easier to take wherever you would like to go, to work or to play, than she will ever be again. As long as she isn't hungry, all adults and everything they do are fascinating to your baby. When somebody is doing simple jobs around the house or garden, she will enjoy being part of them from the vantage point of a sling, and if there's nobody to carry her, she can watch and feel part of grown-up activities if she's semi-upright in her stroller, or carried in her car seat to wherever the adult activity she finds most interesting is going on. That may be somebody practicing the piano, picking up fallen apples, or hanging laundry to dry. Boring for the adult maybe, but not to her.

Your baby shouldn't be propped up for too long at a time, though. A mat on the floor makes an interesting change, in fact as long as you can keep her safe from over-enthusiastic dogs or toddlers on tiny trikes, it's the ideal playground. But perhaps the best of all entertainments for older babies, whether wakeful or not—and indeed for all babies—are baby bouncers or stationary activity centers. These safe alternatives to baby walkers support babies in an upright position with only their toes touching the product base. The baby is surrounded by toys, and can bounce and spin freely. They give babies an upright and 360° view of the world and wonderful freedom to move and spin. If your baby is miserable, equipment of this kind will make her happier, if she is happy, it will delight her.

Comfort habits

Your baby depends on you and other adults to comfort him when he is frightened or frustrated, angry or sad, but as he gets older he also begins to be able to comfort himself.

People often think of "comfort habits" such as thumb sucking, as *bad* habits, but there is a lot that is good about them. While your baby relies entirely on you for comfort, the amount he gets is up to you. He can't make you go on rocking him. But once he has developed self-soothing, self-comforting rituals, they are under his own control. He can have as much as he wants whenever he wants it, and there's very little that adults can do about it.

Comfort habits are good in that they help babies begin to be able to rely on themselves and leave them less at the mercy of the adult world. But they're not good if a baby comes to rely on them instead of the kinds of comfort that should come from adults. If he keeps rocking alone in a corner, you need to ask yourself whether he is shutting out an available world of people and play or if he is comforting himself as best he can because nobody else is offering.

People may call it a "bad habit," but a baby who sucks her thumb has comfort under her own control.

Typical first-year comfort habits

Sucking is the basic comfort habit of human babies. Your baby may have started sucking his thumb in the womb and have been sucking his fingers or a pacifier for weeks, but around now, sucking combined with other comfort habits may take on a new significance as a protection against emotional distress. If he is not sucking when you leave him, he cries. But if you leave him when he is sucking he will suck harder, using the comfort of sucking to cover the distress of your departure.

◆ **Transitional comfort objects:** Those pieces of old blanket, fuzzy blue rabbit, or other "cuddlies" are many babies' most precious possessions. Your baby may not take to a cuddly—not all children do—but if he is going to adopt something to use in this way he will probably do so in his second half-year. Cuddlies symbolize love and security. It is almost as if those grubby pieces of fabric stand in for loving people in children's minds. Your baby cannot make you stay by his crib, but he can hold on to his cuddly when you leave him, and it will be there for him when he wakes in the night and you are not. Different babies use cuddlies in different ways, but however they are used they are of real emotional importance. Your baby may get attached to a conventional soft toy and simply hold it as he falls asleep. But he may adopt something that had no nursery connections and use it in elaborate ways, some of which would be considered risky for a newborn, such as draping a scarf across his face so that he can suck his thumb through it, or holding your old teddy bear in such a way that its ear is under his nose. Its particular smell is probably part of its magic for him, so don't wash it unless you really have to.

A baby's "cuddly" is her most important possession.
Losing it would be a disaster for the entire household.

If your baby takes to a cuddly it will be his most important possession and a real responsibility for you and anyone else who takes care of him. It must not be left in the park, thrown out with the trash or lost on a trip to the supermarket: if it is, your baby will be heartbroken until or unless it is recovered. You can never duplicate a cuddly exactly because daily use contributes to its uniqueness (that smell!). But if disaster strikes, something is better than nothing, so it's worth taking precautions. If the cuddly started out as a blanket or a soft toy, you might be able to buy a duplicate and hide it away. If it was a special shirt or scarf of yours, you might be able to halve it without your baby noticing and put the second half away somewhere safe. It won't be the same, but producing it may comfort your distraught child enough that going to sleep begins to seem like a possibility.

◆ **Rituals:** Going-to-bed routines help most babies to settle peacefully, and "off to work" rituals help many to release parents in favor of caregivers. When you help your baby build a ritual, though, beware: he may take what you offer and then build on it until a routine that took five minutes each morning when he was nine months old takes 15 by the time he is a year. You also need to make sure that anyone who ever cares for your baby at one of these ritualized times knows every detail.

◆ **Soothing rhythms:** You "rocked" your baby when he was in your womb, and ever since he was born you have probably used rhythmic movements to soothe and comfort him: walking with him, rocking him, dancing with him, and patting him. As they get older, most babies still find physical rhythm soothing, and many find ways, some more desirable than others, to provide it for themselves. Your baby may rhythmically stroke his face or pull on his cuddly, and that's obviously harmless. Pulling and twisting his hair isn't exactly harmful, either, but it's not desirable because it can tie fine baby hair in knots or even pull it out. Many babies get onto hands and knees in their cribs and then rock. He may manage to move the crib across the floor and that's no more than a nuisance, but if he also bangs his head on the end of the crib, you need to know why.

◆ **Head banging:** Babies who bang their heads rhythmically on the end of their cribs as they

rock usually do it for the sound and the jarring sensation, but a few do hurt themselves—and seem to need to. The easiest way to find out whether pain is part of your baby's pleasure is to fix cardboard to the inside of the crib-end so that he can still hear and feel a thud but cannot hurt himself. If he rocks himself to sleep as usual, there's nothing to worry about, but what if he transfers his head banging to the unpadded side-bars of the crib, or cannot settle as he usually does? If your baby seems to be missing the pain aspect of his head-banging habit, you need to think about why he might want or need to hurt himself, and discuss it with anyone who cares for him when you are not there. If the head banging only reached these somewhat worrying levels when he started with a new caregiver, a chance to get used to the new person gradually may bring it to an end. If nobody can identify a particular stress in his life, the older baby's cure-all—lots of extra individual attention from you—is worth trying. If nothing helps though, and especially if your baby head-bangs more often, and hard enough to mark his head, consult your pediatrician. Ignore people who tell you this is a common habit. It isn't.

◆ **Masturbation:** It's natural and right for babies to explore all parts of their own bodies when diapers and sleep sacks don't foil them, and to discover that touching feels good. But it's also natural to be taken aback if you find your baby rhythmically pulling on his penis or rubbing her vulva against the crib bars, and obviously excited. Try not to be shocked; if you are shocked, try not to show or express it. This kind of infant body-play is entirely harmless, but an over-reaction from you might not be.

Milestones not race tracks

All babies' physical development follows the same path and all pass the same milestones along it, but not at the same rate. Every baby goes from one to the next at his own particular pace.

Some babies travel fast from start to finish; some start out rapidly but then slow down for a while and speed up again later, while others go slowly but steadily all the way. What this means is that out of a group of healthy, active babies, some may be weeks ahead of or behind others in achieving any particular skill, although they are all developing entirely normally and acquiring the same new accomplishments within the same developmental time-frame and in a similar order. Your baby may start to sit alone long before his cousin of the same age, but they will both learn to sit before they stand, and if your son is happy to sit for a while and the cousin is eager to move on, she may stand before he does.

Living here and now, within our individualistic and achievement-oriented society, parents' desire for their children to achieve not only individual excellence but excellence relative to others is readily understandable. However, determination to demonstrate it from day one in an endless series of comparisons is

unfortunate. The evaluation of developmental accomplishments by the speed with which they are achieved, rather than by their quality, range, or utility, contradicts much of what is known of the nature of human development and is demonstrably counterproductive.

Physical milestones like rolling over, sitting up, crawling, standing, and walking are useful reminders of what you can expect your baby to do next, but they tell you very little about when he will do it and even less about when

1   2

The earlier your baby tackles stairs the less sensibly she'll do it. (1) She's going up all right but (2) she's come down faster than she meant; and can't yet do it safely.

From research

Climbing stairs. Recent large-scale studies have found that the age at which babies were first able to climb stairs ranged from 6–18 months and was not dependent on the achievement of other physical milestones. Some of the early climbers had not yet pulled themselves to standing while some of the later climbers were already walking independently.

he should. Development is an orderly process, it is not a race. There are no prizes for getting there first, wherever "there" may be. And getting quickly from one milestone to the next is not necessarily better than getting there more slowly. Try to believe it.

Major landmarks such as walking and talking are important and exciting, because in the first months and years of his life each baby repeats at lightning speed the evolutionary stages that produced humanity. But that does not mean that it is better for your individual baby to get to them and through them faster. The modern infant is human (not just evolving toward humanity) and therefore will become a biped and communicate in speech. He is not a better example of his species because he does these things at an earlier age than its average, nor does infant precocity predict adult excellence. We sometimes behave as if the child who walks earliest will run fastest; as if exceptionally early single words predict especially meaningful later sentences, and as if children's prospects as intelligent, independent, and socialized people can be improved by speeding them through age-appropriate illiteracy, dependence, or incontinence. It is not so, and there is abundant research evidence to prove it.

Age and accomplishment

Just as adults seem unable to interact with each other until each knows what the other "does" ("He's a lawyer and I'm a stay-at-home mom") so they seem unable to accept any child until he or she has been slotted into an age-bracket. Parents are not surprised to be asked how old their baby is; exact answers—"three months and four days"; "four next week"—trip smoothly off their tongues. Their children's position on the calendar is never far from their consciousness, being used, from the beginning, to judge the legitimacy of their needs, the appropriateness of their demands, and the adequacy of their progress. A new baby's cries at 3:00am say she is hungry, but it is the calendar that says whether or not she ought to be. An older baby crawls across the floor or gets to his feet and again, it is the calendar rather than his face that

From research

What is "normal"? Most developments have a "normal range." That means that any point within that range is just as normal as any other. For instance, walking independently at 10 months is normal, and so is walking independently at 14 months. The outer limit of normal for walking is 18 months.

tells his parents how to react. If he is "only" six months or nine months old they will be triumphant; if he is "already" 12 or 28 months old their dominant emotion will be relief at this evidence that their beloved baby is catching up.... Catching up with what or whom? With "age-norms" from a book or developmental c hart; with the expectations of a daycare center or grandparent, or with the "superior" performance of a niece or neighbor who, horror of horrors, is younger than he is.

Your developing baby is all of a piece

First-year development is sometimes described as if it was a set of measuring tapes, one for physical milestones (rolling over, cutting teeth); another for using hands (reaching out, touching, grabbing); and yet another for listening and talking (responding to his name, joining in a song). But the developments that will carry your baby through to his first birthday are far more like one of those skeins of multicolored knitting yarn—each color spun into the rest. What matters most about each of your baby's individual accomplishments is not being able to check it off a list but the effect it has on everything else about him. When your three-month-old baby begins to roll himself over, he is not just demonstrating a milestone in neuro-muscular control, he is also experiencing the vital new autonomy of being able to change his own view from the crib or changing table, to release an arm that has been trapped beneath his body, or to keep you in view as you move across the room.

Teeth and teething

Like so much else in babies' development, the order in which teeth are cut is pretty predictable, but the age at which each appears is not. Cutting teeth "early" or "late" has no bearing whatsoever on any other aspect of development. If your baby has three teeth on his half birthday, don't assume that he's "ahead"—or that he'll bite you when nursing. Likewise if he's still toothless on his first birthday, it doesn't mean that he's behind, or that he can't chew food.

The likely order and approximate ages in which first-year teeth will appear are:

◆ Around six months: one of the two middle incisors in the bottom jaw.

◆ Very soon after the first: its next door neighbor.

◆ Around seven months: one of the matching pair of top incisors.

◆ Very soon after: its next door neighbor.

◆ Somewhere around 8–10 months, the top teeth that are neighbors to the middle pair, so that the baby has a row of four teeth at the top and two at the bottom.

◆ Around 9–10 months, the remaining two lower incisors appear so that the baby has a row of four at the top and four at the bottom. Because of their sharp, flat shape, the incisors come through more easily than the molars, though having two or three on the move at the same time may make your baby inclined to be fussy.

◆ Somewhere around a year—but usually after a pause—one of the four first molars that take up the "corner positions" at each side of each jaw will come through, followed by the other three. A baby with a molar on the move may have "toothache" and a bright pink cheek. Lots of dribbling may give him a sore chin, too, so protect his face from cold winds and keep it moisturized.

The following might help:

◆ Smooth toys to bite on. The kind of teething ring filled with a gel you can cool in the refrigerator is a popular remedy.

◆ Rubbing the sore patch of gum with your finger.

◆ Rubbing the sore patch of gum with teething gel can be very effective, especially if your teething baby wakes in the night. Ask your pediatrician for advice regarding preferred brands and the right amount to use.

You may hear...

Once a baby starts cutting teeth you need to stop nursing her or she'll bite you.
First teeth are bottom teeth with nothing to pincer against. Late in the year when there are teeth top and bottom, you may have to stop your baby from playing with the nipple at the end of a feeding, but there's still no risk that she'll bite when she is sucking as she takes the nipple well behind those teeth.

Teething accounts for much of a baby's fretfulness and crying.
Since the first tooth probably won't come through before six months, it's very unlikely that it could cause discomfort before, say, five months.

Teething may cause fever, diarrhea, seizures...
This is dangerous nonsense. A few parents every year wait too long to seek medical help for a baby they assume to be "just teething." If your baby has any of those symptoms, she is ill (whether or not she is also teething) and should be seen by a doctor immediately.

From research

Teething gels. It's important not to confuse pain-relieving treatments for adult conditions such as mouth ulcers with sometimes similarly named formulations produced specifically for teething babies. Britain's Medicines and Healthcare Products Regulatory Agency has recently reported serious adverse reactions in several children linked to the use of oral gels containing choline salicylate. This substance affects the body similarly to aspirin and is equally inappropriate for children under 16.

Taking charge of his body

When you look at your new baby, all scrunched up and crumpled, it's almost impossible to imagine him running around all over the house in little more than a year.

Muscle control starts at the top (with babies quickly learning to balance their big heads on those wobbly necks) and then moves downward at astonishing speed. In less than six months your baby will be able to hold his back muscles steady enough to enjoy being pulled to sitting—and soon to sit unsupported. In another three months his muscle control will extend down to hip level, and he may be getting across the floor in some kind of crawl; and over the next three months he will gain control of his knees and then his ankles and his feet so that he's able to pull himself up to standing.

This is the age when babies start to enjoy physical fun—and rolling over is part of it.

Kicking and rolling

Somewhere around three months, when your baby can lie flat on his back and therefore see what's above him—including his own waving hands—and kick both his legs freely, he will rather suddenly begin to look like he is happy in his body and having fun with all the things he can do with it. If he is awake he is moving, and many of his movements are much more controlled and rhythmical now than even three weeks ago. "Kicking" no longer means little jerky movements: It means that he lies flat on his back and bicycles his legs smoothly one after the other. When he is lying on his tummy he practices a new kind of head control, bobbing his head up off the mat higher and higher and eventually taking some weight on his forearms, so that not only his head but also his shoulders are raised. He can't yet hold this position for very long at a time, but it's a big advance.

Soon he'll begin to roll over. If you put him on his side he probably already wriggles himself onto the broader base of his back without really meaning to, but deliberately rolling the other way, from the stability of lying on his back to the comparative instability of lying on his side, is much more difficult. Beware: Once he can roll, he will roll, and it won't be many weeks before he can roll all the way over from back to front and vice versa.

If you compare your baby with a gymnast in training, your baby's physical developments and the changes in what he can do are minute. But if you think of him as a helpless newborn, anchored and curled around his over-large and heavy head, you can see what enormous differences these tiny physical developments make to his entertainment and his independence. Instead of relying on you to move him around and change his position, he can shift and roll enough to get comfortable by himself. He can watch his hands and catch a glimpse of his feet. Lifting his head means he can get a different view of the room, look at different objects, even keep you in sight when you are moving around the room. If you understand how important these tiny accomplishments are to him, you'll also understand how easy and how sad it would be to spoil them. Tucked-in blankets can prevent him from kicking; a crumpled mat can stop him from rolling, and a bare white wall gives him nothing to look at.

Getting ready for sitting

By three months, your baby can hold his head steady as you carry him gently around, and hold it clear of the floor when he lies on his tummy. Now his muscle control gradually progresses downward from his shoulders to his upper back so that if you pull him slowly to a sitting position, he will hold up his head and shoulders instead of curling over so that his head almost touches the floor, as he did earlier.

Once he has reached this stage—perhaps between three- and four-months-old—your baby's determination to sit up may become almost an obsession. If you take his hands he at once tries to use your hands as handles to pull himself up. If you don't take his hands he will try desperately—and fruitlessly—to get himself to a sitting position without you, craning his head up as he lies on his back, and soon managing to lift his shoulders clear of the floor as well, giving him an amazing glimpse of his own feet.

From then on your baby needs to spend at least some of his waking time propped up rather than lying flat on the floor. Once he is propped up he can not only see his feet and other interesting sights, but also see and be part of whatever's going on in the room. People are more likely to stop and chat to him as they pass, too. Propping your baby up emphasizes the fact that he is a real person.

First sitting

He'll become more and more like other people as his muscle control moves downward. By the time

Staying safe

Safe rolling. The only places it is safe for your baby to roll are on the floor or in his crib or playpen. The changing table that has always seemed so safe and convenient may become a real hazard between one diaper change and the next, and even the center of your big bed is no longer safe without supervision.

If she had her way you'd spend all day pulling her up to sitting.

he is five to six months old, he'll be able to hold his back straight from his neck to his still-saggy hips, and when you take his hands to sit him up he'll need them more for balance than for power. By the time he is six months old you may be able to sit him firmly on his bottom, spread his legs, get him balanced, and then take your hands away. Your baby is actually sitting. Only for a few seconds, though. His muscles are sufficiently under control for him to sit, but not to balance.

Some babies "solve" the balance problem for themselves, discovering, by seven to eight months, that they can stay sitting if they lean forward and put their hands flat on the floor in front of them. If your baby adopts this position he will be quite stable and he will certainly be sitting, but he hasn't really found a useful solution. Bending forward with both hands on the floor, he cannot look up or around, and he cannot use his hands to play with anything or even to suck his thumb.

A bit of support and a soft landing make sitting fun.

Practice makes perfect sitting

Sitting is part of being human. You don't have to motivate or teach your baby to sit—he's been trying to for weeks—but you do need to give him opportunities for safe practice.

Your baby may be ready and eager to try balancing on his bottom when he's six or seven months old. But he'll probably be nine months old before he can get into a sitting position by himself and in the meantime, he will almost beg you to help him. Every time you come within his reach as he lies on the floor, he will stop craning his head and shoulders up in vain attempts to sit up alone and grab your hands to use as levers.

Unless you want to spend much of your day playing the sitting game, you need to help him practice balancing alone, too. Daycare centers often have foam or inflatable "playrings" for babies to sit in. They can get a little bit of back support to help them balance and a soft landing when they topple. You can provide the same sort of support and protection with pillows or rolled blankets.

If he gets lots of practice it will probably only be about a month before your baby can actually sit, all by himself. There's still a snag though: He can only stay balanced if he stays perfectly still, which is not at all his idea of fun. Keep using the padding. It will save him bumps and scares when he stretches out for something and goes over forward or makes a big gesture with his arms and goes over backward.

Safety on the way to sitting

Your baby is so determined to sit that he will use any "handle" he can grab to try to pull himself up, and work at balancing himself wherever you put him in a sitting position. Be careful where you do put him. Some of the equipment you have been using isn't safe anymore.

◆ Use lightweight strollers only for transport, if at all. If your baby goes to sleep in a bassinet-style stroller, perhaps while you are out shopping, make sure you're actually there when he wakes, otherwise he may find himself wedged against the side of it, grab the edge, haul himself nearly to a sitting position and turn the whole thing over. The same thing might happen if you leave him propped sitting in such a stroller while you are busy, and he wriggles forward to practice his sitting balance, or to look for you, and then loses his balance.

If you have been using a bassinet-style stroller as a portable bed for your baby to start his night in when you are having a sociable evening at his grandparents' house or with friends, you might need to think of another option. A fold-up travel crib is a good one that will be useful whenever you are away from his regular crib and all through toddlerhood.

◆ Beware of lightweight chairs—and, temptingly sociable though it seems, never, never put your baby in a chair that's on a table or work surface. Instead of sitting with his weight well back in the seat, wriggling only from above the waist, your baby now struggles to sit forward from the hips, moving his center of gravity away from the junction of the chair's back and seat. For a few seconds there is no weight on the back of the

From research

The importance of lying flat. Although it's good for babies' social development to spend some waking time propped up, it's also important that they spend time, especially sleeping time, lying flat. Contemporary lifestyles and equipment mean that some babies spend most of their time in car seats, strollers, and bouncy chairs, and rarely get to lie flat in the daytime. And because they sleep on their backs for safety reasons, they almost never get to lie on their tummies.

chair, but as he relaxes his muscles he thumps back against it. If the chair tips over when it is on the floor your baby will be frightened—and so will you. But if it tips off the kitchen table the fall might be serious. It's not worth the risk.

◆ Always use a five-point safety harness on every piece of holding equipment—chair, stroller, or car seat. Waist and crotch straps alone aren't enough. In the next few months your baby is almost as likely to try to stand and fall right out as he is to tip it over. Safety harnesses are built-in to most modern baby equipment, but do check, especially if you've retrieved a family heirloom high chair from the attic. You need a separate safety harness on every piece of equipment you regularly use. If you have to switch one harness around from one to another, a day might come when you don't.

◆ Don't put your baby to sit on armchairs, beds, or sofas unless he's on an adult lap. There are bound to be tumbles when your baby is practicing sitting, but the best tumbles are from floor to floor rather than from furniture to floor.

◆ Your baby cannot safely be left on the floor with no adult in the room. If he's lying on his back he could roll or rock into trouble; if he's practicing sitting, surrounded by cushions, he could tip himself face down into them. If he did, the chance of him smothering is miniscule—he'd lift his head and free himself—but the moment he crawls you'll need to watch him every minute so why not start now?

Moving toward crawling

Your baby may look as if he is going to crawl before he is six months old, but it's unlikely that he will. Babies very rarely crawl before they can sit steadily and often not until several months later.

How early you see preliminaries to crawling largely depends on how much of his play time your baby spends lying on the floor on his tummy. Contemporary babies are often unaccustomed to being face down because unlike earlier generations, they are all put to sleep on their backs. But there have always been some babies who strongly object to lying on their tummies, perhaps because in that position it's more difficult for them to look around.

If your baby is happy lying on his tummy, taking his weight on his forearms so as to lift up his head and shoulders, you may soon see him begin to pull up his knees so that his bottom is in the air. By four or five months he may have discovered that he can lift his shoulders higher by pushing with his hands instead of his elbows, and learned to pull his legs right up under him, pushing on the floor with his feet instead of his knees. In a matter of two or three months then, your baby has got both ends of himself organized for crawling, but he can only do one at a time. He won't be able to get onto his hands and knees until he can put both ends together.

If your baby is trying really hard to put these two positions together he may look as if he is see-sawing: head-down-bottom-up and then bottom-down-head-up. A see-sawing baby often covers enough ground to go off the edge of the bed or over the top of that flight of stairs—so it is high time for safety precautions.

Becoming mobile

Independent mobility is crucial to babies' development. Only when they can travel from place to place on their own and of their own volition can they start actively exploring their environment. Now they can go to see what is around the corner, or find the person they can hear speaking behind the door, and they can find out about surfaces, places, and paths between them.

Although crawling is a later development than sitting, many babies learn both skills during the same months, the two paralleling each other closely. At six months your baby may be able to sit alone for a second but not balance, and get into a crawling position, but not progress. At seven or eight months he will probably be able to sit steadily enough to play at the same time, and a month or so later he'll be able to crawl.

Soon after six months you'll probably be able to see that your baby really wants to crawl and is actually trying. You can see that he is "thinking forward," though he probably won't go forward just yet. By eight months or thereabouts, as soon as he is put on his tummy, or rolls into that position or gets there from wobbly sitting, he will get himself onto his hands and knees. Then he rocks back and forth and swivels around and around, following your movements around the room or the cat's escape from his attentions. All that rocking and swivelling, along with rolling over, may mean that one way or another he does actually get from one side of the room to the other. It's not useful progress, though, any more than sitting with his hands on the floor for balance is useful sitting. Your baby cannot yet choose the direction he wants to go in, and if he tries to go toward something he has seen, he will have lost all sight of it by the time he's stopped rolling around.

Although a baby's first self-initiated locomotion is usually referred to as "crawling,"

(1) Bottom-shuffling is so efficient that some babies never change to a "real" crawl. (2) A baby who rolls and squirms can't control her direction. (3) Most babies adopt a "classic" crawl on hands and knees. (4) A baby who "walks like a bear" on hands and feet may go fast but not see where he is going.

it may have little to do with getting around on all fours. Some babies begin moving quite long distances by various combinations of rolling and wriggling. Babies who have learned to balance themselves in a sitting position by leaning forward on their hands may get about by bottom-shuffling in a sitting position, pushing themselves along with one hand and one foot, while still others lie on their backs and get around by arching like a wrestler (or a caterpillar). Most

babies—probably about 80 percent—do eventually adopt some kind of crawl, but at least 25 different kinds have been described, including "walking like a bear," which involves crawling on hands and feet instead of hands and knees.

Of all the alternatives to conventional crawling, "bottom shuffling" is probably the most efficient, especially for a baby who sat steadily at an early age. So efficient is it that babies who get moving by that method don't usually adopt a "real crawl" later on, but go on bottom-shuffling until they are ready to cruise and walk. A sitting baby is already in position to bottom-shuffle—no struggling onto hands and knees—he has a hand free to carry things along with him and because he's sitting up he has a good view of the world.

Once your baby can get around the room on his own, his life will never be the same again (and neither will yours!). Eager crawlers may begin to progress in the ninth month but, to their fury, it is often backward. Fixing his eyes on something on the other side of the room and making a mighty effort your baby sets off, but because he's got more control of his arms and upper body than of his legs and hips, he tends to push harder with his hands and arms than with his knees, and instead of getting closer to the thing he wants, he finds himself getting farther away. Your baby may be furious, but luckily this phase does not last long. Once he can crawl at all he will soon get his pushing power and direction right.

Unlike sitting, which your baby couldn't practice without your help getting him into position, crawling needs nothing from you but the opportunity that comes from spending plenty of time on the floor. You can make crawling safer and more enjoyable for him, though.

Encouraging crawling

◆ **Protect the skin of your baby's knees:** It is still soft and can easily get rubbed by carpets or grass. Even in summer he'll be more comfortable if he wears cotton overalls or long pants.

◆ **Look out for new dangers:** Learning to crawl doesn't bring extra good sense with it, so watch out for steps between rooms and, of course, for hot fireplaces or radiators. Be cautious about your crawling baby's approach to any household pets. Cats usually escape unwanted attention, but a dog who gets irritated when his ears are pulled or his chew-toy taken can be a real danger.

◆ **Gate any stairs:** Top and bottom, before it even seems necessary.

◆ **Watch out for pre-crawl mobility:** Your baby may roll and squirm himself out of the safe corner where you left him, long before he can deliberately cross the room.

◆ **Check what objects are now in reach:** Part of wanting to crawl is wanting to get hold of things. Make very sure that when something attracts him into an extra effort, it is not a pen or a paper clip that has caught his eye.

◆ **Don't try to keep a crawling baby clean:** It's fine to fuss about hygiene in the kitchen and the bathroom, but ordinary cleanliness is quite enough elsewhere when your baby is playing on the floor. If you are someone who minds when nice clothes get grubby, try to keep them for special outings and let him wear durable, easily washable play clothes when he is at home.

◆ **Your baby cannot now be safe if he's left alone and free:** But he can't enjoy his crawling as he should if he's imprisoned in a playpen. He needs a safe piece of floor, safe interesting objects, and constant supervision. (See p. 258.)

From research

Why crawling is valuable. Crawling is not as integral and necessary a stage in infant development as sitting or standing, but recent research does suggest that it plays a valuable part in a baby's grasp of spatial relationships and mapping.

◆ He discovers that things that are far away from him exist (even if he couldn't see them until he moved closer) and he learns how to calibrate how far away things are where previously, far away things all looked the same distance away, rather like stars in the night sky appear to us. Now he discovers that the more crawling it takes to reach something, the further away it is, and that objects don't literally shrink or expand as they move further away or nearer.

◆ He learns to navigate: "Head for the sofa, turn toward the big chair, turn round the back of it, and you get to the toy box."

◆ Just as someone driving a car notices more than a passenger, so a crawling baby notes more and more detail in his surroundings.

◆ He learns to make good decisions about whether or not to keep crawling, for instance over the top of that flight of steps....

Beginning to get onto his feet

Just as learning to sit up and to crawl follow each other in that order, often with a rolling, squirming stage between the two, so standing and walking follow on, with a "cruising" stage in between.

The order of all these milestones is pretty well fixed, but the length of time any baby takes, or should take, getting from one to the other is not. Chances are your baby won't actually walk this year, but you probably will see signs that he's destined to be a biped!

Preliminaries to walking start as early as three to four months, when, held in a standing position on your lap, your baby goes from sagging pathetically to pushing down with his toes to take at least a little of his own weight while he practices straightening his knees. By four to five months the knee-straightening has become rhythmical so that it feels as if he were "jumping." From then on your baby probably chooses standing over sitting. The moment you pick him up and try to sit him on your lap, he will turn to face you, clutch a handful of your clothes or hair and struggle to get himself upright. Once your baby is standing against you, face to face, he's in his favorite kind of warm contact with your body and able to gaze into your eyes. What's more, he has a new view of the world over your shoulder, and it goes interestingly up and down as he "jumps."

In the next few weeks it may become impossible to get your baby to sit on your lap at all. The moment you sit down with him he grabs whatever he can reach—tie, necklace, hair—and uses it to haul himself onto his feet.

Soon jumping turns into dancing, and somewhere in the seventh month your baby will begin to use alternate feet instead of both together, often putting one foot down on top of the other, pulling out the underneath one and then doing it all over again. Is being a dance floor better than being a trampoline?

Your dancing baby still cannot take anything like his own full weight and is not yet "thinking forward" as he did when he was first trying to crawl. He'll probably be at least nine months old when he first gets the idea of placing one foot in front of the other to go forward, "walking" along your knee. Held securely, with his feet on the floor and you taking most of his weight, he'll probably now enjoy some wobbly walking practice.

Babies begin to be able to take their own weight standing up when (and only when) their muscle control moves on down from hip level to include their knees and (flat) feet—usually at around 10 months. Even then, the fact that your baby can take his own weight with braced knees and only a small sag forward at hip level does not mean that he can stand, because he still cannot balance. Fortunately, once your baby reaches this stage it won't be entirely up to you to help him practice, because he will soon learn to pull himself up to a holding-on standing position. He may start by pulling himself, hand over hand, up the bars of a crib or stair gate. Or he may take every opportunity to use people, hauling himself up the legs of anyone who sits down within crawling reach.

Parents talking about...

toddle trucks

❝ One of those little push trucks, with specially angled handles and wheels that don't run away, meant our baby had something safe to pull up on wherever we were. ❞

Standing and cruising

Once your baby pulls himself to holding-on-standing, the assisted walking we call "cruising" will start before long—perhaps within days; almost certainly within a few weeks. When the time comes, your baby will pull himself up as usual, but instead of standing still and hanging on tightly with his hands, he moves both hands together a few inches along his support. Now he's off balance, so he steps sideways with one foot so that his legs are wide apart and he'll probably sit down quickly. Babies sometimes look surprised at their own first sideways shuffles, and no wonder. That sideways shuffle was your baby's first step.

Safety when pulling up to standing

A crawling baby who is ready to pull himself up to standing will use anything he comes across: furniture if he's free in the living room; bars if he is in his crib; the slippery edge if he is in the bath, and the family dog's collar if nothing else is within reach. The more unsuitable his chosen support, the more likely he is to fall. You can't prevent all tumbles, of course, but a lot of falls from standing height can damage his confidence, and at this stage in his life they are likely to hurt his still-heavy head as well. In another six months when he is walking freely he will learn to put his hands out to break his falls, just as older people do. But right now he can't protect himself because his balance isn't very good and his hands are occupied with hanging on. It's worth doing what you can to protect him.

Newly standing babies often go through a phase in which they get to their feet as soon as they are let free to find a support, but having gotten themselves up, they cannot figure out how to sit down again. As soon as they have been rescued and put to sit down they get up again, and as soon as they are standing up again they shout for help. This phase may be equally tiresome for your baby and you. You can help to keep it short if instead of simply plucking him off whatever he is holding onto and unceremoniously dumping him back on his bottom, you help him to slide his hands down his support while you lower him to the floor. Every time you do that you help him feel safe, either letting go with his hands and plopping himself down, or sliding his hands down his support until his bottom reaches the floor. In the meantime, extra car or stroller rides may help you both. He will not yet even think about standing when he is out on an expedition, but will happily sit and watch the world go by.

Once your baby *can* pull herself up, she *will*: Bare feet and a solid support make for safety.

Safety when standing

◆ Your baby will (try to) pull himself up on anything, so pieces of furniture that are too light to withstand his leverage or are tall enough to fall toward him when he is almost up and pulling— and may actually fall on top of him—are definitely unwelcome in a room where he is often going to play. Can you wedge them in place or put them where he can't get to them? If not, you may have to banish them altogether until your baby regularly gets to his feet without holding on.

◆ If your baby is one who loves to climb, chests of drawers with all those lovely knobs can seem temptingly like ladders, and of course if the whole structure tips, he could be badly hurt. You may need to move such pieces or screw them to the wall.

◆ A standing baby is twice as tall as when he is sitting, so things that were previously out of reach may now be in grabbing range. Don't leave dangling tablecloths or trailing cables or cords where he might try to pull himself up on them and bring down dangerous objects on his head.

◆ Sleep sacks are fine for babies in this age group and tend to prevent climbing out of bed for months to come. But if your baby hasn't worn one before, don't start now. If he tries to stand up in it in his crib he will certainly fall and may hit his head on the bars.

◆ Your baby will be safest in bare feet. Shoes are to protect feet, not to "support" them. Your baby doesn't need shoes until he is walking freely on all surfaces including outdoors. In the meantime, wearing shoes will make it far more difficult for him to balance, because they will cut down the sensations his feet receive from the floor and the sensitive adjustments of his toes. They can be slippery, too. As for socks: Only the kinds with non-slip bottoms are safe for a newly standing baby unless every single floor in your home is carpeted.

◆ "Baby walkers" are really dangerous. Don't, please don't, use the kind of baby walker where your baby half-sits half-stands in a canvas seat on wheels and pushes himself around on his toes. Yes, he may love it. Yes, it may keep him occupied. But babies in walkers can bang into things (fireplaces for instance) and tip over, fall down stairs or over steps, or reach things you thought were at a safe height, such as table lamps. And no, these walkers do not help babies learn to walk. They are bad for your baby's posture and encourage him to walk on his tiptoes.

Beginning to cruise

Most parents regard walking alone as the most important of the physical milestones babies pass, so they get more and more excited as their baby pulls himself to his feet, starts to cruise, and eventually stands unsupported. It's fine to be excited of course, but don't let it make you pushy. Learning to stand and walk isn't only part of your baby's physical development, it's also dependent on other aspects of growing up, especially his motivation and his confidence in himself. If you try to hurry him from one stage to another you may provoke falls that will frighten him enough to slow his progress. If he's achieved one stage—pulling himself to standing, for example—but shows no desire to cruise, it may be that he is taking huge pleasure in being able to crawl freely and doesn't feel ready to move from standing on his own two feet toward walking. There's no hurry—for him or for you. While many babies cruise before their first birthdays and a few actually walk, a lot won't get onto their own two feet at all in this first year.

Getting good at cruising

Early cruising is slow and inefficient compared with what's to come. When they first haul themselves upright, babies don't entirely trust their legs, so they feel they have to take some of their weight on their hands, moving both together. Progress is slow. Within a week or two though, your baby will come to trust his legs with his whole weight, so he'll be able to stand farther back from his support and instead of sliding both hands along it together, he'll pass himself along it hand over hand. Each time he moves a hand, he follows it by moving the foot on the same side one step sideways, and then he brings the other foot up to join it. For a few days you may be able to see that the moment when all his weight is on one foot while the other is in the air still worries him, but a few more days of practice and he'll be standing back and using that support only for balance.

Stages in learning to walk

Between the day when they first haul themselves into a standing position and the day when they set off across open space, all babies progress through several distinct phases.

Phase 1: The baby pulls himself to a standing position. He holds on tightly, not trusting all his weight to his legs and feet. First attempts at cruising consist of moving both hands together a few inches along his support. Since he's now off-balance, he moves one foot so his legs are spread wide. With or without help, it's time to sit down and start again. With both arms and legs apart he's stuck.

Phase 2: This is a much more efficient type of cruising. The baby now trusts all his weight to his feet so he can stand back from his support and move along, hand over hand and foot after foot. By the end of this phase he is moving hands and feet in rhythm so that at critical moments he is relying only on one foot and one hand for support, the other member of each pair being in motion.

Phase 3: In this third phase, the baby discovers that she can cross small gaps—no wider than her two arms can span—between one support and the next. She will not let go with one hand until the other hand has caught hold of something, but if furniture is conveniently arranged, she will now be able to get around a room moving along a sofa, crossing to a windowsill, cruising along it and then crossing to a chair.

Phase 4: In the fourth phase, when the child faces a gap that is too wide for him he finds a brave solution: his first unsupported step. Facing the gap, he holds tightly to the first support while he shuffles his feet toward the middle of the gap, lets go, and lurches the single step that lets him grab the second support with his other hand. He has walked across, and what's more he can now stand alone, although he may not realize it.

Seeing and doing

Babies look and see from the beginning, but it's during this second quarter year that your baby will begin to link looking with doing, and seeing with understanding.

As your baby differentiates the people she sees around her from each other she'll begin to understand who is who, and as she differentiates the playthings and other objects she sees, one from another, she'll begin to be able to do something about each, adding action to looking.

These are vital developments, because as long as a baby's looking and touching systems remain separate—as they were in her first months—she is a passive observer rather than an active participant. She has to learn to connect looking and touching so she can reach out and touch and take the interesting things she sees.

Finding her hands

By three months of age or thereabouts, your baby will have taken possession of her hands. She no longer needs the sound of a rattle to draw her attention to them *(see p.155)*; she knows where

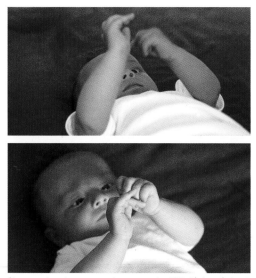

Her own hands are your three-month-old baby's very best playthings—better than any toy.

> ### Parents talking about...
> #### keeping dangerous objects out of a baby's reach
> ❝ One of the most difficult things about having a preschooler and a baby is making sure that the small parts of preschool toys don't get left where the baby can get hold of them. We used a floor mat for the baby, and weeks before she could actually roll over and pick things up we started teaching her older sister never to leave anything on it. ❞

her hands are and she can bring them up to look at them as well as touch them. Her hands are her favorite playthings, and she may occupy herself for several minutes at a time waving them around while she watches them, grasping one with the other and pulling its fingers, letting both hands drop so they go out of sight, then bringing them back up again to suck a finger, take it out and inspect it, and put it back in along with a thumb.

As soon as you see your baby putting her fingers in and out of her mouth, you'll know that she's going to put everything else in her mouth, too. Don't try to stop her from exploring things by putting them in her mouth—nothing you can do *will* stop her, and trying would delay her development. If you are worried about hygiene, make sure your baby has toys that are suitable for sucking as well as for holding and looking at, and wash them from time to time. If you are (more realistically) worried about her eating something dangerous or choking, start now to involve everyone in the household in making sure dangerous objects aren't left in her reach. She can't reach out for things yet, but she soon will.

Reaching out and touching is fun, taking hold is even better, and two at a time is a triumph.

Staying safe

Mouthing unsuitable objects. Since mouthing things is a big part of finding out about them, all babies sometimes put unsuitable objects and substances into their mouths—worms, charcoal, cat food, dirt—and although their parents are nauseated, the babies seldom come to any harm. However, a few things your baby might get hold of are so dangerous that you may want to ban them from your home.

◆ Tiny magnets used to put up cards and pictures. They are horribly easy to swallow, and two or more will attract each other and may do dreadful damage to the stomach or intestines.

◆ Map pins, used instead of thumbtacks but even more dangerous because smaller (and therefore more likely to get swallowed) and sharper.

◆ All batteries are poisonous if eaten. More and more gadgets now use the coin-shaped shiny batteries that used to be confined to watches, and are attractive to suck and easy to swallow.

◆ Pill boxes and their contents. Don't keep pills in anything except the childproof and labeled container in which they were dispensed, and don't put them anywhere to which your baby has access (such as your purse on the kitchen floor).

◆ Curtain and blind pulls long enough for a crawling or standing baby to reach and put around her neck.

Touching and taking

Learning to put what her hands do together with what her eyes see—the beginning of hand-eye coordination—is as important in the first half of the year as standing is in the second, and lastingly so. Good hand-eye coordination will contribute to many skills later on, such as playing sports, dancing, and driving.

Adults often don't realize what a complicated business getting hold of things is for a baby; after all, we do it without a moment's thought. Your baby has to do a lot of "thinking" about it though. First she has to see something, focus on it, and decide she wants it. Then she has to make some sort of estimate of how far away it is, move her arm so that her hand gets close to it, and finally open her hand and make sure it's the right way up for grasping it.

You can't teach your baby to coordinate her hands and eyes until she is ready, but rich opportunities for play will certainly encourage her.

Stages in using hand and eye together

Your three- or four-month-old baby probably won't be content any longer just to touch what she sees; she wants to get hold of things. When you hung interesting things above her a month or so ago, she swiped at them and was obviously pleased if her hand made contact. But now, instead of swiping wildly, she looks at the object she wants, looks at her own nearest hand, lifts the hand toward it, "measuring" the distance by eye, and then goes on repeating this until she actually manages to touch the toy. She won't manage to grasp it just yet though. She almost always misjudges and closes her hand before it quite gets there.

A baby who is trying to grasp things doesn't want mobiles or swinging toys. She'll be better off with a baby gym for solitary play at this stage, provided you can arrange the playthings so that most of them are within the reach of such a young baby. She'll get the best hand-eye coordination practice (and the most fun) when

an adult can play with her and offer her lots of different objects to touch and hold; not just rattles, but toys of different shapes and textures and some objects that aren't toys at all, but look and feel interesting.

Reaching out and taking hold

Your baby needs to have her back supported and both arms free if she is to reach out slowly, bit by bit, adjusting her arms and hands until she can reach the thing she wants. When you hold things for her to touch, be patient of this long, slow effort. If you help her—put the toy in her hands too quickly—you spoil it. Your baby will soon reach out for things you are not offering to her—and maybe would prefer her not to have, such as your best scarf. Removing her father's glasses may be her first obviously intentional mischievous joke.

Around the middle of the year, developments of both hand and eye make it easier for your baby to use them together to reach out and get hold of things. Visually, focusing on things at different distances and following them with her eyes in any direction gets easier for your baby. When she is propped in her chair, she'll now watch as adults move around the room, and even catch sight of interesting things through the window. Manually, your baby now knows where her hands are at any point in time, so she does not need to look from hand to object when she reaches out, but instead can keep her eyes on the thing she wants and lift her hand straight to it. She'll become more efficient at grabbing what she touches, too. You'll see that she now keeps her hand open until it makes contact, and then closes it around the object. You'll also see that if the object is too large to grasp in one hand, she somehow knows it, approaching instead with both arms open and clutching it to herself.

The more different kinds and sizes of object you show your baby, the better. You can help her learn which of the things she sees can be touched or grasped and which cannot. She can see a big truck through the window, but she can't touch or grasp it. She sees flowers on her dress that she can touch, but she can't get hold of them as she can the geraniums in the flower pot. Picture books and her own little experiments will help her to understand.

Around her half-year birthday, she'll begin to experiment more and more as her manipulative skills rapidly improve. She doesn't only want toys and other objects to hold and suck; she wants them to bang against each other or on the floor. She's likely to be more enthusiastic about foods she can put into her own mouth than foods that are spooned into her, and she'll want to hold her own bottle or the breast. And she'll pick up everything she can reach so quickly that you may be too slow to stop her, and everything she picks up will go in her mouth—pens and scissors as well as rattles and snacks.

Touching and taking hold

There's a lot more to manual skill than reaching out and grabbing, though. And by the middle of the year, your baby will not only know where her hands are, but be doing all kinds of things with them, like waving. She won't be able to do really complicated things with her hands, though, until

Your baby will want anything you've got—suitable or not.

she's learned to use different parts of them separately. It's the pincer grip of forefinger and thumb that enables us to pick up minute objects and tie delicate threads in complicated knots, and it will take your baby the rest of her first year to acquire that key to human dexterity.

Still, now, in the middle of her first year, your baby is already beginning to realize that grabbing and mouthing toys is not the only way her hands can explore them. Increasingly she'll discover that she can also use her hands to stroke something or to pat it, and that means she can explore things that can't be grasped or sucked, such as a carpet or a cow.

A world that can be touched and stroked is richer than one that can only be grasped and sucked. You'll probably find that your baby gets increasingly interested in stroking—her high-chair tray and your hair—and that she loves "texture toys" with surfaces of velvet, sandpaper and silk, and playing on different surfaces, too—grass, carpet, soft mats, and wooden floors.

The pincer grip of thumb and forefinger, unique to humans and apes, lets your baby pick up minute objects.

Using arms, hands, and fingers separately

When babies first start to reach out and grab things, they behave as if their arms and hands are all of a piece, holding onto adults by wrapping their arms around the nearest part, rather than by holding on with a hand; and gesturing at things they want adults to look at with a sweep of their whole arm from the shoulder. Gradually, though, your baby discovers that she can use different parts of her arm separately: just her lower arm (from the elbow) and just her hand (from the wrist). By eight or nine months she'll probably delight in waving good-bye.

In parallel with learning to use different parts of her arms separately, your baby is also beginning to do the same with her hands. Instead of using her whole hand to get hold of objects, picking small things up by using her hand like a scoop and larger things using both hand-scoops together as if they were tongs, she begins to use her fingers and thumbs for grasping and for holding on to things. By around nine months your baby may have enough control of her separate fingers that she can use just one on its own—usually an index finger—to poke something or to point.

Opposing fingers and thumbs

Only humans and apes can oppose their thumbs and fingers, and babies develop the skill at around nine months. Your baby will stop using her whole hand as a scoop and use a delicate pincer grip instead. The pincer grip is part of the unique heritage of being human, but right now be wary of it because your baby can—and will—retrieve the one tiny pin you dropped on the living room floor.

Letting go

As she learns more ways to pick things up, so your baby has to learn to let them go again—and that's a great deal more difficult than it might seem. Although your nine-month-old baby understands the idea of letting go of something, and will hold it out if you ask her to give it to you, she finds actually releasing it, uncurling her fingers so that it drops from her hand, very difficult unless the object and her hand are both

Thoroughly exploring shapes and textures requires hands, eyes, and mouth all working together.

flat on a firm surface. For instance, she has no problem putting down finger foods on the table of her high chair, but if there's no table available, she probably won't be able to uncurl her fingers in mid-air. She may manage it, though, if you put your own hand flat under hers.

By about 10 months your baby will probably have discovered how to let go of things in mid-air—and you may wish she hadn't. Once she can do it she will. For a while, all her favorite games (her favorites, not necessarily yours) will probably involve dropping things: food from the high chair, groceries from the cart, toys from her crib, and washcloths from the bath. Increase her fun and reduce your frustration by fastening some of her small toys onto her crib or stroller so that she can drop them and fish them up again. Make a chain of plastic rings that clip together and use it to attach the toy to her stroller or high chair. (Avoid using strings or yarn, which may pose a strangulation risk.)

The passion for dropping things at random won't last long. By the time your baby approaches her first birthday, she'll be more interested in "managing" toys and other things: throwing an indoor ball on purpose, lining up farm animals or blocks, and filling and emptying any bags or boxes you will give her. Purpose-made small toys are fine for this (as long as they are too big to be a choking hazard), but potatoes or oranges with a paper or cloth bag to pack and unpack will probably keep her happy for longer.

Helping your baby to use her hands

Although beloved adults are still your baby's best playthings as well as playmates, she is beginning to need and want to find out about the world itself and the objects as well as the people in it. For that she needs playthings.

Your baby cannot yet go and get things for herself, so she has to rely on you to bring her bits of the world. Bring her plenty. Even while she is too young to do anything much with objects, she is ready to learn about them by looking and sucking and feeling. Rattles, rings, and soft balls are fine, but your baby can make use of the widest range of objects you can possibly offer her, including many household things she sees you use. At six or seven months though, while your baby will enjoy lots of playthings, she will enjoy them more one at a time than if a whole lot are dumped in front of her together, because at this stage in her development she can only pay attention to one thing at a time. If she is holding one block in her right hand and you try to put a second one in her left hand, she won't take it and hold them both: She'll switch her attention to the new block and drop the first.

A month or so later she probably will hold two things, one in each hand, but she still won't bang them together or combine them in any way. It will be another couple of months before that occurs to her.

Your baby will probably be beginning to hold two toys at once at just about the time that she learns to use her fingers and thumbs separately. Those two developments together suggest that she has reached a point where she needs more complicated objects and shapes to explore. Lend her some bracelets to practice threading on her fingers (or buy her a threading toy). And find her interesting surfaces to poke with her index finger—a mat with a raised pattern or a solitaire board (without the marbles of course).

Everyday objects for play

Your baby has seen so little of the world you share that she'll be interested in almost anything you are prepared to lend to her. Try to find her objects of different colors and shapes, sizes and weights. Objects that make different sounds when she bangs or drops them are interesting,

too. It doesn't matter what the things you give her to play with are *for*, because she doesn't yet understand that things have functions, much less being able to make them work.

It won't be long before your baby learns how some things work, though, even how to use them. She learns by watching other people. By around nine months she may not only watch, but also try to do as she sees you doing, even imitating deliberate demonstrations. Try offering her a chunky crayon and a piece of paper when she's watching you make a "to-do" list. She may not actually make a mark this time, but she'll try to copy what you are doing, and next time she may succeed.

She begins to understand the whys and wherefores of favorite games, too, and she can

From research

Treasure baskets. Invented by Elinor Goldschmidt, a Treasure Basket provides a world of opportunity, choice and independence for a baby who can sit but not yet crawl. In a low, rigid-sided round basket put 50 or so objects, natural, household, or play, offering the widest possible range of textures, weights, smells, tastes, and appearances. You might include a pine cone, a large shell, a pastry brush, a wooden spoon, a purse, a soft brush. It is a basic human urge to make sense of our world, find meaning in it and to feel some control over it. When babies begin to play, they first of all examine the characteristics of any objects that come within their reach. They do this by looking, holding, shaking, banging, or mouthing them. If a baby had language she would be asking, "What is this object like?"

The Treasure Basket provides scores and scores of possibilities that excite, interest, and satisfy a curious baby, while at the same time the baby is constructing the connecting neurons in her developing brain, which is the foundation of all intelligent thinking. The Treasure Basket gives a developing baby the opportunity to develop intelligent thinking about the concrete world, which is the first vital step to later abstract thinking.

Make sure you are comfortable with the safety of all the objects in the basket and that you are sitting by your baby while she finds things and takes them out. Don't offer her particular things though, this is her Treasure Basket. How she explores and plays with it is up to her.

"What's this?"—not "What is it for?" but "What does it look and feel like?"

repeat them on purpose. For instance, for several weeks she has probably enjoyed the random movements of pull toys when she waved her arms while holding their strings. But until now she showed no sign of realizing a connection between what she did and what the toy did. Suddenly—literally from one day to the next— she sees the cause and effect; her face lights up with pleasure and she'll pull that car toward her as many times as you will push it away.

Copying what other people do, children as well as adults, becomes a more and more important way for your baby to learn what things do and how to make them do it. Take her where other children are playing and she will watch intently and try to imitate. Show her what you or other grown-ups are doing and demonstrate skills like unscrewing a toothpaste tube or jelly jar; putting a new toilet paper roll on the rod; putting the key in the lock, and filling a glass with water. The skills involved in everyday actions like these—actions we undertake without conscious thought—are generic. Your baby will not only try to copy what you are doing at the time but will also be getting good ideas for things to try to do on other occasions, gradually generalizing what she has seen you do with the toothpaste tube to what she might do with a screw-ring toy.

Once your baby begins to be able to do these things, help her practice all the time on many different tasks—even if her efforts make far more mess and take far longer than it would have taken you to do it yourself. Of course she can't really feed herself with food that needs a spoon, but if you each have a spoon, she can do some of it and feel involved. You can also make a game of directly teaching her a manual skill such as washing her face with a washcloth, turning the pages of her board books, and putting apples in the fruit bowl. All these mundane-sounding experiences, and thousands more, are new to your baby, and doing them with adults will also help her to feel involved in the family in a way that special baby games and toys cannot. The more patient everybody in the household can be, slowing down what they do and tolerating her messes and mistakes, the more skills she will learn. *(See p. 264.)*

Staying safe

Everyday objects as playthings. The more different objects your baby has to play with the better, and toys meant for babies are not always as interesting as the "toys" adults use. Sharing household things with babies adds to parents' responsibilities, because without the regulations and inspections that toy manufacturers are subject to, their knowledge, vigilance, and common sense are the only guarantee that those things are safe for play. You don't just need to be alert to possible hazards yourselves, you also need to alert anyone else who cares for your baby. A mother's helper—even a grandmother— who arrives and finds the baby playing with something of yours might assume that you'd passed it as safe and not realize that it was something she should check, and keep a special eye on.

Remember that the baby will suck and bite at everything, so anything he plays with must be safe for him to put in his mouth. Check apparently harmless objects like sieves for sharp edges and remember that things that are safe when whole, such as yogurt containers, can become dangerous when cracked or broken, so you need to keep checking and be quick to throw things away at the first sign of disintegration. Sucking sometimes means swallowing by mistake or on purpose; watch out for unexpected poisons, such as batteries, and newsprint (assume it's all newsprint), as well as for obvious ones like remaining drops of cleaning fluid in a plastic bottle you thought was empty. It's best never to use for play any empty container whose original contents would have been dangerous to your baby: If you want plastic bottles, stick to well washed-out empties that held fruit juice or baby lotion. And remember that whatever the baby holds, he is certain to drop. Avoid anything heavy enough to hurt if he happens to drop it on his face when he is playing lying down, or on his fingers if he's sitting in his high chair.

More listening and more and more talking

From around the time of her quarter birthday your baby gets more and more excited by her own developing skills, and produces streams of babble-sounds to celebrate.

As she kicks and rolls, plays with her hands, swipes at objects and triumphantly touches them, hugs you and laughs at your jokes and games, she comments with waterfalls of talk. Although she still talks most of all when an adult talks to her, she is seldom silent for long even if she is alone.

At this stage most of the sounds a baby makes are open vowels: "Aah" and "Ooh." People often call this "cooing," and when you hear your baby "talking" to herself first thing in the morning, she really does sound a bit like a dove.

When babies first add consonants to cooing, they are usually K, P, B, and M. They turn cooing noises into sounds which might almost be words, so parents sometimes think the baby has added them on purpose. In fact those "choices" of consonant just happen to be sounds that are easy for babies' immature vocal tracts. Although Western mothers are thrilled with the sound "Maa" and fathers are sometimes saddened by the absence of the sound "Daa," in the real world of babies' development, the explanation has nothing to do with preferring one parent over another and everything to do with the "M" sound being easy, and the "D" sound more difficult. In the first six months of life, no baby is naming anybody; yours simply adds consonants and makes more and more complex sounds because she's programmed to do so. That innate "programming" is important because it ensures that although babies babble more, and more fluently, if people talk to them a lot, they make some sounds even if they never hear any at all because they are deaf. Do be aware that it's only in the second-half of the year that any hearing loss will show in your baby's voice. Until then you can only identify hearing loss from your baby's lack of reaction to sounds. If she never turns her head to look toward the source of your

If your twins talk more to each other than to you, you may not be talking enough to each of them.

Twin tip

Talking to twins—and to each individually— is especially important to their language development. People used to think that "idioglossia" or "twin talk" is an actual language developed between them, but contemporary research has established that it is not a different language at all but an incorrect or disordered version of ordinary language that one twin uses and the other copies.

talking voice when you're speaking quietly, and does not jump when someone drops a book directly behind her, consult your doctor, no matter how much she talks.

Although your baby will go on enjoying face-to-face conversation (don't we all?) by the time she is four or five months old she can listen and watch your face, even if you are talking to her as you move around doing other things. Perhaps the most exciting change in her "talking" is that she is beginning to turn listening and babbling into "real" conversation, putting in a spurt of her own sounds whenever you leave a space in yours, and then pausing to make space for you to reply again.

Your baby is not imitating

Many parents assume that children learn to talk by imitating adults. As soon as they notice the conversational pattern in their baby's babbling, they set out to make it easy for her to copy words, by using simple ones and heavy emphasis. But a baby's speech doesn't come from imitation (she's a person, not a parrot). What babies who are learning to talk need from adults is not easy words to copy but lots of two-way conversation. It's the joy of communication that stimulates her to play the talking game, and talking to your baby as if she understands what you're saying is the very best way to help her toward doing so.

Universal speech sounds

It's very clear that imitation plays little part in babies' word-learning when you consider that their sound repertoire doesn't even depend on the particular language or accent people use in talking to them. All human babies use some of the same wide range of babble-sounds. Which particular sounds your baby makes right now depends on how talkative a baby she is, and on the progress of the physiological development of her sound-making apparatus: the mouth, tongue, larynx, and so forth. Of course, your baby will eventually learn the language of her family and your community as all babies do, but less because she will imitate other people's words than because of the way they will select and react to her sounds. If you are English speaking, you will

Watching you, copying what you do, and taking turns is joyful play and high-quality learning.

Why it matters...

that you take turns. Turn-taking is important not only to developing speech but to every aspect of babies' social development. Whatever rhythmic actions an adult performs—patting the table, nodding her head—the baby will wait for a pause, take a turn, and then wait for the adult to do it again in rhythmic reciprocity.

greet English-sounding noises ecstatically, assuming them to be attempts at words and dismissing the rest as just babble. Japanese or Italian or Czech parents will select and celebrate different sounds, but the truth is that baby sounds are universal and no baby's sounds will become truly different from those of babies from other language backgrounds until she starts to make word-sounds later in the year.

Just as your baby learns to distinguish familiar people from strangers, and one familiar person from another, by looking at them (*see p. 165*), so, during this age period, she learns to distinguish them by listening, too. Babies usually know their mothers' voices from everyone else's because they have been familiar to them from before birth, but from six months on that familiarity extends to other relatives and friends. It's not only the sound of her father's voice in the front hall that will make your baby smile and wriggle, but also the sound of your friendly neighbor or her caregiver.

Helping your baby's language development

Parental pressure tends to slow or dampen babies' development in almost any area, but especially in language. For your baby, making sounds is part of play, and making conversation is one of the best of all games. She'll do most of her talking—to you, another adult or herself—when she is pleased and excited, and she won't talk at all unless she is at least content. If your baby is frustrated, angry, or sad, she won't "talk," she will cry. When you hear her talking to herself in her crib—making sounds, pausing as if someone was going to answer, and then making another set of sounds—what you'll hear will sound like interested or even joyful speech. She'll produce her first real words when she is happy, too. If "Bear" is her first word, it won't come out as a demand for her teddy bear or as an anxious question as to his whereabouts, but as a loving comment on him.

Talking is play, and making conversation with someone beloved is the best game of all.

From research

Developing babble sounds. By six or seven months those open-throat consonants—K, P, B, and M—begin to give way to strings of consonants made with the palate or the lips: tata, nana, dada, mama. Before her birthday she will probably be mixing syllables ("Tada!") and will pronounce most of the vowels and perhaps half the consonants of her family language. Unlike earlier cooing—which is sound-making gymnastics—babbling has recently been shown to be part of actual language: When a baby babbles, it activates the language-control center in the brain's left hemisphere.

From babble to jargon

Although the timetable for developing speech is not rigidly fixed and no one should worry if their baby's sound-making follows a different pattern, the "usual" sequence, set out below, may help parents and caregivers to notice where a baby has gotten in speech development and where she is likely to go next.

◆ At around six months most babies carry on lengthy babble conversations with any known adult who will concentrate on talking to them. Your baby will say "Paaa," pause for you to answer, and then say something else. Most of her sounds are still single syllable cooing noises like "Maaaa" and "Boooo," and she intersperses them with laughter and gurgles of delight. She'll talk to you for as long as you'll go on looking and speaking directly to her, but she'll stop at once if you move out of sight. Calling to her across the room will get no response.

◆ At around seven months she'll become increasingly alert to speech sounds and begin to be able to respond to a voice whose owner she can't see. If you call her when you're out of sight, she'll look around for you. She will even look for the source of a voice on television, ready to talk back just as soon as she can discover who is talking.

◆ Early in this seventh month, you're likely to hear your baby's first two-syllable "words." The first ones are still based on those cooing sounds, so you'll hear her say "Baba" and "Mumum" and "Booboo." Gradually, though, the "words" get separated out from the background of cooing sounds. When that begins to happen, you'll know that a new batch of sounds very different from the earlier ones is on the way.

◆ Around the eighth month, new two-syllable "words" emerge that are more exclamatory and less dovelike. Your baby says "Imi!" "Aja!" "Ippi".... These "words" are as exciting for your baby to say as they are for you to hear. From this point on your baby "talks" more and more and will often wake you with a dawn chorus of what sounds exactly like one half of a cheerful conversation.

◆ As the eighth month progresses, your baby is likely to begin to take an interest in your conversation even if it's not addressed to her. If both her parents are talking to each other over her head, she will turn from one speaker to the next and back again, but when she's had enough of being ignored she can shout for your attention. The shout is new. It is not a cry or a yell or a squeak: It is a definite shout and probably her very first effort to use her voice to communicate a specific message.

◆ Once she can shout, your baby can sing. It's not an aria, of course—a four-note scale is as good as it gets at this stage—but it's clearly song rather than speech and it's usually set off by music—a song from you or a CD or a familiar television jingle.

◆ Between nine and 12 months (or around that time) your baby's sound-making changes rapidly. She'll elaborate those double-syllable exclamations until they become long, drawn-out, multisyllabic "sentences." Gradually she puts in changes of inflection and emphasis until in unwary moments you think you are hearing arguments and jokes. The forms of her speech change, too. She doesn't just go on adding repetitions of the same syllables to her strings of talk, she puts all the different syllables she knows together. "Ah-dee-dah-boo-maa." Now she really does sound as if she is talking (though in a foreign language!), and with half your mind on something else, you may find yourself asking her "What did you say?" She hasn't said anything yet, of course, but she very soon will.

Moving toward actual speech

Almost every parent waits impatiently for their baby's first real word. Relax. Its timing isn't entirely in your hands—it has more to do with genetics than parental behavior.

But if you can't teach your baby to talk or hurry her first real words, it's clear that her fluent, enthusiastic babbling now is linked to the ease and speed with which she learns language, so making sure she gets all the word-play she can use is clearly worthwhile.

Not everybody finds talking to babies (even their own) easy. There are chatty people who talk to anyone who's around including the baby, the dog or even the newscaster on television. Less chatty people who wouldn't talk to a pet (let alone the television) are so aware of a baby as a person that they wouldn't ignore her any more than they'd ignore an adult visitor. But there are other people who are the opposite of chatty, and feel as awkward and silly talking to a baby who can't even answer properly as they would feel if they were talking to themselves.

Parents talking about...

finding conversational care providers

❝It was easier to find care than conversation. In the first six months I was back at work, our baby had three different caregivers and although they were all kindly, none of them really talked to her as much as she needed. She had long daily hours with a bored young au pair who spoke no English and not much of anything. We tried a "stimulating" childcare center but it had too few adults to the numbers of babies and therefore no time for much talk. And then there was a relative who kept the TV on all day as a matter of course.❞

If you are naturally quiet, you can't just change yourself into a talkative person, and if you try to force yourself to chat you may sound so unnatural that your baby doesn't respond as she does to real communication. If this is the case, it may be helpful to set up a few situations that help you to talk easily to your baby, because her responsiveness to your engineered conversations is likely to ease you into more and more spontaneous talk.

Engineering conversation with babies

◆ Picture books can get anyone talking. Look at the pictures with your baby and tell her what the people in them are doing and saying, just as you would if she were three years old. Of course she won't understand most of what you're saying, but she will still enjoy the pictures and the talk. It's good for babies to have their own books, even from this early age. Luckily your baby doesn't need new books at the rate she needs new playthings, because she'll like having the same book repeated again and again. There's always your local children's library, too.

◆ A running commentary on what you are doing is also an easy kind of talking. Tell her about the meal you're cooking; name the vegetables you are peeling and let her hold one; ask her if the casserole smells nice and if she thinks Mommy will like it.

◆ Questions get your baby involved in communication with you. "Is that pretty?" "Where did it go?" "Is that warm enough?" Even "Who's Daddy's girl?" Written down it may look silly, and of course your baby won't understand the words or answer in words. But that doesn't

Modern technology has done nothing to lessen the sheer joy of books for babies.

From research

The how and why of language learning.
Just as many people assume that babies learn words by imitation, so they often assume that babies learn to speak so as to say what they feel or ask for what they want. Neither everyday observation nor research supports these simple ideas. Imitation plays only a very limited part in language learning; if you doubt that, ask yourself how a typical early toddler phrase, such as "See mans" can possibly be imitation when it's not something you, or any adult, would say. As to expressing needs, the first words your baby produces are very unlikely to have anything to do with what she needs or wants. She won't say "Bottle" or "Hug" or "Up." She may start with protest words: "Mine!" or even "No"—but chances are she will start with the name-labels of people or things that she cares about.

mean she won't answer at all: You may be surprised by her range of facial expressions, gestures, and intonation. There's no need to simplify what you say or how you say it. If what's interesting you is climate change or a sale at the supermarket, talk about those. Your baby will be just as interested as if you tell her about the darling little squirrel.
◆ Talk in whatever way comes most naturally to you. If that's baby talk, fine. If it's not, that's fine too.
◆ Some people feel more self-conscious chatting to a baby in front of other people than they do when they're alone. That's one good reason for trying to have one-on-one talking-time with your baby.

Another is that if she's one of twins, part of a big family, or has a somewhat jealous older sibling who is determined to direct most talk at himself instead of her, she may otherwise miss out.
◆ If you find it really difficult to chat to your baby, don't despair. It's not a constant flow of words she needs but conversation. Let her start it: Listen to her and respond, in words, every time she smiles and makes noises at you.

Communicating without words

Shortly before your baby is ready to speak (yes, that first word!) her use of language will become more and more sophisticated so that by her first birthday she may be talking to you in every way short of controlling her vocal apparatus sufficiently to produce spoken words. Hers is a language of gestures, so precise that any interested person can understand them. She nods and shakes her head for yes and no; she tells you where things are or what she wants handed to her by pointing; she hugs for hello, waves for good-bye, and sometimes enlarges those into hugging for sheer love and waving for "go away."

From research

Sign language. Babies who use American Sign Language or British Sign Language typically produce their first recognizable signs between seven and nine months, about three months earlier than most babies in hearing households produce their first spoken words. The explanation is probably part-biological and part social. Gaining control over the hands and fingers is easier for babies than gaining control over the vocal apparatus. Additionally, it's easier for parents to model, decipher, and manipulate babies' signs than their sounds.

Passionate proponents of baby-signing theorize that the demands of forming spoken words holds up the development of language, and suggest that earlier communication by signing is a real advantage. It has even been said, though not proven, that because signing babies can "say" what they want, they get less frustrated and have fewer tantrums.

How many signing and rhyming and tickling games do you know? How many does he?

If you want to teach your baby to sign it will do her no harm unless you become impatient with her progress. But bear in mind that whether they are taught or not all babies "sign," pointing to something they want; holding up their arms asking to be lifted; turning your face toward them with their hands when they want your attention. First-year communication without words between well-attached babies and parents is already good, so perhaps any extra effort you want to put in should go to language rather than signs. At this age your baby will probably love the kind of rhymes and songs and games that combine physical signing, words, and a dramatic climax. Have you tried "Itsy Bitsy Spider" or being "…a little teapot, short and stout"?

When is a word a word?

That's a straightforward-sounding question that's of interest to all parents, but it can only be answered approximately. We know that most babies produce their first "real" word during the 10th or 11th month, but there aren't credible exact figures because first words themselves are surprisingly difficult to identify, and researchers don't all make the same decisions. If a seven-month-old baby says "Mama" (see p. 230), nobody will classify the sound as a word because babies that age are not expected to produce any. But if that same baby makes the same sound when she's 10 months old, you may easily think she just said a real word because you are expecting words; waiting for them; looking for them among all that babble. Celebrating her first word, calling to report it to your mother and begging for your baby to say it again for Daddy to hear, it's easy to forget that the actual sound you've just elevated to word-status is one that she's been making for months.

There is no particular point in trying hard to identify your baby's first words, because it really isn't important whether she uses any or not at this stage. Much more important is how actual words emerge out of the fluent, expressive jargon-sounds and lots of gestures she's communicated with so far.

Talking in words means using one particular sound or set of sounds to refer to a particular person, object, event or action. Toward the end of this year your baby may go through a phase when she uses one word-like sound (let's say "Boo-bah") to refer to anything and everything that she wants or finds interesting: A snack, book, favorite game, and the family dog may all be called Boo-bah for a week or two. Meanwhile she will be trying to "decide" what sound to use as a name for any one particular object. She may ask for something important, such as her cuddly, by two or three different names. It will be clear from her behavior that it is her cuddly she is referring to, but she behaves as if she doesn't need any particular word. Any old word will do.

It will probably be around her first birthday that your baby gets the idea of using one sound to refer to one object and a different sound to refer to another. Even then the sound she uses may still not be a "word" in the conventional sense. First words are often what are technically named "own-words," word-like sounds that babies invent and attach to particular things or particular people. Is an "own-word" that isn't in the least similar to the correct noun really a word? It is a word if you know what she means by it, and if unlike that "Boobah" that could mean almost anything, it always means the same thing.

How babies pick out first "real" words

Babies live in an ocean of word sounds, rippling and crashing around them through almost every waking hour. Your baby doesn't copy them, she grabs hold of individual words that she has particularly noticed. The words she notices usually crop up in relation to things that interest her, are exciting, make her laugh. They crop up frequently, too, and in many different situations and contexts. It's that variety that gives her clues to what words mean. Your baby hears a word like "coat," for example, over and over again all winter as the one constant sound in a mass of different sentences. In one single day she may hear "Where's your coat?" "Oh, your coat is dirty!" "Let's take your coat off." "It's time to put your coat on." She may hear the same sentences from her father and her caregiver as well as from you, and whoever says it, that word "coat" is always associated with going in and out of the house (which she enjoys). Over days and weeks she will come to associate the sound with the coat and then she will know what the word means.

When she understands it, will she use it? Not necessarily, or not right away. Babies know the meanings of many more words than they actually say. Your baby is most likely to use that word "coat" when it suddenly means something joyful to her: You buy her a new one that is bright red and show her how it looks in the mirror. "Look at your new coat," you say: "COAT!" she exclaims.

From research

Learning to talk in two languages. Although early sounds are universal, the same for a Chinese as for a Norwegian baby, when children learn to speak they do it in the languages that are not just around them but actually spoken to them. If yours is a bilingual family and from the very beginning your baby is spoken to equally in each language, she will learn both. What's more she will reach milestones in both languages at about the same ages that a monolingual child would reach them in her only language.

Being brought up in a family where everyone speaks the same language at home but that is not the same as the language spoken in the community—at nursery and so on—is different. Some children acquire the "second language" remarkably quickly, but others, suddenly faced with a new language spoken by everyone but themselves, and nobody who speaks their "home language," stop speaking altogether for a while. If a baby or toddler cannot use the "community language," finding a friend who will play and talk with her in that language in a home setting is often very helpful.

Talking to your baby
so she talks to you

The more affectionate, interesting, two-way conversation your baby gets, the more easily her language will develop. But as we've discussed, not every adult is equally chatty, especially with a baby, and furthermore some types of talk are more positively useful than others.

Good circumstances for good talk:

◆ Be alone with your baby so you can talk directly to her with nobody to interrupt or compete for your attention. At this stage, when she is fishing recognizable words out of seas of sound, she cannot listen to general conversation or keep track of which adult is talking when everyone interrupts, trails sentences off unfinished, or uses expressive shrugs instead of words. Younger children of big families are sometimes actually delayed in their language development because they get so little opportunity for uninterrupted conversation with adults.

◆ Make sure that most of your baby's talking time that isn't with you is with someone she knows well. Since babies learn the meanings of words by hearing them over and over again in different sentences and with varying tones of voice, facial expressions, and body language from the speaker, it is not surprising that they learn best from beloved, or at least familiar, and

From research

Baby DVDs and videos. Although these are supposed to boost babies' language learning they may actually delay it. A large study published in 2007 showed that for every hour per day spent watching videos such as *Baby Einstein* or *Brainy Baby*, babies understood six to eight fewer words than babies who did not watch them. The reason is thought to be that babies are awake and alert for only a limited number of hours per day, so if they spend those hours in front of a screen instead of interacting with a real person they do not get the same linguistic and social experience.

friendly people. Even when she's a toddler your child may be unable to understand a stranger's words because the accompanying body language and tones of voice are unfamiliar. Think hard before you employ anyone to care for your baby who is not fluent in your language.

Good subjects
for good conversation:

◆ Talk about things that are physically present (the tree in the yard) so your baby can make an immediate connection between the object and the recurring key word.

◆ Talk about books. Big, clear illustrations in picture books make the same kind of immediate connection, but over a wider range of scenes than you could find in your daily life.

◆ Talk about anything that is making her interested, happy, or excited.

Good techniques
for good conversation:

◆ Help your baby to understand what words mean by using the nouns that are key labels when you talk to her: "Where is Toby?" rather than "Where is he?"

◆ Use your baby's own name ("Would Mary like one?") even if it does sound like baby talk. It's a vital label for her to learn because she will think of herself as "Mary" rather than as "me" or "I." English grammar makes pronouns horribly difficult for a baby to learn, because the correct word depends on who is speaking. I am "me" to myself, but I am "you" to you.

◆ Ham up your message, using lots of gestures and expressions. Babies with vocally outgoing parents sometimes learn exclamations among their very first words because they hear them so often and with such excited inflections. Let's hope the exclamations are "Oh dear!"; "Here we go!"; or perhaps "Zow-ee!"

◆ Take your baby's word-attempts seriously so she stays motivated to communicate in any way she can. If she says an own-word and gestures toward something at the other side of the room, look to where she is pointing, and list for her all the things that you can see that she might have meant. If you hit the right one, she'll repeat her

The more you talk to your baby the better; nobody else will ever listen to you with quite such affectionate concentration.

own-word with enormous pleasure and probably accept the correct version you then offer her.

◆ Respect your baby's own-words. Say the correct version, too, by all means, but don't try to make her say the word again "correctly." It will bore her (she wants to say something different now) and it won't teach her anything, because she is not imitating language but developing it. Her own-word will evolve into something more correct in its own good time,

but only in its own good time.

Pretending not to understand your baby until she uses a correct word is cheating. You are rejecting a piece of language that was the best she had to offer, and pretending that it wasn't good enough to make you understand when you did. Early speech is motivated by affection, excitement, and pleasure; you undermine all that when you refuse to hand her the ball she is pointing at because she calls it "bibee."

Not exactly a baby
—nor quite a child

The wiggly path from baby to toddler

During the months around your baby's first birthday he may seem to be changing so rapidly that you can hardly keep up. In fact being a loving parent may seem more and more demanding because you have to stay on your toes all the time, ready to alter the way you interact with him.

Learning to move around under his own steam often seems to give a baby's morale and confidence in himself a real boost, and learning to stand, maybe walk, and becoming able to understand a lot of adult words and say a few, are such dramatic developments that your baby may seem like a different person. He isn't, of course. The almost-toddler who crawls after you, holding up his arms to be lifted, is the same person as the baby who cried when you left the room leaving him on his play mat. He's bigger and more mobile, but he is still a baby: your baby. Don't expect too much of him too soon.

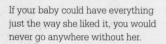

If your baby could have everything just the way she liked it, you would never go anywhere without her.

Do you sometimes feel you are being loved too much?

As we've seen, the last months of the first year are a time in a baby's life when his attachment to parents typically becomes so intense that he is very reluctant to be separated from them—for minutes, let alone hours. If you've managed to stay home with your baby so far but your financial situation now dictates that you go back to work, you may have to reorient yourself toward the adult world and away from the nursery. The baby clings, the outside world beckons, and parents are caught in the middle.

Balancing these demands is never easy, and it's made more difficult by the ever-deepening closeness that develops during your baby's first and most completely dependent year. By now you probably care at least as much about his feelings as about your own. Chances are that you cannot be happy if he is not, and that if he is unhappy, you'll feel responsible.

Keep self-blame under control

Babies are 100 percent dependent on parents and other adult caregivers, and those grown-ups have an alarming amount of power over babies' well-being and happiness. It's fine to take your power and the responsibility that comes with it seriously, but try not to be one of the many parents who always assumes that if things aren't perfect for their baby it's because they have done something wrong.

You are not all-powerful. However hard you try to protect your baby from danger and distress you cannot force the outside world to behave as you would wish, and sometimes misfortunes will strike him. Of course you desperately want the virus that is making him feverish to clear without giving him an earache; of course you're longing for the stalled train to start again so you won't be late enough home for him (or the nanny) to notice. But there is nothing you can do to make those things happen, so it is not your fault if they don't.

Sometimes things will happen to your baby that are your fault. You are people as well as parents, and people sometimes make mistakes. Feel responsible, by all means; feel guilty if you must, but don't wallow in it. It's far more useful to figure out what you can learn from a mistake and how to avoid a similar one in the future. When people become parents they tend to feel more guilty more often than ever before, but a little short-lived guilt goes a long way.

However hard you work at being a good parent, things will sometimes go wrong for your child and you will regret them whether you were responsible or not. But don't waste your energy castigating yourselves or each other for things that have already happened; instead use that energy to support him through the next problem and the next, helping him to cope in an age-appropriate way.

Helping your baby to manage without you

At this stage your baby probably can't cope calmly with being left with people he does not know, and shouldn't be expected to—especially if those people have to share their attention between him and other children. It's never good for a baby to be left with someone he doesn't know, but it's far better for him to be left with an experienced caregiver who can devote herself to talking and playing with him than to be left in

Parents talking about...
guilt
❝I left Joe with his dad while I went out with my girlfriends. He was still breast-fed but he ate lots of solid food, too, so I thought he wouldn't really need me till 6:00 or 7:00pm. I ran late, though, of course. There truly was a train delay, but I was already cutting it close when I should have allowed for delays. Of course the moment he started to nurse Joe forgot about two miserable hours crying. But my husband didn't. He says it was the worst time he's ever had as a father because nothing he offered Joe helped and he felt so completely helpless. He still hasn't quite forgiven me, and I certainly haven't forgiven myself.❞

a group. The baby room at the gym might be fun for the two of you together but not for him alone, and while any visit to the emergency room may be very upsetting for him, it will be much, much worse if you are not allowed, or can't find the courage, to stay with him through whatever must be done.

Babies only flourish when they are being cared for by people with whom they have close, friendly, and eventually mutually loving relationships, so the best way to make sure that they never need to be left with strangers is to make sure they have several of those. You are your baby's primary people. He loves you best and it's very unlikely that anything will ever change that, but if you are the only people in the world he trusts and feels close to, he's at constant risk of a huge upset if a car accident or other disaster takes you away from him. Loving a few other people as well makes life safer, so even if you don't plan on leaving him in daycare any time soon—because one of you plans to go on staying at home with him, or you mean to divide his care between the two of you—you'd be wise to help your baby get close to at least one other person, maybe a grandparent or a family friend, whom he comfortably accepts if you are not there.

Eating

Older babies and toddlers need to eat a lot—and that means that they need to eat often. Very rapid growth requires a high energy intake; much higher than you might expect of someone so very small.

Your baby may need half as many calories as you need yourself when you are not breast-feeding, but his stomach is still so small that he can't cope with three meals a day big enough to provide those calories. Can you imagine your baby eating a plateful of dinner half the size of yours? Like all babies and toddlers he needs to get those calories by eating much more often than adults, and his small meals and snacks should consist of energy-rich foods rather than foods that take up a lot of space for relatively few calories.

That means that a lot of the contemporary "healthy eating" messages that are aimed at families—and especially recommended to very young children to prevent them from becoming obese during the elementary school years—aren't appropriate for babies, or indeed for children under five. Sweet foods should certainly be limited, since although sugar contains lots of calories it brings no useful nutrients along with it, and is damaging to teeth. Sugary drinks—even "pure fruit" juices—are best avoided as much as possible.

From research

Juice-damage. Several studies of trends in American eating behaviors have reported a "substitution effect" such that babies and toddlers who are allowed fruit juice and sweetened fruit drinks and sodas come to "exchange" them for milk, with damaging effects on their overall nutrition. Obesity, failure to thrive, chronic diarrhea, cavities, and shortage of vital nutrients, especially calcium, have all been linked to free or excessive consumption of these drinks.

However, a "no snacks between meals" policy would be disastrous for a baby, and he needs a high-energy rather than a high-fiber diet. In fact babies and small children don't need much "roughage"; it takes up space in those small stomachs that is better occupied by higher-calorie foods, and too much of it may prevent him from absorbing necessary iron from his food and may even give him diarrhea. So don't feel that it's always better to give your baby brown rice and pasta, and whole-meal or whole-grain bread instead of white. He should not have a low-fat diet either, since fats are the most concentrated source of calories, and also contain essential fat-soluble vitamins. When you buy cow's milk to cook for him or dairy products such as yogurt, cheese, or ice cream, choose full-fat versions.

What about protein?

Everyone needs to eat foods that provide protein, but children especially need protein because their bodies use its constituents not just for bodily repair and replacement as adults do, but also as the building materials for growth. However, nobody needs as much protein as adults in rich Western countries usually eat, and although food manufacturers use "high protein" as an advertising point in baby and toddler foods, they vastly overplay the concentration and total amounts children need.

The protein that we need in our food isn't a single ingredient, like sugar, but consists of different amino acids. Our bodies can make most of those amino acids out of the others, so as to arrive at useful protein. Bread, potatoes, beans, peas, and grains, for example, contain amino acids that complement each other, so eating a mixture gives an adult—a vegan, perhaps—a complete protein intake. However a child's growth

demands some particular amino acids that his body cannot manufacture out of others, so he needs to eat them ready-made. These amino acids, vital for growth, are in foods that come from animal sources—like meat, fish, eggs, milk, cheese, and other dairy products. Those used to be thought of—and named—"first-class" protein foods, as if protein from all vegetable sources was second best. It isn't, of course; it is simply incomplete for a growing child until a small quantity of animal protein is added to it. The animal protein can be from animal products such as eggs, milk, cheese, and yogurt, rather than meat or fish. That's why a vegetarian diet that allows dairy is fine for growing children. When your baby eats a combination of vegetable and animal proteins—such as oatmeal and milk, or egg on toast—the result is a dish in which the protein is just as "first-class" as it would be in a helping of meat or fish.

Making sure your baby gets what he needs

Milk is an (almost) perfect food and perfects many other foods that are eaten at the same time. So as long as milk is the major part of your baby's diet, you don't have to worry about his going short of anything except iron. Once milk has become secondary, though, figuring out exactly what he should eat is somewhere between complicated and impossible. Total food needs and requirements for specific nutrients vary both from baby to baby and from one day to the next, and figuring out what he gets from specific portions of food is even more complex; in fact it's impossible. There are books that will tell you exactly what is in 1 oz (25 g) of potato, but did you weigh the potato you cooked for him? How did you cook it: plain boiled or mashed with some milk and butter? And how much of it did he actually eat? If you offer your baby a wide range of foods—for snacks as well as for meals—and in the course of a week he eats at least a tiny bit of each of them in various combinations, he is willingly eating that much-recommended (but not always chosen) "balanced diet." You can be confident that he's getting everything his body needs; anything that isn't in breakfast will be in lunch.

A baby who doesn't eat much of a mixture day by day may still do so week by week. A lot of older babies and toddlers go through food jags, wanting nothing but plain bread (and their milk) for days at a time. But if your baby sticks to bread for three days he will probably switch to something else on day four, and the new passion may be for cheese or fruit.... Stay calm: he doesn't

Babies like to be together but can't begin to understand each other's feelings.

need to have every nutrient at every meal or even every day. Just keep *offering* various foods at mealtimes so that there's something different available when he's ready for it.

Not all babies (and even fewer toddlers) eat anything and everything that is put before them. Quite a lot dislike and refuse almost everything that is conventionally regarded as good for them, especially the first six times it is offered. Their parents decide that they cannot be properly nourished and the seeds of anxiety (and therefore of eating problems) are sown.

While eating a wide variety of foods is the easy way to make sure of getting enough of everything, it is not the only way. No food is essential to a child's health and wellbeing because any nutrients that are in the food he rejects will be in another food—which he may love. Even milk, which used to be thought absolutely necessary for children and is extraordinarily useful at this stage of life, is just another good food, and some children actually do better without it because they do not easily tolerate lactose (milk sugar). The valuable proteins, minerals, and vitamins milk contains are all in other foods, too, especially the many foods made from it. There's nothing useful in a cup of milk that isn't in a cup of yogurt, and there's nothing better about the hard-boiled egg your baby hates than the egg-containing pancake for which he has a passion (this week). Still, if your baby does not seem to eat enough, eats too few foods to make you feel sure that he's getting the vitamins and minerals he needs, and doesn't like any other source of animal protein, milk is the first line of reassurance. As long as he has two breast-feeds per day or a pint (16 ounces) of baby milk, he will not go short of anything, except possibly iron, no matter what else he does or does not eat.

He doesn't have to drink all his milk straight, of course. There's milk in foods you cook for him; and foods you buy: yogurt, ice cream, and cheese. Given the chance, your baby may develop a passion for cheese: in cubes to eat in his fingers, grated over vegetables, in sauces, or spread on bread.

With that much milk in his diet, your baby will not go short of protein or essential fats. The

> # From research
>
> **Vegan diets.** Vegetarian diets that allow dairy products, and perhaps eggs, are no barrier to a good diet for growing children, but vegan diets that exclude all animal products, including milk, are dramatically different, especially if the baby is not breast-fed. Soy-milk formulas are an imperfect substitute for cow's milk; Vitamin B12 is found only in animal products; providing enough calcium without dairy products is difficult, and an adequate intake of protein probably depends on using tofu and other soy-based products. Unless you yourselves are very knowledgeable about the implications of strict vegetarianism for growing children, you will need ongoing dietary advice from an interested health professional.

minerals other than calcium and iron that he needs—such as phosphorus—are widely distributed, so he is bound to get enough, whatever he eats or drinks.

He will not go short of calcium, either. This mineral, vital for the proper development of growing bones and teeth and for the functioning of muscles and for blood clotting, is more widely distributed than many people realize. There is calcium in bread, for example, and in all cereals. However, milk is a more concentrated and universally accepted source, and that pint a day will ensure your baby's or toddler's intake.

Milk doesn't help much with the provision of iron. If your baby has adequate stores in his body they will be used and re-used, so he doesn't need iron-rich food every day. However, the stores of iron a healthy full-term baby is born with are often running low by the middle of the year, especially if he has been fed with formula rather than breast milk. Breast milk is not rich in iron, but the type of iron in breast milk is far better absorbed than the iron with which baby formulas are fortified. After the middle of the year, or whenever he is weaned from the breast, your baby's diet will need to ensure that his increasing iron needs are met.

The type of iron found in meat ("heme" iron) is better absorbed than "non-heme," the type found in vegetables, legumes, cereals, and fruits, but if you or your baby prefer a vegetarian diet, non-heme iron from foods such as fortified cereals, green leafy vegetables, fruits such as apricots, and peas, beans, and legumes, should provide entirely adequate quantities of iron. Babies absorb iron more efficiently if they eat something rich in Vitamin C at the same meal. If your baby has a daily drink of fruit juice, give it to him with his cereal at breakfast or his cheese sandwich at lunch. And of course vegetables and fruits automatically provide both together.

Vitamins

The essential vitamins are widely distributed, so individuals who eat enough food will usually get enough vitamins. However, babies and toddlers who are having a very un-hungry phase, or eating very oddly, sometimes benefit from having three vital ones in (carefully rationed) daily drops.

◆ **Vitamin A:** Apart from liver—which not many modern babies eat—the main sources in the diet are milk (especially baby formula, which is fortified), butter, or fortified margarine. Many children like carrots, which, although they do not themselves contain Vitamin A, do contain "carotene," from which bodies can make their own. Your child will probably get enough from these sources, but if he is having a multi-vitamin supplement it will include Vitamin A as a safety measure.

◆ **Vitamin C:** Although it is widely available in fruits and vegetables, not only green ones but also roots such as potatoes, Vitamin C is destroyed both by light and heat. That makes it surprisingly difficult to ensure a steady supply—which is why it will be included in multivitamin drops. Vegetables that have been long-displayed or overcooked may contain very little Vitamin C. It is easier to provide from fruit, which is often eaten raw and therefore protected from heat, and if it is cooked, the cooking liquid is usually drunk as juice. Citrus fruits are the best source of all, of course, because as well as being served raw, they have skins that keep out the light, but delay introducing citrus until after the first birthday, because the acidic fruit can cause painful diaper rashes. Of course a daily serving of a Vitamin C–enriched baby juice will serve the same purpose, but be aware that if you offer juice at all it may become difficult to avoid giving it to him more and more often when he is old enough to know what he wants and beg for it.

◆ **Vitamin D:** The only concentrated food sources, apart from fortified baby formula and baby cereals, are egg yolk and fatty fishes. Pale skin (even just on hands and face) makes its own Vitamin D when exposed to sunlight, but supplementation may be essential for dark-skinned children, especially in winter.

Fussy eaters

Problems over an older baby's or toddler's eating dominate the lives of whole families for months. In some families, mealtime conversation consists entirely of nursery rhymes and games designed to "fly" a spoonful of food into the baby's mouth, and others never go out to eat because they can't face food battles in public.

You can do a lot to avoid those battles by cultivating relaxed and accepting attitudes now. Try to help your baby feel that eating is something pleasurable that he himself does because he wants and enjoys the food, rather than something he has to do because adults want him to. He eats, actively, rather than being fed, passively. And he eats for himself, not for you. It's far too soon to expect much (if anything)

From research

Iron absorption. Although breast milk does not contain large amounts of iron, approximately 50 percent of its iron is absorbed, compared to only about 7 percent absorption of the iron added to formula, and about 4 percent absorption from infant cereals.

Animal foods, like red meat, fish, and poultry, are excellent sources of iron because they are most easily absorbed by the body. Iron from other sources will not be as easily absorbed. The body retains only about five percent of the iron from non-animal sources.

If you want to avoid irritation now and eating problems later, let your baby eat what she wants however she finds easiest.

of him in the way of "table manners," and demands that he manage a spoon and not use fingers and fists are liable to make him lose interest in the meal altogether. He needs to feel that getting the food he wants is what matters, not getting it in any particular way. Rigid rules about what he may eat with what may spoil mealtimes too. If he wants to dip cheese in chocolate pudding or stir bread into jelly, why should you care? Every society has its own conventions about what goes with what. He will adopt yours in the end, but this is the beginning.

A surefire cause of eating problems is using food as a bribe or reward or withholding it—or threatening to—as a punishment. Above all, avoid making sweet foods seem more desirable than savory ones by saying "no dessert until you finish your meat." Your baby should eat as much as he is hungry for of whatever is available. If he is not hungry, he should not eat.

If you ever find yourself getting exasperated over your baby's eating (or non-eating) habits, make the decision to go to less trouble over his food. If you spend half the morning preparing something special for him and it goes right onto the floor, you're bound to get fed up. Give him either the baby-friendly version of the same dish the rest of the family is eating, or something really simple—bread and butter with grated cheese and grated carrot, for example—and don't even think about cutting the bread into

From research

Food fights. Trying to make your baby eat when, or what, she doesn't want is not only psychologically but also physiologically contraindicated. Any kind of excitement, especially the anxiety or fear that builds up when a parent is angry, blocks hunger and may even close down the digestive process. The more you urge, the less she'll eat.

animal shapes. As long as a baby is reasonably well and happy, he will not starve in the midst of plenty (i.e. milk and manageable solid foods). Try to trust him to know how much is enough, because worrying about how much he eats will set you up for problems later on. It might help you to look at his growth on a chart: If the upward curve of weight and length is steady over time, he is getting enough to eat. Also look at his energy levels: If he is lively and active, he's not wanting for food.

If you are still tempted to push food at him, take him to be checked by his pediatrician. Even if she can see at a glance that your baby is well-nourished, she should be happy to give you the reassurance you need. She will know how important it is for you to relax about your baby's eating before he enters opinionated toddlerhood!

Growing

Your baby's growth rate slows to around half what it was in the first six months as the end of his first year approaches. It would be pointless to weigh him every week if he is in good health, but if you did you'd probably find that he gained only around 2 ounces (55 g) a week.

The increase in the circumference of your baby's head and his length (or height) gains are so gradual that accurate weekly measurement at home would be impossible as well as unnecessary; in the course of the half year he will probably grow taller by 3–4 inches (8–10 cm).

Unless he was born pre-term, has been ill, or had serious feeding troubles earlier in the year, three-monthly weighing and measuring will be enough, enabling you to see his overall growth.

If you enter your baby's measurements on his growth chart, you'll find that they still follow the general shape of the percentile curves, and he may still be in or close to the segment where he began. His growth curves may be less steady than they were a few months ago, though.

A severe illness or a succession of minor ones may mean that he gains no weight for a while but that when he is well again he gains extra fast to make up. Similarly, he may gain rather little during a period when he does not eat much solid food because he is resisting being weaned from the breast, but gain rather fast when he develops a passion for cheese sandwiches. These minor ups and downs are of no significance, since it is only the shape of his overall weight gain that matters. The more often you weigh him the more likely you are to notice, and worry, about them.

You may find yourself worrying not only about your baby's weight and height, but also about the shape and proportions of his body. When he first begins to pull himself to a standing position, his body is still that of a baby who lives on all fours, rather than that of a child living on two legs. All this will gradually change during your baby's second year, but right now you may think he looks distinctly odd. His head is still very large for his small body (although the contrast is not quite as great as it was when he was a newborn) and he seems to have almost no neck between the two. His tummy is large and protuberant, especially in comparison with his shoulders and chest, which are thin. His legs seem bowed, and his feet are flat to the floor, with no arches. The point, of course, is that he is still the right shape for crawling rather than walking. It will take him the better part of a year to become the right shape for life as a child on two legs.

Twin tip

As the first year comes to an end, parents who were told that their pre-term, low birth-weight twins would "catch up" may become worried all over again because their babies' development still lags behind that of other babies born at full term on the same day. Pre-term babies' real age is a conceptual age rather than a birth date. On that basis, babies born six weeks pre-term are and will remain six weeks younger than full-term babies with the same birth date. Such babies do indeed catch up, but in the sense that a six-week age difference at one year is far less significant than a six-week age difference at six months, and will be less and less significant as the children grow older.

Babies like these, healthy and growing well, are so different from each other in both height and weight that comparing them will leave somebody anxious. Check your baby's growth on his percentile chart.

Changing sleeping patterns

As your baby moves toward the end of her first year, you will probably notice changes in her sleeping. The main difference is not so much in her sleeping hours (though they may diminish a little), but in their changing pattern.

Instead of dividing her sleeping time more or less evenly between night and day and tending to fall asleep after feeds, your baby is now likely to sleep 11 or 12 hours each night and for two separate nap periods, each lasting anywhere from 20 minutes to 3 hours.

The separation of sleeping from eating, and the concentration of most of her sleeping into a long period at night will both tend to make your lives easier. But don't expect too much. That 12-hour night is still quite likely to be broken by at least one awakening, and often by several. And now that your baby is older, she can no longer be counted on to sleep whenever she needs to and wherever she finds herself. By around nine months she'll become able to keep herself awake, or be kept awake, by external noise and excitement or by internal tension about separating from you by going to sleep. And once she is capable of keeping herself awake, she often will.

If you have trouble putting your baby to bed at night, don't add to your exhausted irritation by assuming that her behavior is your fault or her naughtiness, and that most babies go to bed and to sleep without a murmur. On the contrary: This is one of the leading problems of parenting as the first year comes to an end, and you will be lucky if you avoid it completely.

Once your baby can—and at least sometimes does—keep herself awake on purpose, you can no longer assume that she will sleep if she is tired and that if she does not sleep she is not tired. The reverse can be true. She can now get overtired and too wound up and tense to relax into the sleep she badly needs.

Immediate triggers for new going-to-bed problems

If you are going to have going-to-bed difficulties, they are likely to begin when your baby stops having a bedtime breast- or bottle-feed, whether that is when she is eight months or 18 months old. Problems may have nothing to do with your baby's feeding, though, and everything to do with general upsets such as being in the hospital, or traveling away from home. Whether it's a trauma or a treat, breaking your baby's routines can leave her feeling disoriented and unable to fall easily to sleep. Since bedtime trouble is easier to prevent than to cure, think carefully before you make any optional change to your baby's surroundings during this age period. Even being moved out of your bedroom to a lovely new bedroom of her own can cause trouble.

Protecting your baby's external environment won't always avoid going-to-sleep trouble because that trouble may come from inside your baby. A common source is the passionate desire to be with you, which comes with the growing attachment that is typical of the last months of the year, and her resulting anxiety about being separated from you. Your baby may cry bitterly when you start to leave her alone, but even if you stay with her she may struggle to stay awake because going to sleep takes her away from you.

The more successfully you managed problems with going to sleep alone earlier in the year (see p. 192) the less likely you are to encounter them now, and the easier it will be to manage them. But be alert and take action as soon as you realize that trouble is brewing.

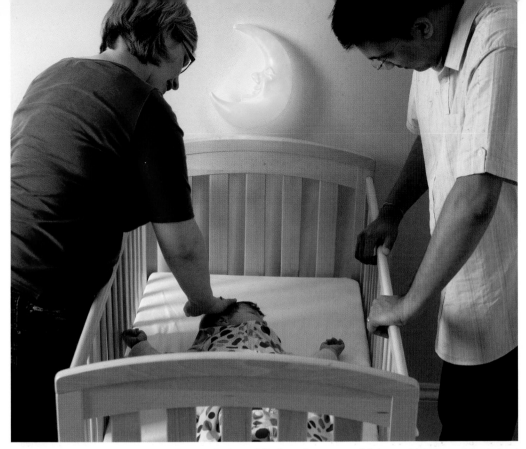
Routines and rituals help prevent as well as cure bedtime difficulties. A two-person lullaby put this baby straight to sleep!

Coping with going-to-bed problems

Try to narrow the gap for your baby between being awake and with you and being asleep and without you. If she is suddenly carried from the friendly living room to a cool dim bedroom, put in a crib she knows she cannot get out of and left alone, it's not difficult to understand why she cries. We don't know what she thinks, but her sobs sound desolate.

Start her bedtime routine long before the actual parting and try to make it such an enjoyable part of her day that she recognizes it with pleasure. Maybe it starts alone with you, having supper in the kitchen, but continues with a rambunctious bath time when her father gets home from work, and then some ritualized wind-down time of stories, songs, and good-night visits to people, pets, and pictures, which gives her a count-down.

When the moment comes, your baby is more likely to accept being in bed if she doesn't feel herself completely cut off. She will probably settle more comfortably if the door is open, letting in both light from the hall outside and sounds from the grown-ups. And she's far more likely to be able to let you go away if you do it gradually, withdrawing a bit at a time, than if you just walk away from her. "Hanging in there" or "popping in and out" are still good solutions. *(See p. 194.)*

If, like many nine- to twelve-month-old babies, yours finds it even more difficult to separate from mother than father, try adding her father into the bedtime mix. If the baby has both of you for a couple of minutes (time for a duet perhaps) you may then be able to withdraw, leaving her father to sing the last song and give her the last kiss.

Eventually your baby is going to be on her own, of course, but even if she would rather if one of you stayed, that's not at all the same as being left feeling stricken and bereft by your departure. If you can keep the whole nightly business peacefully low-key, these are months during which she will learn to use whatever comfort habits she has developed *(see p. 203)* to help herself cope with being without you.

Night-waking

Although babies can, and often do, sleep solidly for a 12-hour period, some wake frequently (even if only briefly).

◆ **Disturbances from outside:** Your baby no longer sleeps as deeply as she did when she was younger, so you can't assume that once she is asleep, almost nothing will disturb her. External events—such as visitors or parents tiptoeing into her room—may easily wake her, so leave her door open and a nightlight on so you can check on her from a distance.

If your baby is being woken by outside stimuli, it will probably be worth your while to spend time and imagination on reorganizing her sleeping arrangements to minimize disturbance. If you are short on space, you may need to take a particularly hard look at the family's shared bedrooms. Once your baby passed the six-month mark, it may have seemed obvious to move her

If it's you rather than your baby who needs reassuring visits, make sure you can peek without disturbing her.

out of your bedroom and in with an older child. But while such an arrangement often works well for everyone, it sometimes does not. If your older child is having nightmares, the baby may be woken by his crying and by your soothing visits, and then take longer to settle afterward than the older child. Would you rather move her back into your room? If the room your baby sleeps in is right on a main road with traffic passing all night, secondary double-glazing on its windows would make a big difference, heavy curtains would offer some help, and both would be best of all.

A very cool room isn't dangerous to her any more, and getting chilly probably won't actually wake her. However it will make her more liable to wake up if something else—internal or external—disturbs her. If you want your baby to stay snugly warm all night even when the heating goes off, consider using a sleep sack, which will keep her warmth insulated in.

If you are going to use a sleep sack, though, start it before your baby learns to stand up in her crib. If you put her in a sleep sack for the first time when she is used to pulling herself to standing, she might do so all the same, find her feet trapped, and fall.

If your baby has a diaper rash she may keep waking because every time she pees the urine stings. If her bottom is even pink, put a thick coating of a silicone-based protective cream on it at night.

Unless you are very lucky, teething pain when she is cutting her first molars, and the discomforts of colds in the head will also contribute to some bad nights for you both toward the end of the year. You won't be able to prevent this kind of waking, but you can probably help her sleep peacefully for the rest of the night by giving her an appropriate dose of a children's liquid acetaminophen.

From research

Night-waking. Studies have been made using video cameras installed in babies' rooms overnight. These have shown babies waking and going off to sleep again without anyone knowing, far more frequently than parents imagine.

From research

Nightmares and tantrums. A nightmare is more likely following a tantrum during the day. It's not clear whether the stress that triggered the tantrum also triggers the nightmare, or whether the stress of a tantrum triggers the nightmare.

Twin tip

Twins are more and more likely to disturb each other's sleep as they get older, especially if one is more wakeful than the other. If they have always slept together, you may dread the upset that separating them might cause—but if you have space to give them separate rooms, the long-term gains might be worth short-term upheaval. Having their own space will not only allow each of them his own sleeping pattern, but also reduce the extent to which either twin depends on the other for going to sleep.

◆ **Disturbances from inside:** Most of the night-crying in this age group is caused by disturbances that come from within the baby, and they are usually far more difficult to deal with. A baby may wake whenever her sleep lightens. If she does not depend on action from you to put her to sleep and finds herself awake but perfectly comfortable, she may drop off again without telling you about it. But if your baby expects to be put to sleep with feeding or rocking or patting, she will have to call for you; if she finds herself not only awake but also anxious or afraid, she will cry for you.

Waking in the night, obviously terrified, is not unusual around this age. Your baby has clearly had a "bad dream"—a nightmare—though of course there is no way you can discover what she has dreamed about, because she doesn't have the words to tell you. Despite her screams on awakening and her obvious fear when you reach her, your baby will probably be easily reassured and quick to drop back to sleep.

A quick return to sleep may not be the end of it though. Some babies wake in this way several times each night and every night for months. If your baby seems to be falling into this pattern, it's possible that something in her waking life is stressing her, and that lessening the stress would reduce the night-fears. If her father has been working away from home, for instance, the baby may be missing him more than either of you had realized. If she has just started in daycare, she may be finding the separation from you and home hard to manage, or, she may be missing the one-on-one attention she has been accustomed to.

Moving toward the end of babyhood can put a lot of strains on your baby, and slowing up on any you can identify may help. If you are trying to wean her from her bottle, for example (see p. 186), you may be going faster than she can easily bear. A return to some sucking—perhaps a bedtime feed—could bring you all more peace.

Above all make sure that bedtime is a relaxed and enjoyable part of her day so she goes to sleep feeling surrounded by love and protection. That's no guarantee that she'll stay asleep all night, of course, but it may help. Certainly the opposite kind of bedtime—the kind that ends with her crying herself to sleep—tends to go with frequent waking.

Parents talking about...
broken nights

❝We were determined not to have our baby sleeping with us when she was tiny. Although she's never been a good sleeper, we managed, and we thought we'd successfully moved her out of our bedroom and into her own. Wrong. She's been waking again and again every night for the past two weeks, and I'm so exhausted I can't see straight. Finally two nights ago I took her into our bed the first time she woke and she slept like an angel for the rest of the night. I'm human again. We sleep in a family bed, but hey, what's that compared with sleep deprivation?❞

Patterns of night-waking

If your baby wakes several times each night, you may feel as exhausted as you did when she needed frequent night feedings. A lot of parents cope by taking babies into bed with them, and certainly doing that the first time she wakes may bring peace for the rest of the night. Try not to do it out of sheer desperation and against your own intentions, though (see p. 131); once she has started sleeping with you she isn't likely to go happily back to sleeping on her own when her cold is better or her bad dreams have stopped. Being taken into bed with you in the middle of the night may eventually make problems with bedtime too. If you hold her closely snuggled while she goes to sleep at 3:00am, why should she be content to drop off alone at 7:00pm? Trying to persuade or even force her to sleep in her crib rather than your bed may give you the worst nights of all....

You're more likely to manage without taking your baby into bed with you if you go to her as soon as real crying begins. If she's just muttering to herself, it's worth holding back in the hope that she'll settle again, but once she is really crying delay will only give her time to get more upset. If it was a nightmare that woke her, she'll probably settle as soon as she's aware of your presence. With practice, you can murmur and stroke her back to calm sleep and roll back into your own bed without entirely waking up.

If she's definitely—loudly—awake but not for any obvious reason, you could try to get her back to sleep with the same techniques suggested for bedtimes. As before, these are compromises between ignoring your baby's crying, leaving her on her own to exhaust herself and give up all hope of getting you to come to her, and picking her up and taking her to sleep with you.

Those approaches, especially the one called "popping in and out," can be dressed up so as to dignify it as a "method." But how can a complete and absent stranger really help you to decide how many minutes you should stay away for the first night, and whether or not you should pat your baby's back on night three? Your only real guides are your baby and your own feelings. If she cries hysterically when you try to leave after what was meant to be a one-minute reassurance visit, you'll probably want to stay with her until she calms down, and you'll be right to do so. But if a few minutes later her crying sounds whiny and fretful rather than frightened or sad, maybe you won't go in after five minutes but will give her a bit longer to settle herself.

There's often a big part for fathers in all this, especially if your baby is breast-fed or has been until recently. Weaning from the breast can easily get muddled with separating from the breast bearer. Your baby is less likely to mind being left if she doesn't think about nursing, and she's less likely to think about nursing if she doesn't smell breast milk. Even if nursing is long forgotten, or your baby was always bottle-fed, she may find separating from you even more difficult than separating from her father. Leaving her father to cope in the night is worth a try, anyway.

Wakeful babies

Having a baby who needs less sleep than most may sometimes feel to you like a negative, but from the point of view of your baby's development, it's actually a positive. More hours awake and playing mean more hours of exploring and learning and practicing. As we saw earlier though (*see p. 202*), the more of their daytime hours babies spend awake, the more adult attention and companionship they need—and the more bored they will become if they don't get it. If your baby is cared for partly by somebody else—in a daycare center or with a nanny, for example—you will need to be sure that her wakefulness is accepted and extra company and play is forthcoming.

Don't abandon daytime naps just because your baby only dozes for a few minutes and sometimes not at all. She may enjoy a rest from her demanding life just as you enjoy a rest from her, and be happy to spend half an hour or more comfortably settled in her crib with toys to play with and interesting things to look at. Go to her as soon as you hear the first grumbles of boredom, though, even if she's only been on her own for 15 minutes. Otherwise she is bound to begin to feel that her crib is a prison, and be less happy to go into it next time.

Sometimes a baby is busy and happy alone in her crib. If so, it's fine to leave her until she calls.

However passionately you love your baby, you're a rare parent if you don't sometimes long for her to go to sleep so that you can just be yourself—or be by yourselves—for a while. A one-year-old who can be relied upon to go to sleep by 8:00pm, stay asleep until 7:00am and then nap from 2:00 to 3:30pm is very much easier to care for, be patient with, even love, than a baby who wakes a lot at night and stays awake all day. In the long run, though, wakeful babies have a great deal going for them because they live much fuller lives, need adults' help in doing so, and therefore learn and develop as fast and as far as they possibly can. You, and any other caregivers, have to find ways of getting on with adult life while sharing it with the baby, rather than dividing the days and evenings into periods of babycare and periods of adult activity. It isn't always easy, but your motivation and your reward will be that plenty of waking time spent with interested adults doing interesting things will probably turn her into a particularly sociable and competent toddler.

Learning through play

During the second half of the first year, play as we usually think of it—especially play with toys—often takes second place in the daily lives of babies who are putting most of their energy into sitting up alone, managing to cross the room by some idiosyncratic "crawl," or getting onto their own two legs.

Practicing and eventually reaching those milestone abilities costs babies more physical effort and takes more sheer physical courage than most people realize. If it's "play," it's only "fun" in the same painful sense that learning to dance in pointe shoes or ice-skates is fun. Unlike older children who choose highly demanding physical activities, no baby gives up. Some move along more rapidly than others, but none of them just decides that it's too difficult and stops trying, not even those who have physical or neurological problems to overcome. Fortunately for their continuing development, babies have a powerful built-in drive for mastery that keeps them moving on. Once your baby can crawl, he will crawl, and keep on crawling. Only being confined in seats and cribs will stop him. A baby who can pull up to standing position will keep on doing so no matter how scared he was when the floor lamp he chose to pull up on toppled onto him, and once he can stand holding on, he'll go on trying and wobbling and falling and trying again until he can stand alone and begin to walk.

Your baby has built-in motivation to press on just as far as he can. Don't plant your newly cruising baby on his feet in the middle of the floor because you think "you don't need to hold on; you can walk; try it." He would if he could, and when the time comes when he can, he will.

Babies do not begin to crawl or walk because they want to go to particular places under their own steam or to do particular things; these new physical achievements are their own reward. They do gradually earn babies huge increases in autonomy, though. Instead of having to rely on adults to take them to see things and to bring them things to explore and experiment with, they can begin to go places and get things for themselves, acting on their own ideas about what they want to do. It will be a long time before your baby is able to ask you to bring him a particular throw pillow so he can examine its fringe, but it won't be long at all before he can go and get it. The fact that your baby becomes more able to go places and do things without adults does not necessarily mean that he wants to, though. In fact if your baby could have everything exactly as he chose, he'd probably have you with him all the time, watching (though not interfering with) everything he does. His attachment to you is growing as the year passes, and he is even more likely to be clingy now than three months ago.

Safe physical freedom

Your baby is more eager to practice crawling or standing for its own sake than he is to get to somewhere or reach something. For him, sitting, crawling, standing, and eventually walking, are occupations in themselves, so what he needs for his play, more than any toy, is safe floor space and freedom to use it. If you haven't yet organized a play space for him, you need to do so now. Provided you and your family are not very short of space overall, it's not difficult. You may need to pad your baby's knees and head (and your nerves) with carpet tiles or matting over "his" part of a stone or tiled floor. If he'll use part of the living room floor, you may want to protect its carpet with a washable rug or the kind of playmats that are printed with road systems, farms, or other backgrounds—a good investment because they will soon contribute to play with toys and go on doing so for years.

Nothing gives a nearly-walking baby more pleasure than this kind of baby walker.

In many households, the kitchen is the adult center of operations. If yours is too cramped to be safe or practical for the baby to play in, you may be able to commandeer a piece of floor in a dining room that opens out of it, leaving the door between the two open but with a safety gate across it so he can see in, but not get in. With thought, though, a larger kitchen can itself be made safe enough for play as long as it is supervised. It's not only the obvious dangers like sharp knives and poisonous liquids you need to think about, but also less-obvious dangers, such as recycling bins (he'll unpack them, complete with sharp tin cans, if he gets the chance) and disgusting cat food, which he'll sample…. This floor space will be absolutely basic to all your lives for many months, even if there's a beautifully equipped playroom or nursery just waiting. Babies and young toddlers don't want their own special places out of sight of adults, they want to be where you are. If you leave your baby in a playroom alone, he will be extremely lonely and bored, as well as at risk, without your constant presence. You will probably either abandon using it altogether, or move in yourself, taking your laptop, your phone, and whatever else you need to get on with your life while keeping him company.

If you are already very short of living space, don't let that make you feel that setting up special space for your baby is somewhere between ludicrous and impossible. The less space there is for everybody, the more crucial separating it out becomes. If a baby or toddler plays in an already-crowded family living room, he is bound to endanger himself, other people's possessions, and the patience of any older children, unless his needs have been provided for. A playpen provides a small space where he is safe both from wrongdoers and from wrongdoing, but is not a complete answer because a baby who is constantly confined cannot do and learn all that he should, even if he goes into the playpen without protest.

Your baby will feel less restricted in a play corner marked off less formally, perhaps behind a sofa that he can eventually use to pull up on. And since what your baby needs is safe space to move around, the most unexpected and unprepossessing areas of hallway can often be useful provided any stairs are gated. As for outdoor spaces: Any porch, yard, or balcony that you can make safe can expand your baby's horizons—and perhaps enable you to let him have finger paints or sand—even if they are not large enough for crawling around in.

Parents talking about…

playpens

❝ I couldn't have managed without a playpen, but I didn't put her in it: I let her three-year-old sister use it as a place of safety for drawing and playing with dolls that otherwise got grabbed. ❞

Twin tip

A playpen can be invaluable if your twins are at very different stages of development—so that one can literally walk on the other—or during times when they can neither "play nicely" nor leave each other alone. Put one baby in the playpen and let the other play outside it so that they can see each other, even pass toys if they want. Be sure to offer fair turns, so that the pen does not come to seem like a punishment or a privilege.

Playthings

Your baby probably doesn't need new toys as much as he needs freedom to move around and explore. He needs playthings, of course, but many of the toys he's had for months will seem new and newly interesting to him once he can handle them while sitting up, and get them for himself by crawling. However, there are a few categories of plaything that he may not have had before and that he will especially enjoy because they fit into his current stage of development.

Things that roll along are frustrating to babies who can't crawl, because they keep escaping. But now that your baby can chase after them, he will probably enormously enjoy

"I do this, and *that* noise happens…" Discovering cause and effect and his power to make things happen is thrilling.

Staying safe

Toys. Remember that anything your baby holds or even touches will be sucked or chewed. Watch out for things that are safe when whole but sharp when cracked, such as yogurt containers. Choose large objects (no marbles or beads, however much she would like them) and check all wheeled toys for sharp or protruding parts, especially around the axles.

balls, little wheeled toys, and household things that roll, such as toilet-paper rolls or apples.

Once he has learned how to let go of things without there being a table or adult hands underneath them, your baby will enjoy dropping things out of his high chair or stroller—even if you wish he wouldn't. He will learn to throw things too; not only permitted "indoor" balls but games that are hilarious and forbidden, like throwing things out of your shopping cart as fast as you put them in.

The more he handles different objects, the more your baby will learn about cause and effect. Adults feel like they've always known that when

you drop something it falls down—never up. But that most basic law of gravity is something everyone has to learn, and your baby is learning it now. He's also discovering that he can actually make objects do things. Unless he is still alarmed by sudden and unexpected noises, he may now very much enjoy simple musical instruments, such as drums, tambourines, maracas, and xylophones, reveling not only in the sounds, but also in his own power to make them happen. Even if your baby is not yet an enthusiastic musician, you can give him a similar sense of personal power with a toy that does something when he pushes a button or pulls a lever. A push-along toy that makes a sound as he pushes it may become a favorite.

It will be several months past his first birthday before your baby begins to remember what toys he owns (although he'll certainly notice if a special "cuddly" goes missing). Right now, though, you cannot assume that he'll know what he wants and look for it unless it's in full view. Toys that are put away in cupboards out of sight will be out of mind too. Somebody needs to get out a small selection for him whenever he's put down on "his" floor, and pick things up and replace them in between sessions. Leaving everything he currently plays with permanently strewn on the floor may save adult effort but actually spoils baby play. Babies are most interested in objects that are similar to things they've seen before but novel. Leave all the toys out all the time and your baby will lose interest in them just because he has seen them all so often. If your baby has a lot of toys, more than you feel he needs, you may like to put away toys he is not quite ready for, or toys that make so much noise you have to be in the mood, and produce them only from time to time, perhaps on special occasions, or when a run of bad weather is keeping you confined to the house. Those toys may keep their play value for longer than most others.

At this stage a toy box kept in a corner of "his" floor is a good compromise. It doesn't have to be purpose-made for toys, and you don't even want it to have a lid. A big wicker basket might look nice (but beware of sharp parts) or maybe a large smooth plastic storage tray like the ones designed to go under beds; some even have casters. If everything in current use ("real" toys

and loaned household playthings) lives in there, cleaning up between play sessions will be easy and quick, and your baby will be able to see some of his toys and will quickly learn where to go when he wants something. Don't be surprised if he sometimes gets almost everything out and plays with nothing in particular. Emptying out is today's game. With encouragement, filling up again (call it cleaning up if you like) can be part of it!

However many toys your baby has, though, and however carefully you organize them, no supply of "real toys" can keep up with your baby's desire to see and explore and learn about things he hasn't met before, nor should it. He needs pieces of the adult world to explore.

A shopping expedition can be fun, but as long as the groceries and bag are both safe for her, unpacking is the best part.

You can provide a lot from shopping trips and by rescuing interesting cast-offs you were going to throw away. Watch for things he might like and save them, out of reach, until you have time to turn them into temporary playthings:

◆ A collection of washed-out yogurt containers or plastic plant pots will be fun for him to pile up and knock down, and can also be used for filling and emptying games.

◆ Cardboard boxes have innumerable uses: from a doll's bed or horse stable to a container for toys. Small boxes are more scarce, so hang onto any you find—they're fun to fit inside bigger ones.

◆ Cardboard tubes serve triple-duty as things to roll, to drop other things into, and to look through (like a telescope).

◆ Shiny ribbons and pretty papers that turn up around Christmas and other special holidays may inspire your baby's first efforts at dressing-up—himself, his doll, you, or the cat.

◆ Lidded plastic containers can be filled with water and a drop of baby shampoo (maybe even a drop of food coloring) so they bubble when shaken.

◆ A squeeze bottle that held something harmless and has been well washed out makes a good bath toy.

◆ The used paper from your printer is ideal for first scribbles (it will recycle just as well next week with scribble on it).

◆ Colorful magazines are fun to crumple and tear, and your baby will enjoy being shown pictures in the gardening, cooking, or parenting sections.

Changes of scene and changes of activity

At this age your baby's attention span is relatively short and what he can do with any particular plaything is limited, so he needs lots of changes of scene and activity to keep him involved in play and prevent him from getting bored. Very little is yet familiar to your baby, so a simple move to another room can be as interesting to him as an outing will be when he's older. The bed you're trying to make can be a gorgeously soft trampoline or place for comforter-hide-and-seek. Playing with toys on the hard floor of the kitchen is interestingly different from playing on the carpeted floor of the dining room, especially

if you show him how differently his wheeled toys behave. And trips out of the house, especially in his stroller rather than the car, are invaluable. The more he can be taken out and about with adults the better, and these trips don't always have to be baby-focused, either. He will love a drop-in baby-and-parent group, but that Saturday morning round of errands and chores that you might once have found boring is full of new sights and sounds and sensations for your baby—and through him, for you too.

Playing with your baby

Babies explore and learn, hone old skills and develop new ones, through play, so hopefully you play with your baby almost all the time you are with him. That doesn't mean that you have to spend all your time on the floor with toys though: There are many ways of playing with a one-year-old, and a lot of the time, play is more a question of attitudes than actions. Your baby doesn't know that having a bath is "care" but sitting in the baby pool is play, or that going to the toddler group is play, but going to the farmers' market is "shopping." What he does know is whether you are engaged as well as present, cheerful rather than withdrawn or stressed, quick to respond to what he does, and happy to demonstrate how things should be done.

Parents talking about...
sociable stroller-riding

❝ A friend I was meeting was making a big thing about how she'd got a stroller that faced toward her so her little boy could see her. I began to feel bad that I had one that faced away, but when I caught sight of her across the park she was talking on her cell phone—and from the number of times it rang while we were together, that's what she does most afternoons. You wouldn't walk along with a friend talking to someone else on the phone, would you? It would be rude. I like to have my phone with me in case of emergencies but I've taken to turning it off when I'm out with my little boy. ❞

Joining in adult games

At this age and emotional stage your baby would probably rather play with you and your "toys," or with whoever takes care of him when you are away at work, than with anyone or anything else. Watching and sharing adult activities helps babies learn about the world, its objects, and people, so the more you can take yours around with you the better. It's not very likely that you'll be able to share much of your work-world with your baby because modern work is seldom suitable to share with children. Unless you are a small-business owner, even professions that sound child-friendly, like growing vegetables or raising chickens, are generally too large scale and mechanized to be safe and interesting for a baby. Most jobs don't even sound child-friendly. They are office-based. You probably can't take your child with you and if you do, most office activity will be incomprehensible and therefore boring to him. Even if he is one of the small but increasing number of children who is lucky enough to have a parent who works at home, computers and printers will not interest him for long, and endless phone calls mean adult talk that is not for him. Combining working with taking sole care of a baby or toddler almost always means shortchanging one or the other—or both.

Domesticity

Whatever the nature of their outside work, almost all parents do domestic chores around the home, and these are the activities that babies and small children find most interesting. In many ways it's regrettable that being companionable with a child and doing housework go so well together because it means that they get lumped together in people's minds, as if parenting and sweeping were the same activity. And since domestic activities *still* tend to be regarded as female, that tends to confine mothers and leave fathers out. They are not all the same of course. Efficient housework—by woman or man—gets necessary routine chores done as quickly as possible. Involving a small child means slowing the pace and deliberately structuring the activity so he can do it too.

If a nanny comes to your home to take care of your baby while you are at work, don't readily

Staying safe

The housework game isn't a good one for babies with a tendency to asthma, since dust (especially dust mites) is a common allergen. The "adult toys" a baby shares need careful thought, too—almost all cleaning chemicals are dangerous. You may want to banish the most lethal liquids, such as bleach, from your home, and replace pressurized sprays with products that are kinder to eyes as well as the environment. Some modern cloths clean with water only so you can abandon almost all house-cleaning products.

accept that she can't do *anything* around the house because the baby ought to have her professional attention, full-time. Likewise, if your baby goes to a home daycare, don't expect the caregiver to do nothing all day but play with the children. Of course your baby needs to spend some of each day in concentrated one-on-one play and talk with a beloved adult, and of course you want to be sure that his needs, whether for a whole afternoon's cuddling or a long walk in sudden sunshine, are always given priority, but adults who do nothing but watch babies play often don't contribute much to that play and may be boring companions. If they get bored themselves, they may withdraw onto their phones or keep trying to persuade your baby to play a different game in a different way, which the baby may experience as intrusive. Your baby will probably enjoy himself more if the days he spends away from you are spent in cheerful, chatty, ordinarily busy company.

Shopping can be a treat for your baby (and perhaps a break for you) as long as it's done in person rather than online. Your baby will enjoy the sociability of strolling to a shop he knows well for two items; equally he will enjoy a major supermarket expedition, riding in a cart and helping himself to things off the shelves.… If you don't want him to open every item and destroy the shelf displays, let him help himself to something innocuous, like a baguette, at the beginning. Struggling with something he knows

Enthusiasm is catching: You may have more of it for gardening than for housework.

is good to eat but cannot easily manage, and something that is also interesting to hold and play with, will (probably) distract him.

The best part of supermarket shopping for your baby is the unpacking. If you're organized enough to pack breakables in a separate bag or can deftly remove eggs, tomatoes, and anything packaged in glass or plastic bags, he will unpack the rest, rolling potatoes and apples all over the floor.

Almost every child likes to cook, and babies and toddlers are no exception. They will enjoy it as "messy" or "water" play long before they make any connection between kitchen activity and delicious things to eat. It is usually easiest to arrange for your baby to participate and stay safe if he sits in his high chair and is handed odds and ends to mix, mash, and taste.

Even "housework," the domestic activity many adults enjoy least, can be made to seem like a game that's played all over the house if the baby is bounced on the bed that is being made, plays peekaboo around the furniture, and has a clean duster to wave.

Not every baby gets a chance to play at gardening, but those that do almost always enjoy it. There are safety issues to think about, but as long as at least half your attention is on the baby rather than the plants, most garden hazards are no worse than kitchen dangers. If you have a pond in your yard though, you might want to consider what you can do to make it safe not only for now but for much later on. A rigid metal mesh installed *just* beneath the surface of the water is one solution. Turning the pond into a pebble pool is another.

You need to be careful not to use power tools —mowers, trimmers, hedge-cutters—while children are in, or liable to arrive in, the yard (blades don't stop turning as fast as toddlers move), and to keep sharp implements and poisonous chemicals locked away. You also need to be aware of the likelihood of toxocariasis infection in earth that is fouled by cats or dogs, especially if you live in a city where there tend to be a lot of pets living in small areas of yard. Your baby should be fine crawling around on a lawn or patio, but wear gardening gloves yourself and take them off before you wipe his nose. Small children should do their "gardening" in fresh soil in their own seed trays that are stored under cover.

Of course your baby should not be exposed to too much sun or to disease-carrying ticks, but these are only hazards in certain parts of the country at certain times of year. As to poisonous plants, they won't be a hazard if you don't grow (or tolerate) any.

Word-play

As he becomes a toddler, your baby must and will learn to use more and more words. Right now, though, even if he says nothing that is recognizably "a word," he will be understanding more and more language. Whenever you talk to your baby about something he can see or feel, you are helping his understanding. And whenever you use language to encourage him to do something, you are helping him to develop skills. This kind of talk isn't something that only goes on when you are deliberately playing with him, of course. It goes on whenever you are together and whatever you are doing, as long as you are sharing it. Think, for instance of the routines and rhythms of his everyday care. Mundane activities like washing and diaper changing, having meals and being settled for naps, all lend themselves to lots of chatter about what you are doing and why, and what he is feeling and why, and they all help your baby to feel securely loved and cared for—which means that they aren't really mundane at all. Gradually he'll begin to understand the care you give him and eventually to share in it with self-care, grabbing the washcloth to wash his own face; pulling off a filled diaper before you can get to it. Day after day, week after week, he learns new concepts and the words for them: learns that a bath can be "too hot" (and what that means); that the hot tap is a "no!"; that plastic ducks float but washcloths don't. Eventually he may surprise you with the amount he understands: He has his towel (white with a hood-corner), you have yours (which is blue), and he goes for the right one when you weren't even aware that he understood the idea or knew what words like "where's your towel?" meant (although he can't say them and is a year or more away from knowing what each is called).

Words in books are special because of their pictorial context. When you talk to your baby about something that is there and touchable—like his lunch bowl—he can link the word with the object. When you read to him about something that isn't there to be touched but is pictured to be seen, he has to link the word with the picture and the picture with the thing it represents. That's a big step toward abstraction and becoming able to understand when you talk to him about something that isn't there to be touched, or pictured to be seen, but is only in his head, like Daddy, who'll be home soon.

Don't for a moment assume that because your baby doesn't talk in words yet he is too young to get anything out of being read to. At this age, books themselves, the pleasure of "reading" them with you and the words they contain and encourage, become an important part of his playing and learning. His understanding of speech is linked to his understanding of concepts—not only "hot" and "cold," but also "up" and "down," "big" and "little," "full" and "empty." As that increases, books and the kinds of talk that go with being "read to" become more and more valuable. "Pop-up" books, offering just the age-appropriate amount of novelty

Picture books are glorious, pop-up books are thrilling: You can see his excitement in his toes.

and surprise, may become his favorites, and it won't be long before he'll be able to follow the instructions you pass onto him: "Pull here," "push," "turn over." Whether they have built-in action or not, the pictures in his picture books really matter, and his first loves will be large, colorful, and clear. If a one-year-old is to recognize a picture of a cat, it needs to be the kind of cat he has actually seen, not an artistic impression or cartoonist's joke of a cat. If the book has a "story," don't just read him the words that are on the page: Show him (ask him) where the dog or the Daddy is in the picture. Tell him (and ask him) what the cat or the cow says. And be prepared willingly to "read" the same book again and again, maybe several times each day for weeks. He cannot get everything out of one or even three readings; repetition is crucial and coming to know the book by heart is part of the pleasure of it.

Your baby won't sit on your lap and share a book that doesn't have pictures, of course, but if you choose times when he doesn't have anything else to do (in the car, maybe, or in his high chair waiting for his lunch) he'll love to listen to rhymes for their rhythms and jokes and he'll realize they are funny from your tone of voice, long before he knows exactly why. No matter how poor a singer you are, sing him songs and nursery rhymes, and hymns and carols too, if you like. If you can't remember many from your own childhood, invest in a CD—but one of the best things about going to a parent-and-baby group is that you'll learn lots of songs and action games that end with a surprise tickle. Games that name fingers and toes and noses and ears will help him both to be aware of different bits of his own body and to learn what they are called.

Given the importance and the fun of words, you may be tempted by talking toys. Toy makers know that they will appeal to parents (who are the people doing the buying) and produce an enormous range, from simple toys where pressing the button with a picture of a cow produces a mechanical voice saying "cow" or making a mooing noise, to sophisticated "baby computers." Any of these might (or might not) amuse your baby, but none of them will teach him to understand language, teach him to talk, or teach him anything else, for that matter.

Beginning to think about discipline

For most parents, life with a nearly one-year-old is by no means all laughter and gentleness. There are bad days, and irritations sometimes get out of proportion.

That's the context in which many parents of babies this age—and sometimes their own parents too—begin to think and talk about discipline. The timing is fine because your nearly-mobile, almost-talking baby is just beginning to be able to understand some of the things you want her to do and some of the things that are forbidden. She can understand what "no" means, for example, and she can begin to cooperate with adults, even

You may hear...

"It's never too soon for discipline: Start as you mean to go on." "Don't let your baby rule the roost." "Giving in to him is just making a rod for your own back." If you don't have the time and energy to argue, or you're in awe of the speaker or you don't dare, at least try not to listen.

From research

Avoiding mess? In the 1990s, influential church-based parenting classes instructed parents that to avoid mess (and enforce instant obedience), a baby who dabbled in his food bowl while they were trying to spoon-feed him should have his hand hit with a small stick every time he moved it out of his lap. In a few instances this policy, taken to extremes, led to babies not only giving up putting their fingers in their food but also giving up eating.

(sometimes) when she doesn't actually want to. But if the timing is appropriate, the bad-day context is not. Your baby is still nowhere near to understanding why you approve and disapprove of particular behaviors, and that means that she is nowhere near ready to cope with your anger or disappointment or sadness when she doesn't cooperate, or when she breaks something or makes a mess. Angry adult reactions will certainly upset her but they'll teach her nothing useful, because the reasons for adult feelings and behavior are a complete mystery to her, and your anger seems to her to erupt out of nothing: an act of god, a thunderbolt. Real anger is as unexpected, inexplicable, and appalling to your baby as it would be to you if the beloved family dog suddenly got up and bit you.

On her feet, wearing a very small pair of jeans and what can only be described as a cheeky expression, your baby may seem much more grown-up than she did last week. The saddest mistake you can make is to think that she actually is, or should be, as grown-up as she seems and treat her that way. Think through one of those "bad days." Your baby had no way of knowing that the particular thing she did— spilling her cereal all over your shoes—was the "last straw" on a really bad morning. She didn't know that it was a bad morning or what that means. If she sensed anything at all as you raced around, late and multitasking, it will only have been your general tension, and although she will have disliked it, she will neither have understood what it was about nor even wondered. She doesn't understand much about your feelings or your affairs: She can't, not only because she

Parents talking about...

lack of support from bystanders

❝ We'd be at the supermarket checkout and I'd be trying to distract Jess from grabbing things out of the cart, and eventually I'd lift him out and hold him so he could see everything. I can't tell you how many times people in the line told me 'What that one needs is good spanking.' Nobody ever said 'what he needs is a good hug—or something interesting to do'. ❞

Despite appearances, he's still a baby.

hasn't had enough experience, but also because the "social" part of her brain that will enable her to empathize is not yet mature enough. And she shouldn't, because they are not yet her concern.

There are parents whose advisors have convinced them that all indulgence is spoiling; that they should indeed "start as they plan to go on," and that that means disciplining babies into instant obedience.

There are even a few parents (fewer, perhaps, than 20 years ago) who punish their babies for crying—even smack them to "interrupt" tantrums. Fortunately, while a lot of parents—perhaps all parents—occasionally lose patience and are cross and negative with their babies, most can see that deliberate punishments are not appropriate, let alone acceptable, at this age.

Most parents try gentler ways of stopping babies from doing dangerous and tiresome things: thinking ahead to avoid conflict and distracting them when there is a clash. They get little support and a lot of criticism, though. To many people those baby-centered approaches still look like "spoiling."

By this time that should have changed, or at least be changing, because the inappropriateness of punitive discipline in managing undesirable (or inconvenient and irritating) baby behavior is no longer a matter of opinion but of scientific fact.

You cannot discipline a baby in the true sense of teaching her how to behave, as you can and should when she is a child. However hard you try to teach her, she won't learn to control her behavior in her first year. She won't because she can't. She can't because the part of her brain that controls her social understanding and behavior, the orbitofrontal cortex, only began to develop after she was born and won't be fully functional for another year or two.

Your baby's brain

Whatever your baby's potential for the future, what she can do and how she is right now depends on her brain development. Human brains are incredibly complicated, but understanding even a little will help you understand your baby a lot.

When she is born a baby has something like two hundred billion brain cells (neurons). That's all she needs, forever, she doesn't need to grow any more cells and will actually prune some out later on. At birth, though, there are very few connections (synapses) between these neurons, and she does need more synapses because it is making those connections that will lead to her higher brain function. The more connections, the better the performance. It is in the second half of this first year, just when the attachment between your baby and you is building up, that these synaptic connections in the prefrontal cortex achieve their highest density thus far. They reach a final high pitch in early toddlerhood.

Shaping your baby's brain

Since most of the growth and development of your baby's higher brain—the almost exclusively human part whose great size eventually sets her apart from all other mammals—takes place after birth, and develops according to social experience, it takes place on your watch with you at the center. The first higher brain capacities to develop, sited in the orbitofrontal cortex, are built up through her early relationships and experiences, which largely dictate the kind of

From research

Brain size. It is thought that the reason human babies are born when they are so much less developed than other mammals is that if their brains were fully developed at birth their heads would have to be too big to pass through the pelvis of a mother who stands on two legs.

brain your baby will have—even the kind of person she will become. A baby cannot develop an orbitofrontal cortex by herself, so it's no use sitting back and waiting for it to happen. Whether you are aware of it or not, you make it happen. Many aspects of your baby's brain are literally created by parents and any other people who are important to her. Instead of "start as you mean to go on," how about "be nice to your baby, for the sake of her brain"?

If a baby is born into a family where very little adult interaction is available to her, where she cannot establish a secure attachment to anyone, or where there are high levels of domestic aggression, even violence, her brain structure and chemistry will start to adapt defensively to that environment. She may become hyper vigilant, and have extra-strong fear and anger reactions, or intense attack and defense impulses in the deep, primitive part of her brain. But if a baby is born into a family where parents enjoy her, cuddle and play with her, listen to her, laugh with her and comfort her when she is upset, the connections that form in her brain will be very different. She'll be on the way to becoming someone who is resilient: can cope with stress, manage anger, and form close relationships with other people.

From research

Brain shaping. It makes excellent evolutionary sense that infants' brains should be highly malleable at birth, because the molding of them by parents means that every new human being in the world is shaped to fit the environment in which he lives.

Brain structure and function—a sketch

The brains of all vertebrate animals—including us, of course—share a core, unchanged by evolution, that controls basic instincts and functions. This "hindbrain" (often called "primitive," for obvious reasons), with the spinal cord carrying messages from body to brain and back, includes the cerebellum, mainly concerned with movement; the medulla oblongata, controlling autonomic functions such as circulation and respiration; and instinctive behaviors related to survival, such as fight-or-flight responses. The pituitary gland, controlling many hormonal processes including growth, sexual maturation and functioning, is here. The next area to have evolved is the lower brain or limbic system, often called the "emotional brain" because it is the site of strong feelings such as rage and fear, love and lust, bonding and playfulness. The region called the hypothalamus has many discrete areas with a wide variety of functions, including linking the nervous system to the endocrine system via the pituitary gland. A vital pair of structures called the amygdalae are crucial to memory and to emotional processing, especially in deployment or moderation of fear responses such as sweaty palms and the release of stress hormones.

Anxiety disorders are thought to be linked to amygdala functioning.

The last part of the brain to evolve, the "neo-cortex" or cerebrum, is partially shared only with other high-level mammals (primates, dolphins). This "rational brain" takes up more than three-quarters of our brain mass and is the site of everything that makes us human, such as language, abstract thought, imagination, consciousness. It develops only after birth in human babies. The neo-cortex is divided into left and right hemispheres. The left side (which controls the right side of the body) contains verbal centers: language and understanding of language; words for feelings. It registers mild and positive feelings rather than emotional pain and does not link closely with the body. The right hemisphere (which controls the left side of the body) is not verbal but emotional. It registers strong and painful feelings, picks up emotional atmospheres, and has close links with the body and with the lower brain's alarm system (the amygdala). A band of nerve tissue called the corpus callosum eventually connects the two sides of the brain, passing information about the individual's experiences from one to the other; it is not fully developed in infants, though.

The higher brain has several lobes, each with specialized areas that must develop to some degree during early childhood. The frontal lobe, for example, is concerned with a wide range of intellectual and creative activities (as well as some muscular coordination, motor skills, and physical reactions including sexual urges). The occipital lobe is responsible mainly for vision and reading, while the temporal lobe controls many kinds of memory. The prefrontal part of the brain (the latest to evolve) links the sensory areas of the cortex with the emotional and survival areas and governs social choices. The first part to mature, the orbitofrontal region, is crucial to individuals' management of strong feelings, inhibiting primitive impulses from the lower brain, interpreting other people's social and emotional cues, and modifying behavior in response to rewards and punishments.

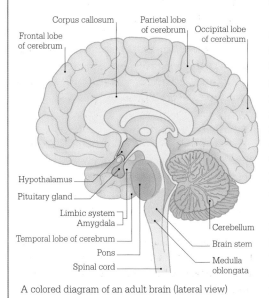

Corpus callosum • Parietal lobe of cerebrum • Occipital lobe of cerebrum
Frontal lobe of cerebrum
Hypothalamus
Pituitary gland
Limbic system
Amygdala
Temporal lobe of cerebrum
Pons
Spinal cord
Cerebellum
Brain stem
Medulla oblongata

A colored diagram of an adult brain (lateral view)

Your baby's brain and behavior

Your baby cannot do, or learn to do, anything that is outside her brain's current capacity. Earlier sections have stressed the uselessness of expecting her to reach for a toy before she has her hands and eyes organized to work together; of trying to hurry her through developments that must come from inside her, such as beginning to walk or to say "real words"; as well as the importance of responding quickly when she is upset so that levels of stress do not rise too high or last too long. The developments of this year have transformed her into someone who can stand on her own two feet, look you in the eye, and do what you've forbidden, but they have not (yet) made her into someone who can understand and remember how she is supposed to behave and control herself, accept a "no" to something she wants without tears, or consider your feelings as well as her own. Don't expect deliberate "good behavior" from your baby any more than you'd expect an opera from an ape. No chance: The equipment isn't there. Real self-regulation will take a lot more higher brain capacity than a one-year-old's, so you are asking not just the difficult but the impossible.

If you ask the impossible of your baby you are going to be frustrated and disappointed, which will be no fun for you, but worse for her. If the development of that rational brain is to proceed as fast as it can, she needs you to enjoy her, to be pleased—often delighted—with her, more than she needs anything else. It's not only because they are "unfair" that you should avoid making demands on your baby that she can't meet today, but also because constant disapproval may mean less than optimum brain development tomorrow.

Your influence on your baby's brain development is uniquely important, but there are other influences, including her genetic inheritance and some prenatal and birth experiences, which your parenting cannot change, although it may modify their effects. Time (and the maturation it brings) is one of them. Even if you are the warmest, most sensitive, and most consistently responsive parents imaginable, you can do very little to hasten brain development. At nearly a year old, your baby's higher (rational) brain is still so incomplete that the lower brain, with its primitive impulses and rioting emotions, is bound to dominate, and sometimes overwhelm, her behavior. It's up to you to deal with it for her, and doing it with understanding will help her to learn, eventually, to do it for herself.

Tantrums

Although they are regarded as typical of toddlers, tantrums are common in babies as young as nine months and neatly illustrate the unkind uselessness of trying to discipline a child for behavior that is not yet under her brain's control, just because adults abhor it.

A tantrum is the explosive end result of a build-up of tension, often frustration, usually with a mixture of fear and anxiety. There may be anger in the mix, but "temper tantrum" is a misnomer that demonstrates the adult world's punitive attitude. "Temper" sounds naughty; tantrums are not. Sometimes the build-up to a tantrum is slow—you may know when you get your baby up from her afternoon nap that there's likely to be trouble before bedtime—sometimes it's lightning quick. Either way a tantrum is something like an emotional blown fuse, and while it lasts your baby is completely overwhelmed by violent feelings experienced and discharged by the lower brain. There is no way she can control these feelings or their results because the pathways between the lower ("emotional") brain and the rational upper brain, and between its left and right sides, are not yet developed. Her brain is flooded by stress chemicals; she is out of control and she feels terrible and terrified.

From research

Causes of tantrums. About 17 percent of tantrums are said to result from conflicts over food and eating. Feeling imprisoned activates the lower brain's feelings of anger and frustration; 11 percent of tantrums take place when a baby or toddler is strapped into a car seat or high chair, and another 11 percent are associated with being forced into or out of clothes.

Your job is not to "discipline" her, even in the sense of "teaching" her, but to regulate her and restore her equilibrium from outside every time until her brain is mature enough to do it from inside. However unpleasant your baby's tantrums are for you (and they may be very embarrassing in public places or in front of guests at home), they are much worse for your baby.

It's important to understand that a baby or toddler in the throes of a tantrum is truly distressed; suffering, in emotional pain. If you really believe that you will see how inappropriate it is to get angry, shout back at her, or even turn away and ignore her. Withdrawing her audience can be an effective way of handling the semi-deliberate tantrums three- and four-year-olds sometimes use to manipulate adults, but your baby is not three years old, knows nothing of manipulation ("if I scream loudly enough she'll give in"), and has no intention or control in her tantrums.

Sometimes it helps to hold your baby in your arms, but only if she will let you, so you are cuddling rather than compelling her, and only if you can stay calm and controlled yourself. Sometimes distraction can help. If you can catch your baby's attention with a toy or a passing fire engine, that can trigger interest and motivation and reduce the levels of stress chemicals in her brain.

Sometimes simple, repeated, crooning words—"OK, you're OK"—may lay soothing sound over her screams and help to reduce their feedback so that she quietens. Don't try to talk, or expect her to talk, about what has upset her, though. If she is having a tantrum, the thinking and talking centers in her underdeveloped higher brain have been temporarily hijacked.

As your baby gets older, she will gradually become slower to melt down into tantrums, because pathways will begin to develop between her frontal lobes and her lower brain. Eventually she will often (or at least sometimes) be able to control and calm explosions of anger, anxiety, and fear, and instead actually express strong feelings. However, even "sometimes" is in the future. It will be many months before your baby-turned-toddler can calm and comfort herself instead of needing a beloved adult to do it for her, and in the meantime her behavior will

often be extraordinarily unpredictable and quick to change. Until the corpus callosum, linking the right and left sides of her upper brain, matures, information—and surges of feeling—from that emotional (and currently furious) right frontal lobe is not readily transferred to the moderate and verbal left. One moment your child may be laughing and talking, using all the words in her repertoire, her left brain dominating her behavior. The next moment, she is kicking on the floor in wordless rage. Her right brain's activity has overwhelmed the left.

Telling your baby she's naughty won't help her to be good

If you want your baby to be good—meaning to behave as you want her to behave—try telling her you love her.

Toward the end of this first year, with the increasing development of the orbitofrontal region of her brain, your baby becomes able not only to recognize and remember faces (see p. 274) but also facial expressions: smiles, frowns, thrilled or appalled astonishment. At first, facial expressions are stored in the brain like separate photos in an album, but gradually, as similar situations get repeated again and again, those snapshots join up, stored in the brain as lasting emotion-loaded images of herself with other people. Your baby will be noticing, cataloguing, and storing often-repeated loving greetings, glorious games, and sensitive and helpful reactions—holding, soothing—to overwhelming feelings. This store of images that your baby is now beginning to build up will play an important part in how she learns to regulate herself when there is no adult present to do it for her. When your baby (as a toddler, a child, a teenager, or an adult) meets a social situation that arouses feelings that are in that store, she will unconsciously use those images to guide her reactions and her behavior. Because that older person looks for guidance to her own inner resources, we think of this as "self regulation," and indeed it is. But how did those loving images she uses get into her brain in the first place? From the ways you are managing her, day by day. They flood her with "feel good" chemicals, such as endorphins, now, and they will make her feel good when she taps into them in the future.

Your baby is also noticing, cataloguing and storing oft-repeated stern, disapproving, angry faces and negative behaviors and interactions. Your unsmiling, disapproving face can shower her brain with stress hormones such as cortisol, even if you don't say or do anything unkind. If you are someone who really dislikes changing soiled diapers, so that smiling, raspberry-blowing play while you are undressing her on her changing table always switches into disgust when the diaper comes off, chances are that feces, or their smell, will establish a negative "trace" in your baby's brain. She may grow up to be as uncomfortable with her own baby's poo as you are with hers.

If negative facial expressions can affect your baby's brain development, it's not surprising that negative behaviors often have a far greater impact than a parent intends and, at this stage, not often a useful one. If your baby starts to do something dangerous—like crawling toward the top of the ungated stairs—and you catch her up and scold her, she is quite likely to laugh at the unexpectedness of your strong reaction and when you put her down she may instantly set off again. Doing what you tell her not to is a favorite joke-game: a baby equivalent of the "Oh yes you do" "Oh no you don't" pantomime. She clearly hasn't learned not to crawl to the top of

the stairs, though, so now what are you going to do? If you yell at her so that "amusingly unexpected" tips over into "scarily aggressive," she will jump and cry. If you lose your cool to a point where you actually punish her physically, shaking her, spanking her, or dumping her in her crib, she will be amazed and horrified. She may not only cry but scream and tremble and she will not have the least understanding of a connection between anything she did and what you did. Your baby cannot learn anything useful from punishment until the reasons for adult anger become comprehensible, and most of her own actions become controllable; when that time comes, she will be able to learn without it. In the meantime it isn't your baby's responsibility to keep herself safe by doing as she's told. It's adults' responsibility to keep her safe, and that means action rather than (or as well as) words: changing the environment rather than trying to change her. With a crawler in the house, why weren't those stairs gated?

Teaching children how to behave is an increasingly important part of your job as a parent, but most of it is positive not negative ("yes" to this, rather than "no" to that), active rather than passive ("try it" rather than "stop it"), and mutual rather than individual ("let's" rather than "you have to"). Yes, children need clear, comprehensible boundaries, but there's no reason why those boundaries should be associated with anger as long as parents make sure that interested, exploring, testing children cannot break them. "No" has to be understandable and it has to mean "no" always. A stair gate that your baby can open is even more dangerous than none; a gate that she cannot open will eventually teach her that the stairs are a "no," and by the time she's a toddler, stairs-lessons can be positive: "Go down on your tummy like this." In the first year of your baby's life, the key is that word "eventually." She will learn when she is ready and able; but in the meantime the more gently you tell and show her how to behave, the sooner that will be.

As we've seen, people who do not know very much about babies' development (and know nothing about your particular baby) may tell you that always (or almost always!) being gentle and

From research

Physical punishments are dangerous. Even if it's a "little smack." And shaking a baby, or dumping him down in a crib, can kill him. His head is still relatively heavy and his neck relatively weak, so he is very vulnerable to whiplash, and it is extremely dangerous. If his head is shaken so that his brain bangs against the inside of his skull, tiny blood vessels can break and bleed between the two. If clots form they can press into the brain and do horrendous damage. Shaking a baby can leave him blind, or deaf, or dead.

Positive limits can be fun: He must not climb in with the breakables, but this compartment has been left empty for him and is perfect.

positive and loving with a baby this age will "spoil" her and create behavior problems later on. That's an old-fashioned view predating the findings of contemporary brain research. It is a matter of fact rather than opinion that a baby's brain develops its full potential through close, secure attachment to parents who are sensitive and warmly responsive, rarely angry, and never punitive. The more consciously and continuously you love your baby (despite those bad days) and enjoy the way she loves you and her inexhaustible desire for smiles and hugs, the better shape you will all be in to face the new learning and the challenges of toddlerhood.

Thinking about working outside your home

Leaving a baby to return to paid work is almost always wrenching, and doing it now toward the end of your baby's first year, as some mothers do, may seem especially hard.

The two of you are even more closely attached than you were six months ago, and he's much more able to make it clear that he doesn't want you to leave him. Tearing yourself away from a baby who clings and cries and may even call for you by name is horrible even if you're just going out to lunch; worse if you're going to be out at work all day and tomorrow and the next day. Once you've made the decision, though, try to focus on making the best possible arrangements for his care and your working hours and ensuring the financial and time fit between the two.

Don't let yourself regret that you didn't leave him earlier. It might have been easier for you but it would have been less good for him. And as long as you can make high-quality arrangements for his care, don't feel guilty about leaving him now. Being cared for mostly at home and by you for the better part of a year has given your baby the best possible start, and however it looks and feels to you, this is a better time in his life to start leaving him than any earlier would have been. If he fusses more about it at a year than he would have done at six months old, that's because he's more conscious of loving and depending on you. He'll benefit for the rest of his life from having had time to establish that relationship with you.

Your baby will flourish without you while you are at work as long as he passes seamlessly from your loving care to someone else's, and back again when you return. So if and when you want to be able to leave him on a regular basis with someone he has not known before, the most important thing you can do to ease the separation for him is to make sure that he and the new care provider have lots of time in advance to get to know each other and begin to trust each other. Ideally your baby needs to get to know this new person well with you, so that he sees that you like and trust her before he has to rely on her without you. Settle them together over several visits. Let the new person see how you do things (including really personal things like helping him with his lunch, changing his diaper, or putting him down for a nap) and then let her do it while you're there to make your baby feel sure that that's OK too. And when you do begin to leave them together, start with half an hour and work up slowly. Although your baby doesn't have much time sense yet, you want him to know, from constant experience, that when you go, you always come back. Above all, don't listen to anyone who tells you to "make a quick getaway before he notices." He'll notice all right, and he'll be even more anxious about being left next time.

Finding good childcare isn't easy, and nobody can give you detailed guidance because the quality of the care depends on the individual care provider, and the extent to which it is good for your child depends on him and what he feels about her. You are going to have to look yourself at any care facilities you are considering, but it may help to begin by thinking about what type you would prefer: If every type of care was available and affordable, what would you choose for your baby?

Live-in caregivers

A live-in caregiver may sound like the nearest you could ever get to cloning yourself. But while she may indeed allow you lots of freedom to come and go, both in the daytime and the evening, she'll also impinge on you. After all, your home will be her home, and she'll have every right to be there when you don't want her as well as when you do.

◆ A trained nanny will be competent to take "full charge" of your baby, but although nannies are increasingly flexible, she may not expect to do much else. Are you going to resent cooking her a meal in the evening even if you only want a snack yourself?

◆ If you can find a mother's help or a housekeeper with plenty of experience with babies, she'll probably be willing to do anything you would do if you were at home: childcare, domestic chores, maybe even watering the plants and taking in the dry cleaning. Even if you can find such a multi-skilled paragon, though, you may not be able to keep her. Like many mothers, their helpers often find being home all day with a baby (who isn't even their own) lonely and boring.

Some babies this age are very shy, but even the most sociable need to get to know people before they are happy to be handed over.

◆ Don't assume that an au-pair will be at least as good as a mother's helper and maybe as good as a nanny, but cheaper. Some au-pairs are marvelous, especially for families with older children where they can take something close to a big-sister or young-aunt role. There are not many who are competent to care for a small baby, though, or eager to do housework, and they shouldn't be expected to work anything approaching full-time hours.

Daily care providers

Care providers who come in daily are often easier to find (not many nannies want to live-in), and you may find it easier to get along with each other because neither of you gets in the way of the other's private life. Of course anyone who comes in every day may have problems with travel, and if your daily nanny has children of her own, she may struggle to get in as early as you need to leave for work and be reluctant to do evening babysitting.

◆ Half a daily nanny may be affordable when a whole one is not. Many nannies like shared arrangements between two families, and some nanny agencies arrange them. A shared nanny may work half the week for each family, or she may care for both sets of children together. In the latter case, think carefully about which house she and the children will be based in (there are considerable wear-and-tear and evening tidying issues), and make sure that the parents can all get along together and that the children are manageable as a group.

◆ A daily mother's helper or housekeeper probably won't have the training or experience that she would need to take full charge of a baby, but provided she has excellent references, she may be a good solution for your family if you work part-time or partly at home. There are often people who are working their way through college, changing careers, or caring for elderly relatives, who are glad to work short hours and able to match them to your needs. If she has children of her own, though, your needs are likely to clash in the school holidays unless you are willing for her to bring her children with her when she needs to.

Family caregivers in your home or their own

For many parents, care by a grandparent—almost always a grandmother and often the mother's mother—is the ideal form of childcare, but not all grandmothers are able or willing to do it, and those who are, and who live close enough, often cannot manage the hours you need or comfortably adapt their approach to yours. Sometimes other relatives offer informal, even unpaid, childcare, but such arrangements need careful thought. "Family" doesn't always spell "kind, knowledgeable, and trustworthy," and a relative who cares for your baby will not be subject to any kind of registration or inspection. Do you know this individual well enough to be absolutely sure that your baby will be safe and happy with her? And has she really thought carefully about this enormous favor, or is it liable to go sour when she realizes just how big a commitment she has taken on? In domestic settings—even a grandparent's home—or in any care that is not inspected, you need to make sure of up-to-date safety habits (such as putting babies down to sleep on their backs) and of child-proofing (including safety and hygiene precautions concerning any pets).

Non-family caregivers in their own homes

(Home daycare or family daycare.) Caregivers care for a very small group of children, including their own. The domestic-scale care they offer is usually more personalized and flexible than in most daycare centers. Experts recommend that caregivers who offer childcare in their own homes should be licensed and get regular inspections. Some offer before- and after-school and holiday care to older children as well as daytime care for babies and preschool children; this means that siblings can be cared for together.

Group care

(Daycare centers.) Some parents think that under-ones are too young to be cared for in a group, while others think that babies benefit from being with other children, and in a more obviously "educational" environment, even at this age. Not all parents who would like a daycare setting for a baby can find one that is accessible and affordable. While some communities can provide places in daycare centers for almost all who want them, elsewhere they may have long wait-lists.

With demand booming, numbers of daycare centers are increasing—but although the highest demand is for places for the youngest children, not all daycare centers will accept babies under one because the regulations and the realities of their care are more burdensome than for older children. Quality (and costs) vary tremendously, so if you want a place for your baby you need to spend time visiting available centers in action as well as talking to the people in charge.

The people doing the caring matter more to young children than the type of childcare. If the quality of his care is high, your baby may be happy with a grandparent or aunt, a nanny or mother's helper, a family daycare or a nursery worker. Once he's had time to get to know her and begin to love her, what matters is that she loves *him* and that you can enjoy the relationship they have with each other rather than feeling uneasy about their closeness or jealous of the time they spend together.

Quality is crucial

It's very difficult to judge the quality of care an individual or a group will give your baby. Word of mouth from other parents may be useful, but their agendas may be different from yours. Watching the caregiving person with children—and with your child—is essential. While you observe, it may be useful to measure what you are seeing against some benchmarks for high-quality care for babies:

◆ The fewer children each adult has to care for, the better, especially when they are under one year. Most authorities agree that where children are being cared for in groups, no one caregiver should ever be responsible for more than three babies, and a ratio of 1:2 is better for under ones, especially at times when they particularly need holding, such as when they are being greeted at the beginning of the day, or when they are being fed or changed.

When very small children are cared for in groups, the groups themselves need to be small. In a daycare center, baby rooms shouldn't have more than six children (and two adults) in them. When a home daycare worker or a shared nanny cares for children of different ages in "family" groupings, she shouldn't have to look after more than two children under two years of age, and if there is a baby under one year, he should be the only one (unless he is a twin).

◆ The physical conditions in which children are cared for are obviously important, but don't let yourself be overly influenced by the decor and the charmingly tiny toilets. They will mean nothing to your child. Much more important is how warm, well-lit, and interesting the playroom is and how much unencumbered space is available. Will your baby be able to lie on the floor and kick, then sit, and eventually crawl, without getting knocked over by people who are getting onto their feet?

Is there outdoor play space that all the children really use on a daily basis? It is difficult to imagine high-quality childcare without it.

◆ Babies need highly personalized, intimate care given always by the same person or the same several people. From the moment he leaves your care your child should be, and be aware that he is, the special charge of one particular adult. In a nursery or daycare center where there are several caregivers, that particular adult will probably be known as his "key worker," and as far as her working hours and shift pattern allow she will undertake most of his hands-on care, especially the highly personal stuff, and be sent for if he should be unwell or upset. A key worker can't be there every moment, but when she goes off duty she shouldn't be replaced by a temporary fill-in whom your baby does not know but by a familiar deputy.

◆ Even if your child is a small baby (and he isn't going to stay small for long) he needs care that is much more than "babysitting." As all the earlier pages of this book have made clear, babies are learning everything there is to learn from the beginning of their lives, so lots of different kinds of play that are stimulating and appropriate to his stage of development, and plenty of talk with adults, are as important as good physical care. Providing lots of toys is the easy part. A whole playroom full of them won't provide good play for your baby unless there is an adult to show him the possibilities and help him do whatever he is trying to do.

Whatever kind of care you are considering, the aim is not that babies should be taught "subjects" such as math or French or even that they should be directly taught skills, but that each should be encouraged in a wide range of play activities tailored to his particular development and changing with it.

Sometimes the home-based care that offers lots of individual attention and affection offers a poor range of play opportunities. There are grandparents who find it an effort to take babies outdoors and may even rely on the television to keep them quiet. Relatives don't need to be "trained" in order to give babies high-quality care (after all, parents are not), but they do need to be interested in the baby's stage of development and the kinds of experience that will help it along. Parents usually learn a lot about infant development from their reading during pregnancy and afterward and, above all, from talking to other parents in pre- and post-birth groups and in the local park. Grandparents and other relatives may not have up-to-date information or parent-networks to get it from, and may not know about, or realize that they would be welcome in, the various caregiver-and-baby groups that may be available nearby.

Your baby is a person; you know that, and so, clearly, should anyone who is going to care for him while you are not there. Caring for him well means doing it with respect, always trying to make him feel good about himself, listening to him and really trying to understand him even if he has no words yet. And it means helping him to manage things for himself rather than saving time by doing it for him. Above all, a setting and a caregiver who is going to provide high-quality care for your baby will avoid punishments, sarcasm, and teasing in all age groups. Dignity is important, even to babies. It's fine to laugh with them but not to laugh at them.

Finally, you matter too. Think whether this particular care provider is someone you yourself are comfortable with. If your baby is to get the best out of the non-parental part of his care, you and the care provider have to be able to work closely together, neither of you competing with the other for your baby's affections.

You and your baby are on the same side

Everyone knows that newborn babies are demanding and that toddlers can be difficult, but what about the months in between: Does being a parent get easier or more difficult?

After the exhaustion of the first couple of months, caring for your baby once she was "settled" but not yet mobile probably seemed easy, and once she got smiley and chatty it may have seemed as good as being a mother or father could get. As she gets older, though, rather to your surprise, you may be finding caring for her more rather than less difficult and demanding, even though she's not a toddler yet.

Older babies go everywhere, get into everything, and do a lot, and not everywhere they go and everything they do is what parents would choose. They have more and more likes and dislikes, which they express loudly, and they cling a lot, which can make parents feel smothered. In the last couple of months you may have had days when everything your baby did (including crying whenever you left the room so that you couldn't even go to the bathroom without an uproar) seemed irritating, and the fact that she wouldn't go to sleep at naptime, so you didn't get that precious hour or two off, felt like a last straw. Don't lose sight of the other days that you've certainly had, when your baby behaved in exactly the same way but you responded completely differently: "Don't want me to go without you? Let's go together." (Yes, it's perfectly possible for both genders to pee while holding a baby!). "No sleep today? All right, we can go to the park nice and early." As to whether you feel smothered or loved, what word are you using today? "Clingy" is a criticism but "cuddly" is a compliment.

Everyone has bad days and good days—and as your baby turns into a toddler you'll have plenty of both—but good days are not only more fun but also better for both of you. If you mostly enjoy the time you spend with your baby, you'll be less aware of the downsides of parenthood—of what being a mother is costing you professionally and personally, at work or at play—and you'll be more inclined to feel that she is part of you and therefore that you are always on her side, unconditionally, no matter what she does. That's enormously important because it matches what she feels and what she needs. Your baby loves you with passionate and uncritical devotion; she cannot ever have too much of you, get bored by you, or wish that you were different, and she's incapable of understanding that you might feel differently.

She cannot understand that you might want a "minute to yourself" because although she may tolerate such minutes, she would never choose them over your company. She cannot understand that you might want to "get something done" because however enjoyable the game she is playing on the floor beside you, she would never choose to go on with it rather than come up on your lap for a cuddle. She cannot understand that there is a separate you, with a life and personality of your own, because there is not yet a separate her. You are her other half, her completion.

As your baby grows up, she will learn that you and she are separate people; that it's safe to be separate, safe to feel differently or to disagree, that even arguments do not damage the love between you. But she is not ready for that yet. Right now she is as dependent on you emotionally as she is physically, attaching herself to you more and more closely, practicing loving for the whole of her life. The more she can love you—and the other people to whom she is attached—and feel herself securely loved back, the more resilient and generous in giving love she will be when she grows up.

Index

Author's acknowledgments

I would like to thank Peggy Vance, Publisher at DK, who talked me into this project, editorial manager, Anna Davidson, and Claire Tennant-Scull, whose editorial judgement I have come to trust on anything from the placing of a comma to the shaping of an argument. It was an unexpected pleasure to watch the enormously talented Vanessa Davies take pictures of everything from squishy bananas to abstract ideas (and babies, of course), supported by Peggy Saddler's expert art direction at the shoot, and to watch Nicola Rodway select, unerringly, the shot that made each point. Carolyn Hewitson has been endlessly patient in bringing words and pictures together on the pages. What a team!

As the author I must take full responsibility for the facts and opinions this book presents but I cannot take all the credit for them. During the three years I have spent thinking and talking about it, hundreds of people have shared with me their experiences and their ideas. I would like to take this opportunity of thanking them all, especially colleagues at The Institute for the Study of Children, Families and Social Issues at Birkbeck, University of London, in the Association for Infant Mental Health (UK), and in The Children's Project, as well as many parents, some of whose voices can be heard in "Parents Talking."

A prime purpose of the book is to bring some important ideas from recent child-development research to readers' attention. The device of the "from research" boxes has been used so that I can encapsulate—though inevitably simplify—some such ideas rather than describing and referencing dozens of individual studies that few parents of babies under a year old will have time or inclination to find. Readers who would like to explore some of these areas of research in greater depth but still without tracking them through the academic literature, may find the following books accessible and of particular interest:

Lynne Murray and Liz Andrews, *The Social Baby*, Children's Project Publishing, Richmond, 2000
Helen and Clive Dorman, *The Social Toddler*, Children's Project Publishing, Richmond, 2002
Sue Gerhardt, *Why Love Matters: how affection shapes a baby's brain*, Brunner-Routledge, Hove and New York, 2004
Margot Sunderland, *The Science of Parenting*, DK Publishing, New York, 2006
Helen Barrett, *Attachment and the Perils of Parenting*, National Family and Parenting Institute, 2006
Penelope Leach, *Child Care Today; getting it right for everyone*, Knopf, New York, 2009

Publisher's acknowledgments

The publisher would like to thank Isabel de Cordova for initial design, Steve Crozier for help with retouching images, Romaine Werblow, picture librarian, Jenny Baskaya for picture research, Debbie Maizels for the illustration on page 271, Joanna Dingley for editorial assistance, Dawn Bates for proofreading, and Sue Lightfoot for the index.
Thanks to the models: Anna Beardsworth; Sarah Brick and Charles Hennessy; Freya Burgess; Richard Carr; Rachel Chan and Niamh; Robin and Gill Clarke; Bradley Clayton, Amy Wilsmore and Toby Clayton; Alex, Sarah and Isaac Cottrell; John and Beatrix Crumpton; Bradley, Grete and Joel Dawson; Beatriz De Lamos and Alexander Walker; Holly Dixon; Bob Katie and James Dockray; Kelly and Lucy Eke; Natasha and Melody Estelle; Hazel Evans; Naomi Fidler and Daisy Wright; Christopher, Bernadette and Alexander Gascoigne; Katherine and Jack Gordon; Penny and Jemima Groves-Berry; Sanjeev, Rachel and Jai Gupta; Tiernan Hicks; Michael Patrick, Emmanuelle Gaëlle, Joachim Roger Michael and Ethan Jean Michael Horsford; Clarissa Isles-Johns and Lakeisha Isles-Joseph; Emily, George, Olivia, Eloise, and Daisy Johnson-Ferguson; Gary, Dorinda, and Bailey Kemp; Olivia King; Emma Kate Leask, Matthew Allen and Holly Elisabeth Leask Allen; Sam Leith, Alice Bowden, and Marlene Leith; Phoebe Teen-Yun Leung; Rafael James Livesey-Howe; Marianne and Jacob Lee; Ester Marney and Ruby and Amelie Read; Jessica and Natalie Marsh; Kryssy and Evie Martin; Ruth Mbegabolawe and Naomi Okundaye; Kirstin and Max McCartney; Catherine, Sophie, and Tess McCormick; Andrew, Jane, and Jessica McManus; Teodora Mihaylova and Alexander Brooklyn Ivanov; Cemre Mirel and Leonn and Kiana-Leigh Meade; Sophia and Teddy Morling; Lois, Matthew, Phoebe, and Layla Oliver; Oonagh Phelan and Emma Rose Hopkins; Emma, Laura, Hannah, and Eva Purnell; Lucy and Micah Reis; Andrew Smith; David Vangasse, Emily Fleuriot, Albert Fleuriot Vangasse, and Frederic Fleuriot Vangasse; Kate Wheeler and Freya Bartlett; Justyna, Majid, and Nicole Zohreh.

Picture credits

The publisher would like to thank the following for their kind permission to reproduce their photographs: (Key: a-above; b-below/bottom; c-center; f-far; l-left; r-right; t-top)
Alamy Images: Chloe Johnson 53tl; **Babybond® www.babybond.com:** 8clb, 13bl, 13br, 13cl, 13cr, 13tl, 13tr; **Corbis:** Owen Franken 6bl, 42; Louie Psihoyos/Science Faction 49; **Getty Images:** Paul Bradbury 17; Anthony Bradshaw 73fcrb; Peter Cade 9cla; Gabriela Hasbun 23r; Noel Hendrickson 275; Photodisc 9cr; Andersen Ross 45; Terry Vine 9tl, 29; **Jenny Matthews:** 73br, 120, 152, 222bl, 222clb; **Mother & Baby Picture Library:** Eddie Lawrence 19; **Photolibrary:** Bananastock 41; **Science Photo Library:** Samuel Ashfield 8t, 21; B. Boissonnet 25; Eddie Lawrence 38; Larry Mulvehill 47; **Tony Sheffield ABIPP Australia:** 91t; **Wellcome Images:** Anthea Sieveking 9tr, 39
All other images © Dorling Kindersley
For further information see: **www.dkimages.com**